A Life's Mosaic

▽△▽

A Life's Mosaic

THE AUTOBIOGRAPHY OF
Phyllis Ntantala

UNIVERSITY OF CALIFORNIA PRESS
Berkeley   Los Angeles   Oxford

Published in 1993 by The University of California Press, 2120 Berkeley Way, Berkeley, California 94720, United States of America, and by the University of California Press Ltd., Oxford, England

First published 1992 in southern Africa by David Philip Publishers, Cape Town

© 1992 Phyllis P Jordan

Printed in South Africa

Library of Congress Cataloging-in-Publication Data

Ntantala, Phyllis.
  A life's mosaic : the autobiography of Phyllis Ntantala.
    p.   cm. — (Perspectives on Southern Africa : 49)
    ISBN 0-520-08171-4 (cloth : alk. paper). — ISBN 0-520-08172-2
  (paper : alk. paper)
    1. Ntantala, Phyllis. 2. Civil rights workers—South Africa—
  Biography. 3. Civil rights workers—United States—Biography.
  4. Anti-apartheid movements—South Africa. 5. South Africa—
  Race relations. 6. United States—Race relations.
  I. Title. II. Series.
  DT1949.N75A3   1992
  323'.092—dc20   92-20587
                                                          CIP

Contents

Photographs on pages xi–xvi

Preface

It was one evening at the Lincoln Center in New York. Pavarotti's voice filled the auditorium with 'Mama', one of those arias he sings so well, and the audience, in appreciation, gave him a thunderous ovation. As he came back for yet another bow, my mind suddenly flashed back, and that other world to which I once belonged came into sharp focus – the bends of the Nqabarha River, the meadows, the animals, the simple country folk, the school kids pouring out of the school-gate at the end of the day. I saw them all, as I had seen them so many times in that far-off time and place. I sat down, cupped my head in my hands and bowed my head, softly saying to myself: 'How strange! Little do all these people know that while I am part of them at this particular moment, I am part of another world of which they know so little. I come from Gqubeni along the bends of the Nqabarha River. That's where my roots are. That's me!'

Some years ago, my daughter-in-law Casey once asked me: 'P, how did you and Joe meet? Just tell us.' .

Laughing, I dismissed her question with: 'You know, where I come from, that is one subject parents do not discuss with their children. Maybe one day I'll tell you how it happened.' We both laughed and left it at that.

After that night at the Lincoln Center, it occurred to me that, perhaps, my other world was part of me in a way that not even my children knew, let alone the friends around me that night. How could my children, born and raised in the city, know anything of this other world? What they knew of this world were snatches gleaned from me and their dad and all those other visitors from the country with whom they came into contact when they were growing up.

Even to answer Casey's question, I had to go back to this other world. It was the only way she would understand why and how I ended up marrying Joe. So I started jotting down notes, recounting my experiences that span three continents, experiences that have shaped and moulded me into the person that I am.

I wanted to leave a record of my life for my children and my grandchildren and all those other friends I have met in my sojourn through life, for them to know and understand that it was because of these far-off roots that I am the person I am. It was to say to them: *'Ndivel' eGqubeni, nindibona nje!'* [You see me here! I come from Gqubeni!] Yes, this is my story.

Like Trotsky, I did not leave home with the proverbial one-and-six in my pocket. I come from a family of the landed gentry in Transkei, the kulaks of that area. I could, like many others in my class, have chosen the path of comfort and safety, for even in apartheid South Africa, there is still that path for those who will collaborate. But I chose the path of struggle and uncertainty.

I trace the foundations of this attitude to my upbringing in a home where the less fortunate and destitute always came and found help and succour. From a very early age, I was made aware of the needs and problems of others and I saw all these people treated with dignity and humanity. This had a tremendous impact on me as a child, even though there were never any lectures on it. And yet I am still very class conscious and, like most people from my class, very arrogant. My arrogance, however, has always been tempered with concern, sympathy and caring for the less fortunate. From this class position, I knew quite early that I was as good as the best, black and white.

This book is not a political thesis. But I have used the story of my life as a peg on which to hang life and events in South Africa and North America as I experienced them. We have here a huge canvas, depicting the mosaic that is South Africa, with all its colours, strong and subdued, its lines long and short, and the dots, large and small. In social life, it is people who make up that mosaic; it is they who make things happen. Their actions and interactions determine the course of events. At the very centre of all this are human relations, and to understand those human relations, we must meet real people, hear them speak, how they speak, and then we shall know why they speak the way they do. A summary of events does not and cannot give the whole picture; the nuances are lost in a synopsis. The whole mosaic has to be seen – lines, dots, colours and all – in its totality, to be appreciated.

In drawing this mosaic we have gone back in time and history; given a lot of background and sometimes in detail, for to understand the present, we must know the past; even to predict the future accurately, we have to know that past, as it was in the past that the seeds of the future were sown. For how can one explain and understand Granny Matthews, wife of the late Professor Z. K. Matthews, so English and yet so African? Of the African women I know, there are none as African and aware of their great African heritage as she is. And yet, on the surface, she is so English. Or how can one understand my husband A.C., peasant in outlook, one who remained suspicious of city ways to the end of his life, and yet, as a Classical and European scholar of literature, history and music, one who could field with the best? One needs to know the roots from which such people have sprung.

Here is also a slice of the mosaic that is America, a country not unlike South Africa in many ways. Both are young and vigorous, the meeting-place of Africa and Europe. Nature has graciously smiled on both and endowed them with riches under and above the ground and with a beauty unsurpassed. Their people are warm, kind, generous and with a concern for others. Bigotry and racism are a curse on both, for in both colour is king. Arrogance of power is a plague in both, power so ruthless and manipulative that it allows nothing to stand in its way. Yes, so much alike and yet so different! There is a promise and a future in America, for the bedrock of her foundation is a constitution that guarantees liberty, equality, freedom and the pursuit of happiness to all her people. For South Africa there is *now* a promise, some hope. But the future is still blurred.

There had been stirrings in me even before I left the University of Fort Hare. The blatant racism at Healdtown where I went to school had opened my eyes. This was not so much directed towards us, the students. After all, the white establishment there was a little distant from us, and the three whites on the High School staff could not be accused of being racists. It was the attitude of the white colony towards the African staff that disgusted me. I resented this with all my soul and could not wait to get out of that place. I strongly suspected that the interests of this establishment were inimical to mine. So by the time I got to Fort Hare, all establishments were suspect.

It was in Kroonstad where I came to teach that my anger was aroused. It was concern for my students whose hopes and ambitions seemed to end in a cul-de-sac that made me ask 'why' and seek answers to the problems of poverty that thwarted the ambitions of such good students. I was not to find answers until I got to Cape Town. Here I learnt that, though I seemed free, there could be no freedom where others were not free and that in fact, nobody in South Africa, or any other country, was free while others were not. I learnt also that it was not the ill-will of any individual white person or group of them, but a system of exploitation that benefited only a few and saw the rest of mankind as units of labour that could be exploited for the benefit of those few who held the economic power. This was what was responsible for the miserable plight of so many people in my country and in other parts of the world. It was brought home to me in Cape Town that not until this system of exploitation of Man by Man had been smashed and disbanded could there be freedom in the world. And it was people who, by taking their destiny in their hands, could change things, turn them around and create for themselves a new world, a humane world of free, liberated people. Having understood this, I could not leave it to others to do. I had to be part of it.

My stepmother, Edwina, with baby
Somikazi on the outside veranda
at home

Below: Tata, my father, as I knew
him in my youth. He was 59 when
this photograph was taken.

Fort Hare Rag, 1935: Phyllis as Harlem girl, Vin Kraai as golfer

Below: My wedding day, eGqubeni, 2 January 1940.

Above left: Phyllis and baby Nandi (15 months), Kroonstad

Above right: Sister Nontsikelelo, A.C.'s sister, with baby Pallo (3 weeks), Kroonstad

Right: A.C. Jordan, Cape Town, early 1960s

Left: Nandi on her way home from the Little Theatre, Cape Town.

Ninzi, New York, 1967

Meeting held on the Grand Parade, Cape Town, 30 March 1952, during the campaign against the Van Riebeeck Celebrations. On the platform from left: Phyllis Jordan, Willem van Schoor, S.A. Jayiya, Goolam Gool, Dan Neethling, Jane Gool.

Lindi (7 years) and Pallo (10) with Bojie, A.C.'s nephew, Cape Town

A.C. with Dr Claggert, Director of Center for Research, University of Wisconsin, Madison, 1962.

Z. Pallo Jordan, London

A.C. and Phyllis photographed for the Capitol Times *of Madison on the day the news broke of Pallo's endorsement out of the USA, March 1967.*

A SALUTE TO

Tata, my Grand Old Man, friend and first teacher
A.C., my husband, comrade and colleague
Granny, Somhlophe and Ntangashe, my wonderful sisters who
protected me throughout my growing years
Nqokothwana (Mzukie), the brother for whose coming I prayed
and Nandi, Ninzi, Pallo and Lindi, my children and
source of my inspiration

AND A LEGACY TO

my grandchildren, Thuli Ofuma, Samantha Lee and
Nandipha Esther

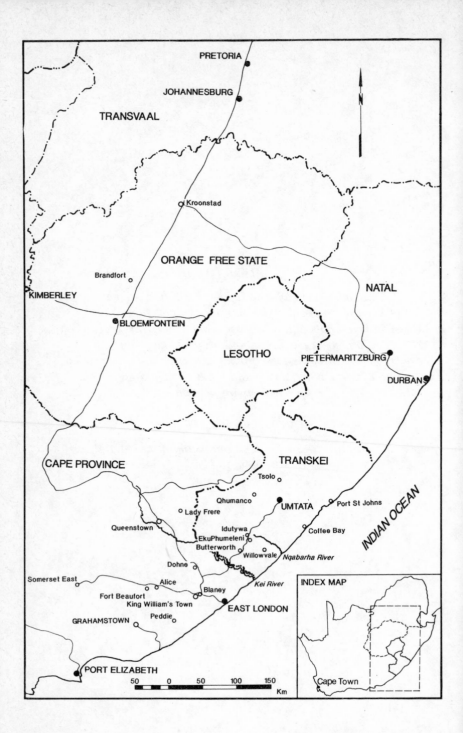

Duff Mission

This is my home. In this mission church I was baptised by the Rev. John Thompson. Some twenty years later, I came down from Kroonstad in the Orange Free State, to be married in the same church by the Rev. J. J. Mdlekeza.

Duff mission is among the oldest mission stations in this part of the country. The first was the station established by the Wesleyan Society in 1827 in Butterworth near King Hintsa's court. Not to be beaten at the game, the Free Church of Scotland established the Thuthurha mission eight miles away in the Centane district and then this one at Duff mission in the Idutywa district.

The Idutywa district was to be the first foothold of British penetration into Transkei. In 1858, shortly after the Nongqawuse or cattle-killing tragedy,* Sir George Grey, Governor of the Cape Colony and High Commissioner, sent a force of Frontier Armed and Mounted Police to occupy the area, to prevent King Sarhili from returning to the area, after he had left it in the wake of the Nongqawuse tragedy. A magistracy was set up to exercise jurisdiction over the Africans there, and Idutywa was declared a dependency of the Colony, to be governed from Cape Town.

The Africans who settled here were offshoots of various groups that had lived in the area before Nongqawuse. These were the Gcaleka, the Mfengu,† who had been settled here by Hintsa when they first immigrated, and the Ndlambe under Smith Mhala, grand-

---

* In 1857, following the prophecy of a young girl, Nongqawuse, the Xhosa people slaughtered their stock and destroyed their crops in the expectation of an act of revenge by their ancestors on the white colonists.
† These were refugees of Tshaka's wars, a period known as *iMfecane* in Xhosa and *Lifaqane* in Sotho.

son of Rharhabe, who had been brought over by the British after the war of 1842 to form a buffer between the Colony and the Xhosa.

As an incentive for Africans to settle in the area, the one-family one-lot system of land tenure was introduced (rather than the more usual system of communal ownership of land). Each family unit was given a title-deed to its residential and arable lot. This enabled polygamists to acquire large tracts of land, as the distribution was on the basis of one lot per family unit. Such a system, however, deprived younger sons of ever acquiring land, for on the death of the original title-deed holder, his land devolved to his senior heir. The property was not divisible among all the children by means of a will.

Duff mission, like most mission stations in rural South Africa, was a land grant mission. It is situated on one of the fertile bends of the Nqabarha River, about seven miles from Mputhi, its source, and seven miles from the town of Idutywa.

The mission house is a typical rural mission house of the nine-teenth century – a square stone building with a zinc roof, with stables for the missionary's horses and Cape cart, a cattle-fold, trees to provide shade and shelter, and a fruit and vegetable garden on the west side. About thirty yards east of the mission house is the church, which serves as schoolroom for five days in the week. Behind the church is the graveyard. Along the riverbend, on the east and west, are the ploughing fields, two for use by the missionary, one for the principal teacher of the school, and the rest, about twenty, hired out to parishioners and others.

Across the Nqabarha River on the west are settlements of school people. To the east, on a knoll on one of the bends of the river, is another village, eRhwantsini. East of eRhwantsini again, across the Foley stream, a tributary of the Nqabarha, is a further settlement of school and non-school people, eziThenjini. In this area is my home, the actual homestead known as eGqubeni by all the local people. It is an imposing rural homestead, facing east, with a vegetable garden in front and a backdrop of wattle and gum trees, beyond which are the ploughing fields. At the foot of the knoll beyond the ploughing fields are the deep pools of the Nqabarha River, as it follows the contours of the land on its long journey to the Indian Ocean. My home is, in fact, three and a half miles from the mission itself.

The African communities always regarded a mission station in their midst as their responsibility. With their labour and contributions, they helped the missionary build it. This duty involved not only the school people but the non-school people as well, whose children attended the mission school. The people taxed themselves to buy the building materials and those who were carpenters, roofers and bricklayers gave of their services free. They saw to it that the missionary's fields were ploughed and that his pantry was never empty.

The school community had been drawn here because they were members of the Free Church of Scotland and, above all, because the land was good. It was a community of people of moderate means who, through diligence, raised their stock, ploughed their lands and were able not only to feed themselves but also to send their children to colleges like Lovedale, Blythswood, Clarkebury and eMgwali Training School for Girls, to become teachers or learn a trade. Because there were not many openings for them when they came back from college, most of the young men left for the cities where there were better opportunities. But all of them kept their arable and residential lots in the country for years. Some of them came back; others never did. All of them left their families behind, and some never saw those families again.

When I was living in the Orange Free State and after I got married, it struck me every time I went home that the girls I had been with in school and had known in these villages, many of them my age and younger, were living the lives of widows as their menfolk were working in the urban areas. In some cases the men had not been back for years and the girls were left alone in the country, raising their children, scraping the bare soil for a living. A few of them had fallen victim to men who could support them and their children – teachers, agricultural officers, ministers of religion, clerks and petty chiefs – and had children by these men. But many were carrying on stoically, working at whatever jobs were available, keeping their homes and raising their children. Today, Duff mission, as with most rural areas, is a place of women without men.

Throughout his stay, the missionary and his family were supported and maintained by the community. My family, since the time of my great-grandfather, had been very much involved in this, so involved that every month my father would send a harmel (or castrated ram) to the mission station, to provide meat for the missionary and his family. I remember occasions when a new missionary arrived; our ox-waggon would be sent to the train station to fetch him, his family, and their belongings. I remember also one of the deacons announcing in church that the mission house needed repairs, and appealing to the congregation for donations. The teachers, too, were treated in like manner. In those days, some of them were not locals; they came from other parts of the country, sometimes as far afield as Ciskei. It fell to the local people to support and maintain them. Because of this community involvement, my home became the second home of every missionary or teacher at Duff mission.

It was in that one-room school hall at Duff mission that I learnt my three R's. I have seen that school hall develop into three rooms – a huge hall for all the beginners up to Standard 2, a wing for Standards 3 and 4 and another wing for Standards 5 and 6. And just before I graduated from Standard 6, I witnessed the building of yet another classroom, a rondavel, for Standard 6. But my beginnings are in that one-room school hall, a church hall on Sundays and a school room for five days of the week.

At Rivermead (kwa Ngqondela) is our local trading store, run by Arthur Venables and his wife Nonqabarha. White traders came to the Transkei, hot on the heels of the missionaries, to provide all the new needs that the missionaries demanded and to satisfy the new tastes that had been introduced. To be accepted as Christians, the Africans had to wear European dress, which they could only get from the traders. The missionaries also brought new foods – tea, coffee, sugar, flour – and through association with the missionaries Africans acquired a taste for these items. Moreover, the traders provided the people with ready-made tools – pots, hoes, ploughs, and dishes. These were much more convenient and the people fell for them, both the school and non-school people. That they were undermining the home handicrafts of the local people was not yet thought of.

They were a hardy breed of men and women, these traders, isolated, lonely and hard working. In order to survive in this sea of black people, they had to learn how to live with people. Very few of them slept with revolvers under their pillows or locked their doors. They knew they were safe among their neighbours. They had learnt who was who in the areas where they lived, ingratiated themselves with the most influential families, and kept friends with the majority of the people. They learnt the language of the people and made sure their children learnt it too. Some of them born in these parts knew Xhosa before they knew English.

When Britain began replacing the civil service personnel in South Africa with locally born whites, most of their recruits came from this class of whites, who knew the Native and spoke his language. Recruits for missionary work too came from this class. Those of them who went on to universities became experts in the areas pertaining to Africans – Anthropology, African languages, Native Administration and Native Law. But though living among Africans, like all white South Africans they never forgot that they were white.

The Venables were great friends of my family. Their eldest child, a girl, was the same age as my sister Granny. She was called 'Miss Gladys' by everybody, including her parents. I did not know the reason then, but I know it now. As a white person she could not be called just 'Gladys' by the Natives. There were two boys, George and Darian, the ages of my sister Ethel and myself respectively. Everybody called them by their first names. There were constant exchanges of gifts between Mama and Mrs Venables – boxes of sweets and biscuits from the shop, or vegetables, fruit and eggs from Mama. When we were sent to the shop carrying these we always went round to their living quarters, where we played with George and Darian. We would play in Grandma's room, Grandma being Mrs Bode (Mrs Venables's mother), who lived with them, and always left it a mess.

Whenever Mrs Venables went shopping in East London, she sent word to Mama, asking if she did not want anything for the children. This was not only because Mama was a friend, but also because she was a good customer.

The relationship between the Venables and the local people was so good that when he went bankrupt, the locals sent a petition on his behalf, pleading that he be given another chance. We knew when the court bailiff was at the shop, for Mr Venables would come home on his horse, and remain there the whole day until the bailiff had gone. My uncles and other local men would come and sit with him, expressing sympathy: 'Child of Venables, how can the whites treat you like this? Don't they know you have been a good friend of ours? But white people are a funny breed!' In this case they did not regard him as a white person. He was one of them and the white enemy was out there to destroy him, and them too.

On one occasion, Tata, my father, on a visit to Johannesburg, heard that George was a manager on a mine. Tata visited him and found him married with a child. George thanked Tata for the support he and other locals had given his father. George told Tata that Darian, also manager at some other mine, was away on honeymoon, but would visit home before coming back to duty. When Darian brought his wife to the Transkei, they visited my parents. Again the locals came to greet Darian and his wife as soon as they learnt that the car standing in our courtyard was Darian's.

This sort of relationship was not an isolated case. The traders Whitfield (kwa Wofa) at Chizele, where my sister Granny lived, had a very good rapport with the villagers there. After Ernest Whitfield died and the son took over the business, there was a lot of friction between him and his mother. The son wanted to run the business on strict lines, suing those who defaulted on their payments. The mother would not hear of it: her husband Ernest had never done that. No one had ever been taken to court or had his property garnished for failure to pay. They always paid when they could, the mother argued.

It was the Africans who, during the Second World War, looked after the families of traders in rural South Africa, once their men had joined up. Again it was these African neighbours and friends who broke the news to the families when sons or husbands died in the war. Because they regarded these areas as home, many traders were upset and refused to move when, with the introduction of the policy of separate development, the government wanted them to sell up and move away. 'I don't belong in Bellville,' said one, Jack Mather. 'I belong here. My roots are here. I am the fourth generation of traders here. I am not going anywhere.'

But for all that, these traders never forgot that they were white. Their children attended white schools in town and not the local African school, just a few miles from home.

My People

My father's grandfather, Ntantala, was a Ngqika, a courtier of Maqoma, warrior-king and Ngqika's first-born son. He came to Transkei a year before the Nongqawuse tragedy. Because he was the son of a mistress, his father advised him to cross the Kei, where there was still plenty of land, and seek his fortune there. So Ntantala, with his two wives and their children, crossed the Kei, put himself at the service of Sarhili, the Xhosa king, and was given a place in which to settle. Because of his keen mind, his wisdom and eloquence, he soon distinguished himself in the Gcaleka court and was admitted to the inner councils of the kingdom.

Then came the Nongqawuse story. Various people – councillors of the court – were sent by the king to go and verify the girl's story of people who spoke to her from behind the reeds in the riverbed, of moving objects in the sea. On one of these occasions Ntantala was among those who went down to the Gxarha stream to see for themselves. He came back unconvinced, it is reported, and in his report-back, he made it quite plain that the whole thing was a hoax. So eloquent was his evidence that doubt entered the minds of even those courtiers who had been convinced by the story. Then the great debate went on and on for weeks, with the people see-sawing between belief and disbelief. In anger and frustration, those who were for the killing of their livestock, *amaThamba* as they were called, turned round and rebuked their fellow Gcalekas for listening to a newcomer, a Ngqika, whose feet were still wet with the dew of the morning of his arrival. Then Ntantala realised that those close to the court could not be moved; they were bent on their own destruction; they would press the king to give the go-ahead. He went to the king and asked for permission to leave Gcalekaland. This was granted. Collecting his family and his livestock, he left for Hohita, one of the outposts of Hintsa's kingdom. He remained there for more than ten years, and prospered.

When Sarhili and some of his followers fled to Hohita after the Nongqawuse tragedy, they found Ntantala there, a prosperous man. After ten years in Hohita, Sarhili was allowed back to his area, now all carved up by the British into Gcalekaland, Fingoland and the Idutywa Reserve. Ntantala sent his king ten heifers to help him start his new life. For this service he earned for himself a place in the Gcaleka court, and to the end of his days he, and his sons after him, became trusted councillors.

Ntantala came back from Hohita in 1870 and settled at Zithenjini in the Idutywa district. In recognition of his services, Sarhili – who, on his return, had been given some limited powers over the Africans in the Idutywa and Gatyana (or Willowvale) districts – appointed Ntantala his overseer in the villages of Zithenjini, Rhwantsini, Cungcwini, Falakahla, Ngquthu, and Phesheya kwe Nqabarha, all in the Idutywa district. He also took a job as policeman, rising to the position of sergeant in the new African police force in Idutywa. Ntantala's two youngest sons – Govan, my father's father, and Mandoyi – followed their father into the police force in Idutywa, also reaching the rank of sergeant.

Because he was a polygamist with three wives, his descendants number hundreds of people, all settled in the Zithenjini village. Most of them became men of means, rich in stock, large and small. And because they had taken advantage of the land distribution in Idutywa, they acquired large estates. Almost every large tract of land, arable and residential, in this area belongs to some member of my family.

It is not clear how Govan, a younger son, became the centre of the family and wielded more influence in the area than his older brothers. We can only surmise that this was because of his position in the white administration in Idutywa. Govan's homestead became the centre of the whole family. Here were the family grain-pits; here the family gathered to observe family traditions; here important visitors from the Gcaleka court were received. The homestead came to be known as kula Mzi Mkhulu (the main homestead) or just eGqubeni (the place of the huge piles of cow manure).

My father, George Ndabakayise, was the eldest son of Govan by his wife Nomaqwelane (NoHanti to her in-laws), a Mpondomise woman of the Majola house. He was born on 9 April 1881, in the year of the final crushing of the Mpondomise, the year of the disarmament of the Sotho and the annexation of Mpondoland. In 1879, the Xhosa had been finally defeated in the War of Ngcayechibi; Sarhili, the king, was forced to flee and seek asylum among his mother's people, the Bomvana. In 1879, too, the Zulu had been defeated and Cetywayo, the King, was arrested and sent to Robben Island.

These events were still fresh in people's minds as George was growing up. The accounts of these happenings made a deep impression on him, and he followed with such keen interest the story of the Wars of Dispossession that later in life he became a knowledgeable student of their history and this period of British expansion in South Africa.

From the local school at Duff, George's father sent him to Zonnebloem College in Cape Town. Zonnebloem, the Eton of South Africa, had been established for the training of the sons of African monarchs and notables, as well as the sons of senior administration officials. He was fifteen years old and was to remain in Cape Town for the next seven years, making the journey home only three times. How his father, a policeman in Idutywa, ever got to hear of Zonnebloem, we do not know.

It was a long journey from home; first on horseback through the Kei Gorge to amaBhele where one caught the train to Cape Town. Or on horseback to amaBhele, then the train to East London, where one caught the boat to Cape Town. Cape Town! In faraway Cape Town, who would look after him when he was not in school? Fortunately, James Tolbatt – who hailed from George's neighbourhood – and his wife were there and they took charge of him. It had been arranged that because of the distance, George would work during the winter holidays and come home once a year. He found work in the house of a Dr and Mrs Waterkant as office boy, helping the doctor in his surgery and also as house-boy, helping in the kitchen. The work in the doctor's surgery taught him a lot about how to treat infection and wounds. A better medical assistant you could not find anywhere. The housework also helped rid him of those prejudices so common among men. Tata could cook, clean house, wash and iron, something unheard of among men in those days and, in some cases, even these days.

The Waterkants liked him so much they wanted to take him back to England with them when they left South Africa, so that he could continue his education there. Grateful as he was he declined the offer, reminding them that he was the first in his family to have come that far for an education; that his people back home had doubted he would ever return when they heard he had been sent to a school in Cape Town. If he left with the Waterkants these fears would be confirmed and it would mean the end of schooling for members of his family, many of whom were not yet school people.

He remained in Zonnebloem and completed his education. Among his best friends and contemporaries at school were Chief Masupha, one of the sons of King Moshoeshoe, after whom Tata named his first grandson. In Cape Town, years later, I was to meet Mr Heneke, ex-principal of Trafalgar High School, who was a junior at Zonnebloem when Tata was there. Mr Heneke was excited to know that the Jordan children he was teaching at Athlone High School were the grandchildren of George, one of the fellows he had admired and respected in Zonnebloem as a freshman there.

George Ndabakayise came home in 1902, after seven years in Cape Town. He was twenty-two years, old enough to take a wife. And the big question was: Whom was he to marry? Were there girls good enough locally to marry this polished gentleman from Cape Town? His mother, Nomaqwelane, did not think there were any. Perhaps in the Colony, across the Kei, among the first families of converts, there might be one.

My mother was Ida Balfour, one of the many daughters of Makhaphela Sangani Balfour, eldest son of Noyi, who, on baptism as a Christian, assumed the name Balfour, after that eminent Scottish scholar Dr Balfour of Glasgow. My mother's mother was Emma, granddaughter of Mhala, king of the Ndlambes. Cyril Mhala, who went to Canterbury for his education, was one of her brothers. My mother was born in 1885 at Lovedale, the home of the Balfours.

Noyi (now Balfour) had helped the Rev. John Bennie alphabetise Xhosa and, in 1822, these two had produced the first Xhosa primer. At the Ncerha station, Balfour and Bennie completed the translation of the New Testament into Xhosa and in 1834 went to Somerset East to print it. It was on their return from Somerset East that they found that the mission station had been burned down during the recent war, the so-called War of Hintsa. Balfour went to Tyhali, the regent, to ask for another site. Tyhali gave the missionaries a thousand morgen of land west of the Tyhumie, to build a school that would be a heritage for African children till the end of time. This is the present Lovedale, from which have graduated some of the most illustrious men and women, white and black, from southern Africa.

When the question of finding a suitable girl for George came up, his mother was adamant that there were no suitable girls locally. The grandfather, Ntantala, then suggested the Balfour family at Theko Springs. No girl could be more suitable for such as his grandson than a girl from the Balfours. So to Theko Springs the Ntantala envoys went. They found there four, all of marriageable age and beautiful. The older two were engaged; the next two, Ida, aged seventeen, and her sister, Annie, aged sixteen, were not. Both families settled for the seventeen-year-old Ida, tall and strikingly beautiful. This was her first year of teaching at the local school, having finished her teacher training at Lamplough Girls' School in Butterworth. Ida and George were married at Thuthurha church in December 1903. She was just eighteen years old.

Ida had hoped that her favourite brother, Menziwa (or Bhut' Mgwenye as they called him), would be there for her wedding. He did not come, for he was running a business in Mossel Bay. However, Menziwa came back a year after her wedding and one of the first things he did was to visit his sister to find out for himself who this 'lucky young man' was. When he arrived, his sister is reported to have said, introducing her husband to him: 'Meet this boy that your father married me to. What do you think of him?' At twenty-two, Tata must have looked a mere boy of eighteen. His looks belied his age. At fifty he still looked a young man of thirty-five. Anyway, what the brother saw pleased him. Here was an elegant, handsome young man, with a keen mind, knowledgeable and sophisticated, a gentleman to his finger-tips.

Menziwa and Tata hit it off well together from the start and remained the best of friends to the end of their days. To us children, no uncle was as loved as Malume Mgwenye, he loved us in return. His wife, Nobani, a Ngcwelesha woman of the house of Tshawe, became one of Mama's best friends. She was an elegant town woman.

I think my parents were a near-perfect pair. My father was six foot two, well built, dark complexioned, dignified, warm, kind, generous, slow to anger, understanding, with a healthy attitude towards women, a gentleman through and through. Many of his female contemporaries often said that in his presence they never felt inferior or inadequate, for he always treated them as human beings. My mother, five foot nine, was a rich pink brunette with a ready laugh, outgoing and outspoken, a balance to my father's rather reserved disposition.

Those who knew of her coming as a young bride into the Ntantala family often told how her mother-in-law was beside herself with pride and excitement. This was the kind of girl she had hoped for for her sophisticated son. Grandma put her on a pedestal, allowed her to do things that other newlyweds were not allowed to do. For example, Mama was allowed to accompany Tata to the places he went to – country fairs, exhibitions, choir competitions; she was also allowed to visit her numerous sisters and brothers who, in turn, visited her. Many of the family customs were waived in her case. All this was done because according to Grandma, 'cultured people' did not have to observe such customs. To be free to run their lives as they saw fit – as 'cultured people' – the young couple were encouraged to move out of the big homestead (Mzimkhulu) to build their own home. On this site they built their modern, three-bedroomed square house, with two rondavels on each side, and stables for the horses and their Cape cart. They gave their home a backdrop of trees, with a vegetable and flower garden in front, some fruit trees at the back, beyond which were the ploughing fields, all fenced in.

This is my home, my birthplace and that of my siblings. It was to this house that the missionaries, their families and the teachers came. It was here that visitors of all sorts – local and from abroad – came. In this house I first met and saw a black American, Dr Wright. And because we had been told that America was a country where the people had freed themselves, I thought America was a country of black people. Because of the Rev. Thompson, many visitors to Transkei would visit our mission station and, invariably, he would bring them home to meet my parents or to meet Mama if they had already met Tata. Besides, all the educated families in the district and beyond knew each other and were very close. Visits among them were common. All this was in addition to visits from Mama's huge family.

Mama soon became popular as seamstress and dressmaker. Wedding gowns were her speciality. (My sister Granny was to follow her in this.) She must have been in great demand, for I remember piles and piles of bridal material in one corner of the room. The girls would come to our house for measurements and fittings, with some

of them remaining there for days if their homes were far. The dress
would be taken to the girl's home a day or so before the wedding,
or her family would come pick it up. Early on the morning of the
wedding, Tata would drive Mama there, for she had to dress up the
bride, accompany her to the door of the church and be with her the
whole day. She came home only in the evenings. But if the girl's
home was not in our locality, Mama had to go to her home the day
before and come back the day after. In rural South Africa, weddings
are not only at the girl's home, but also at the groom's, and Mama,
as dressmaker, had to be at both places. This meant a whole week
from home sometimes. On such occasions, Mam-nci, wife of one of
our uncles, would be left in charge of us. Tata was always there
with us.

There were also the weddings of Mama's nieces and nephews, to
which both she and Tata would go. Mam-nci again would take
charge, assisted by Granny, our eldest sister. Mama was so popular
among her sisters and brothers that her house became the 'finishing
school' for their daughters. As a result, many of our female cousins
have lived with us, on and off, for a year or two before they got
married. I have never been able to find out why this was so.

When my sister Granny and aunt Agnes (Tata's cousin) were students at Lovedale, the first Sunday after they came home for the
Christmas holidays was known as the 'Sunday of the Lovedaleans'.
There were seven of them from our mission station. On this day, they
would be joined by others from Thaleni, Ngcingwane, Chizele and
Good Hope, making a total of about twenty young people, with a
sprinkling of local teachers and older people. After the church service, they would all converge on our house where dinner would be
waiting for them. Sis' Ma-Zangwa, our help, would have prepared the
dinner, with my sisters Somhlophe and Ntangashe running errands
for her. As soon as Mama came in, she would go to the kitchen to
see that everything was all right; then she would return to the
dining-room, put in the two leaves to extend the table, cover it with
a starched tablecloth, invite her guests to the table and feed them.
These were always lively, happy gatherings. Those were the days!

And yet for all these things, some of them so vivid in my memory,
I do not have a complete day-to-day mental picture of Mama. My
picture of her on the Sunday of the Lovedaleans is of her wearing a
dove-grey three-quarter suit, approaching our gate with three other
ladies, also in Sunday dress. Then I see her with jacket off, spread-

ing the tablecloth, with Somhlophe and Ntangashe standing by with
the knives and forks, while I am fluttering around them. In yet
another, she is about to serve her guests. She is wearing a black
skirt, a white blouse with high collar and a black bow. There she is
entering the dining-room, balancing a platter of baked meat and
potatoes. The guests are already seated at the table. After placing the
platter in front of Tata, she steps back and declares 'Let us say
grace', bows her head and says the blessing.

It is such images of her that remain in my head.

Ida and George had seven children, two of whom were twins. The
younger twin, Agrinette Nozizwe, and the boy after them, Car-
michael Makhaya, died in infancy. Their eldest son, Elliott Carlson
Mzolisa, died during the 1918 influenza epidemic. He was fourteen
years old. Then they were left with four girls: Theodora Granny,
Evelyn Nonkululeko (Somhlophe), Ethel Ruth (Ntangashe) and
Priscilla Phyllis. All four girls were different in temperament, positive
and strong, and the pride of their father. Tata told us early in life not
to take second place to anybody, because we were as good as the
best, including men. In these days of women's liberation, I tell
people that I am a charter member of that organisation and it was
Tata who inducted me into it.

I was born on 7 January 1920, with the rising of the sun. My
parents were hoping for a boy, having lost their only son two years
back. They named me Priscilla Phyllis at the request of Dr Lumley,
our family doctor and great friend of Tata, for whom he had worked
when he first came back from Cape Town. The Lumley girl with
these names had died at fourteen and her parents wished that name
to live through me, the daughter of their friend.

The first year of my life was uneventful. But at fifteen months, I fell
seriously ill. I was already walking and running about like most toddlers at that age. I regressed as a result of the illness. I was so sick
that Mama and Grandma had to move to a place in town to be near
the doctor. Even with the doctor checking on me every day, there
was no improvement. So Mama and Grandma decided to go home
so that, at least, I might die at home. I am told that when I saw my
sister Granny at home, I stretched out my withered arms to her and
she took me in her arms. Mama allowed her to hold me just for a
few minutes, saying, 'Give her back, Granny; she must not die in my
child's arms.' Everybody thought I would not live through the night.

Early the next day one of the neighbours, Mrs Mathikinca (aunt Ma-Mpethwana as Mama called her) came over. She had heard that Mama was back with me and I was not expected to live. Aunt Ma-Mpethwana brought with her some herbs. She brewed these and when the brew was cool, gave me a spoonful, telling Mama to suspend all other medicines from the doctor. When she left, she instructed Mama to give me another spoonful of the brew at bedtime. The next day and the next, aunt Ma-Mpethwana was there to make sure I was given this herbal brew. In a week I showed signs of improvement. I became alert again, showed interest in people and things around me. I continued to improve, aunt Ma-Mpethwana making sure that Mama did not slacken in giving me this herbal brew. When I had improved enough, Mama took me to Theko for a rest, which she too needed. Here at Theko I continued to improve, started walking again, started talking and put on some weight. People tell me that I was so active, chasing chickens and everything I saw moving, asking questions, that they likened me to the tiny grass warbler [Nogqaza] and they called me that, a name that was to become my Xhosa name.

All the people who knew me at Theko call me Nogqaza. Members of my family too and all those who knew me as a child growing up use this name, and I like it. A good few call me Phyllie, and others still when they really want to be sweet, call me Nomphyl. Tata used both Nogqaza and Phyllie, and I would not have him call me anything else, to the extent of not wanting him to write 'Phyllis' in a letter to me. When in his old age, with his sight failing, he got someone to write for him and the letter would have 'Dear Phyllis', I would be so annoyed; it would take me a day or two to read that letter and I would write back saying, 'Please tell whoever writes for you that I am not Phyllis to you, but Phyllie or Nogqaza.' In his reply he always apologised, adding, 'People don't quite realise what these names mean to us.'

Nobody except aunt Ma-Mpethwana seemed to know what this herbal brew was. But whatever it was, it was an elixir of life, for I have enjoyed good health ever since. I then became a special child to this old lady. She had saved me from death and this she would never forget. When I was growing up at home, she kept an eye on me. On my way to and from school, she would be standing there looking out for me. Her house was on our way to school. After I had gone to boarding school, she came to see me every time I returned home for the holidays. Big as I was then, she still wanted to nurture me, made me sit by her side and sometimes let me share her plate of food. In her old age, she began to lose her sight and could not see me well. How touching it was when she would make me stand in front of her, feel me all over – my face, nose, ears, arms and whole body. Then she would invite me to sit next to her and tell her about my life at boarding school. As I was talking, she would say: 'Just say that again. I did not quite catch it.' I suppose my voice was music to her ears and whatever I said was beautiful. She was one of those who never called me anything but Nogqaza.

I did not see her much after I got married. My visits home were few and far between. I came back one holiday and she was gone. Tata had written to tell me she was dead. Though she was old, I could not imagine being home and not seeing her. I feared even to visit her grave, because I did not think I would be able to take it. I did, though, for I had come to accept that it had been time for her to go. My aunt Ma-Mpethwana!

The Household

The home of a man of means in the rural areas is a huge establishment, where all sorts of people gather. Ours was such a home. Here
came relatives, close and distant, on short or long visits, sometimes
bringing their children with them. Some of them came to ask for
blankets and clothes to see them through the next winter. One such
was Sis' Dinah, a distant niece of Mama. After she had been bought
this and that by Mama, she always went to the washing-basket and
picked a few more things for herself and her children, especially my
dresses for her daughter Ntombentsha, who was my age. Mama
would discover this after she was gone. Sis' Dinah was able to get
away with it because the washing-basket was in the store-room for
the convenience of aunt Ma-Mlambo, who could get to it whenever
she came to do the washing, so she did not have to wait for Mama.

Some arrived because of some dispute with a husband or a son
and came to ask Tata to intercede on their behalf; others came
because they had not seen us in a long time. None of these people
could not be sent away empty handed. Many of them proved of
great help while they were here. They helped in harvesting beans,
sun-drying the pumpkins, getting the corn into the silos, grain-pits
and tanks. They helped in the ploughing fields, hoeing and around
the home, putting new plaster onto the rondavels. Then on the day
Tata went to sell his bales of wool, those who came for a blanket or
coat were taken along and came back, not only with the blanket or
coat, but with other articles of clothing. There would be joy all
around. They were grateful and pleased. Tata would be pleased too
that he had been able to fulfil his obligations. When relatives arrived
because of trouble at home, and the husband or son eventually
came along, the family heads were called, and the dispute was

settled; and after getting her share of presents for having tarried with us so long, each of these too left at last.

Then there were the travellers, who stopped here asking for water to drink and to rest under the trees. These travellers could not be given only the water for which they had asked, but would be given tea and food before they resumed their journey. It was unthinkable to send them away without feeding them. Some of the travellers were saleswomen or salesmen, hawking their wares from village to village. They were usually women from Mndundu and Rhamrha in Gatyana, Mfengu women selling tobacco, mats, baskets and pottery. Word would have gone around that travelling saleswomen had been spotted somewhere in the neighbourhood. We, the children, would be asked to look out for them, and tell them that our parents wanted to buy something from them. For days we would be on the look-out, and when we spotted them, would run off to call them, asking them to stop at our place. Tata seemed to prefer their tobacco to that bought at the store.

Then these women would arrive, driving their donkeys laden with bags of tobacco, while they themselves carried their mats, baskets and pots on their heads. On the veranda or under the trees their wares would be displayed, and Tata would buy what he wanted, while Mama would be looking at the mats and baskets (seldom the pots, for we did not need them as we did not brew any of the home-made brews from corn). She too would pick what she wanted. While all this was going on, a warm conversation between our parents and these women would ensue. We, the children, would be busy making tea for everybody and getting food ready to feed the starving saleswomen. They, too, could not be sent away hungry.

Engrossed in their conversation, they would forget that time was passing and not waiting for them. Late in the afternoon would be heard exclamations of 'Yho! Is it this late already? It will be dark by the time we cross Thethiswayo [a ford in the Nqabarha River]. We do not want to cross that part of the river in the dark. It is not safe.'

'And even after you have crossed, you still have far to get home,' one of our parents would observe.

'Yes, you are right. We were not aware it was getting this late already.'

'You might as well stop over for the night and resume your journey tomorrow,' one of the parents would suggest.

This would be agreed upon and the saleswomen would be our

guests for that night. Nobody thought it strange. This was as it should be.

Then there were the daily drop-ins who came for a chat and would remain here for the midday meal and sometimes for the evening meal. In addition there were those who came to help with the daily chores – cleaning the yard, plastering, hoeing, harvesting, mending the cattle-fold or the fence, and all the chores around a home. Though this was 'free' help, they all expected to be given something when the chore was done. Another category was those who came to work in the fields to earn cash or kind. These, too, expected to be fed when they had finished and before they went home. This meant a big pot every day for people known to be here and even those who still had to decide whether to stop or not.

Then there was the central core family – the family itself, the helper in the kitchen, the yard-man and the herd-boys (four, aged ten to fifteen). Tata usually had four herd-boys – two for the small stock and one for the cattle and an older one floating between the cattle and the yard-work. This core group lived as a family unit, with all grown-ups wielding authority over the children. None of us dared to say to Sis' Ma-Zangwa, our kitchen help, or to Bhut' Nobhula, our general factotum, 'You are not my parent; you cannot order me about,' or tell them that they were being paid for what they did. Such talk would have meant punishment and they would not have hesitated to take the matter to our parents, for though they were servants, they were not our servants.

The men earned a beast a year (usually a female beast) or ten sheep, which they could send home or keep with our stock until they left. Some of the workers, especially the herd-boys, became as brothers to us. In the kitchen at night we taught them the three R's. Nose, who had come to us at the age of ten and left at fifteen, learnt to read and write in our kitchen. He had become so much part of our family that his mother was concerned he would never want to go back to his home again. Fearing this, the mother came to plead with Tata to release him. 'He is my only child. He is so happy here. I fear he will forget us. You know, whenever he comes home, we cannot eat without saying grace first. These are things he has learnt here and he likes them.' At fifteen Nose left us with four head of cattle and twenty sheep. Tata always said to him: 'Just tell me, how many young men who have been to Johannesburg have as much stock as you?'

Nose was not the only one who learnt to read and write in our kitchen. There were many others who did. Sometimes living with us would be children who had come to our school for Standards 5 and 6, because the schools in their areas only went up to Standard 4. They never paid any boarding fees. Now and again, a parent would send some contribution in kind – beans, pumpkins, vegetables or a harmel – towards the upkeep of the child. In a setting like this, children learn to live with and adjust to all sorts of people. Seldom does one find clashes of such a nature as to make life intolerable.

Each child had a chore to do, and woe to those who neglected their chores. If you had a puppy, it was your duty to feed, wash and clean up after it. If your chore was to feed the chickens, it was your duty to see that they were fed in the morning and given fresh water, the eggs were collected at the appropriate times, and the geese were let out to go to the river for their swim. Those in the chicken yard had the responsibility of opening the gate in the afternoon for the geese to come in. There were pigs to be fed and given water. Sometimes a ewe would die in childbirth and Tata would assign the responsibility of raising that lamb to one of us, with the promise that if it survived, it would be that child's own. The child would then nurse that motherless lamb, feeding it warm milk, cleaning its feeding bottle and finding some ewe that had lost its lamb to suckle it. We earned a few sheep this way.

It was we, the children, who saw to it that the stamped mealies for the next day's pot were ready the night before. In the morning there was no time for that before school. And if this was not done, Sis' Ma-Zangwa would say in the morning, just as we were getting ready for school: 'Hey! I do not know what they will eat when they come back from school. I am going to help in the fields today.' And she would do just that. Sis' Ma-Zangwa, our kitchen help, had more say than Mama about what each of us had to do. She would announce: 'I am going to the stream to do the washing today and Ethel is coming with me. Nonkululeko, you remain behind to make tea for Bhuti when he comes home. You did not make it yesterday, because you were late coming back from school and Ethel had to.' Or she would pick one of the kids to go to the store with her. She nearly always picked Ntangashe, for she was quiet and would not come back with reports of all the people met on the way or at the store, as my sister Somhlophe did. On those days when she was going to cook for the workers in the fields, she would assign the family pot to the children, and there was no questioning that command. This was good training, making children grow up responsible people. None of us ever considered it harsh. It was life, and these things had to be done.

I still remember of a morning during the ploughing and hoeing season Tata, standing early at the kitchen door, saying: 'There are some women in the fields today. Please see to it they are fed before they leave for home.'

'Yes, Bhuti!' Sis' Ma-Zangwa would respond.

'Did you hear what Bhuti said?' – this to the children. 'I am going to cook for those workers in the fields. You will have to take charge of the family meal.' So, saying, Sis' Ma-Zangwa would drop everything and busy herself with preparations for the meal for the workers in the fields. In fact, she never even cooked for them, for once she had set the pot, she would go to the fields to chat with them, leaving us, the children, to mind her pot.

At noon the workers would come back from the fields, sit under the trees, and ask for water to drink and wash their hands. Sis' Ma-Zangwa would join them under the trees, keeping them company. And when her 'pots' were ready, she would feed them. Their work was not measured by hours. Some days they would sit there, chatting until it was time for them to go home. Then they would have their sugar weighed out and given to them, or their bars of blue soap, or kerosene, for which they had come to work. Very few of them came to work for money.

When there was a big job in the fields or around the home – re-roofing the rondavels with new grass or re-plastering them – then a work party would be organised. My parents would delegate one of our neighbours, someone with the reputation of being a good organiser. Days before the party, this individual would come with her helpers, to prepare the food for that day – to stamp mealies, brew *marhewu,* bake bread. Depending on the size of the party, one or two sheep would be slaughtered. It was on such occasions that we tasted *marhewu.* After this beverage had been brewed and fermented well, the woman who brewed it would bring Mama a beakerful, saying to her: 'Please do have some, before it all goes. It is so tasty. It is the best I have ever brewed in all my life.' Because this brew was not part of our daily fare, I never acquired a taste for it. And yet those who know it say it is very nourishing, good for people working in the fields.

My people! How they seemed to take life in their stride.

Starting School

A younger child in a family, I think, is always at an advantage over older siblings. Such a child moves into the world of children sooner, getting to know all the things that the siblings are doing; and if precocious, as I was, absorbs most of the things the older children are learning.

At four years old I was ready for school. Even though I could not write, I knew my alphabet from A to Z and I could count to twenty. Looking at Ntangashe's Standard 2 English reader and recognising the picture accompanying the lesson 'A Garden in a Plate', I would read to Mama the first sentence and translate it as Ntangashe did:

'Ha! Ha! Who ever saw a garden in a plate?'

'Qhokoyi! Mntan' entankumba! Ngubani owakhe wabona igadi esepleytini?

My favourites were 'The Roll Call' in Somhlophe's Standard 4 reader and 'The Soldier's Reprieve' in the same book. Looking at the picture of the little girl who had sent the letter to the President, now just standing outside the door, I would call 'Come in!' as the President did. And with Mama's glasses on my nose, I would ask, 'Who is Bennie?'

'My brother, Sir. They are going to shoot him for sleeping at his post.'

Then the President: 'Oh yes! I remember. It was a fatal sleep.'

To this very day I am very sentimental when I hear the chorus 'Good Morrow to My Lady Fair', for I sang it with Mama and Somhlophe, before I went to school. I can still remember Somhlophe's beautiful soprano:

Wake, my Lady Fair,
Good morrow, good morrow,

Awake, my Lady Fair.

and Mama's contralto:

Lady Fair, awake, awake;
Wake, my Lady Fair, Lady Fair;
Good morrow, good morrow,
Awake, awake, my Lady Fair.

I was ready for school and my parents knew it. So all the rules about age were waived and I went to school. And as Mama said to all those who remarked upon it, 'If and when she gets tired, she will stop and stay home.' I never stopped. Even the three-and-a-half miles to and from school did not deter me. I had walked that distance on Sundays, going to church with my parents. Doing it for five days in the week was not going to be so forbidding. Anyway, what teacher, manager or even inspector of schools could say 'no' if my parents wanted me in school?

Everybody at home was enthusiastic about my going. Somhlophe volunteered to carry me piggy-back part of the way. As she had so many friends, some days I never walked, for her friends took turns carrying me. They liked it and so did I. It was only on my way back home that I would walk those three-and-a-half miles, for Somhlophe, in the upper classes, could not leave with us.

The schoolchildren accepted and welcomed me the very first day I got there. For were they not, most of them, my sister Somhlophe's friends? On that first day, one of her friends, Nozipho Ntshona, came to say 'Hi, Phyllie' during recess, and shared with me some of her wild turnips she had dug up. These wild turnips were very popular among schoolchildren. The teachers, who on many Sundays came to eat dinner at home, were no strangers to me. I knew them and they knew me. School was no strange place to me. I moved into that setting as if I had always belonged there, and I liked it.

And yet for all that, Mama was somewhat apprehensive. I remember her saying, as she was tying up my *kappie* [bonnet] and straightening my dress, 'When the teacher asks you a question, speak up and answer the question. Don't cry, Philli-girl.' She said this because my sister Ntangashe, shy and quiet, took a long time to adjust to the school atmosphere of lively, loud, strange children. However, by the time I went to school Ntangashe had got over her fears and had quite a number of friends, too, among the schoolchildren. Little did Mama know that there was no need to tell me to speak up when spoken to. I answered questions even before they were directed at me.

We were late coming to school that morning, and as the custom was, late-comers had to wait by the door until the teacher-in-charge came to find out why the students were not on time. Miss Dlova was conducting a religious instruction lesson across the hall not very far from the door. 'Who can tell me what the Eighth Commandment is?' asked the teacher. And before any of the class answered, a tiny voice from those by the door called out: 'Thou shalt not steal.' I had taken Mama's advice seriously and was answering the question asked. Anyway, I knew the Ten Commandments from my Sunday school. Later in life, whenever Miss Dlova congratulated me on my achievements, she would say: 'I knew you would do well. You passed with honours even before your name was in the Admission Register.'

I must have taken Mama's advice too much to heart. That whole day in class, whenever the teacher asked a question, my hand shot up, ready with an answer. I do not recall if I knew every answer and I doubt if I did in fact. At the end of the day our teacher, Miss Ntshona, took me aside and asked why my hand went up every time she asked a question. 'Mama told me to speak up and not cry,' I shot back. She laughed, helped me with my *kappie* and sent me home with the others.

One day I had on a beautiful new dress. I must have been proud of myself. That whole morning I never sat for longer than fifteen minutes in the classroom. Whenever any girl wanted to go out, I volunteered to go along with her. We were allowed out in pairs, so we would troop up to the teacher with our 'Please, Miss, may I go out?' (Why we had to make this request in English, I have never been able to understand. I suppose it was part of our education.) As we were coming back from one of these forays outside, the teacher called me: 'Phyllie, you have not sat ten minutes in the classroom. Why?'

Extrovert that I am, I pointed to my new dress. 'Don't you see?'

She had to laugh. Now what teacher does not like a child like that?

Before the end of my first year in school, when I was four and eight months, Mama died. She had been ill early in the autumn, but recovered. Then she went down with pneumonia late in October and died within a week. She had been nursing aunt Daisy, Tata's sister, who had been brought very ill from her home to Grandma's house.

Shuttling between the two homes – ours and Grandma's – Mama caught the pneumonia virus that was to kill her.

The family doctor, Mrs Thompson, was called in twice to see Mama. Her last visit was on the afternoon of the Saturday she died. The doctor told both Tata and the patient that the pneumonia had not peaked yet, but with the drugs she was leaving, it should peak by the next day. She left, promising to come back on Monday.

My cot was in the room where my parents slept. On either side of the room were their beds, with a table in the middle, a dresser on the side of Tata's bed, and my cot between Mama's bed and the dresser. I woke up that Sunday morning, and looked across at Mama's bed. She was lying on the mattress on the floor, and her bed was folded and put behind the door. Tata was sitting on the edge of his bed, dressed, and on one of the chairs in the room Oom Papana, Mama's cousin, was also sitting. Somhlophe came in with a tray of morning coffee, set it on the table, stood at the foot of Tata's bed, and looked across at the mattress on the floor. Then Tata broke the news to her: 'Nonkululeko, Mama has left us, my child. She died early this morning.'

Somhlophe stood there for a few minutes, turned round and quietly went out. To this day I do not know who broke the news to Ntangashe and what her reaction was. Nor do I remember seeing either of them crying. I do not recall who helped me dress, nor what the reaction was when we three met. What I remember next is the three of us sitting on the steps in front, eating *mvubo,* which Tata gave us. I do not even recall finishing eating and what we did after that. But I remember Grandpa, coming from Mzimkhulu, breaking down as soon as he entered our gate, and Tata going up to him, leading him to the room where Mama was. Then our cousin Nqalolo, who lived at Grandpa's, brought out the oxen, inspanned the ox-waggon and headed for town. Throughout the day, people came – our relatives, neighbours, Mam-nci Nopitoli, uncle Solomon's wife, and others. It was a strange and funny day.

Early in the evening, the ox-waggon came back laden with supplies and planks. In it was our aunt Agnes, whom we called 'Colosa', my mother's widowed younger sister who lived at Colosa, about seven miles from our home. Aunt Colosa immediately took us under her wing, saw to our comfort, moved me to the rondavel where my sisters slept and slept there with us. She took out some of our best dresses, sewed black bands on the sleeves and did everything possible to make us comfortable. Colosa was very much concerned about Ntangashe, she told us afterwards, for Ntangashe would steal away from Somhlophe and me and from her, to go cry all by herself. Colosa also told us that of all her children Mama feared more for her quiet, shy Ethel, in case of her death. Throughout her life, Colosa was to show this concern about Ntangashe. She was the only person who could separate me from Ntangashe, when she would invite her for a holiday to her home and leave me behind.

As I grew older I understood why a quiet, shy and reserved child like Ntangashe was always misunderstood. In school such a child is often accused of being cheeky and unfriendly by the teachers and other people. Even at home, the only people who understood Ntangashe were Tata and I. My two sisters, Granny and Somhlophe, would sometimes rub Ntangashe up the wrong way. And Tata would caution: 'Leave Ethel alone. Do not rush her. Don't try to bend her your way. She is very understanding.' How very true. We never had any major quarrels, for if she did not accept my point of view, I always backed down, giving her time to sort things out her own way. Throughout our life, she was my supporter and shield, and no younger sibling was protected by an older as I was by my sister Ntangashe. This bond of understanding between us grew stronger as we fended for ourselves at a very early age under a neglectful stepmother.

They buried Mama the following Saturday. As we left the graveyard, Somhlophe put her coat over her head and started crying. Aunt Ma-Miya, Mama's friend and one of the neighbours, went up to her: 'Nonkululeko, wipe off those tears, wipe off those tears!', put her arm over her shoulders and walked home with her. In front of the house was a bath full of water and according to custom everyone washed hands; Colosa and aunt Ma-Miya helped us wash ours. Then we went in. Colosa remained with us for two weeks and then returned home.

A month after Mama's death my sister Granny came home from Lovedale for the summer holiday. She had not attended the funeral as this was examination time and she could not afford to miss her finals. Colosa came down to be there when Granny arrived home. Not once did I see Tata wipe a tear during all this period and yet Mam-nci Nopitoli, uncle Solomon's wife, says: 'Never in my life have I seen a man who has lost his wife weep and grieve as Bhuti did.' I believe it. Looking back, I think they were happy together. They did things together, and when she was gone, his life was a void. And then there were their children, the eldest of whom was seventeen and the youngest barely five, children who knew no other home but their mother's, children who had never spent a night even at Grandma's next door.

To lose a parent is a very traumatic experience for children. It can make or destroy them, depending on their ages and where they live. We were fortunate in our case for we had Tata, loving, patient, understanding, generous, tolerant. Tata played, as much as is humanly possible, the role of father and mother towards us. Even in our case the loss of a mother affected us profoundly, perhaps not so adversely for Ntangashe and me, as we had to learn quite early in our life how to cope, fend for ourselves and, above all, how to close ranks. We knew what solidarity was and what it could do for us. This lesson was to stand us well in later life.

Sis' Granny, though not quite out of her teens when Mama died, was by country standards grown up and that was why at nineteen she could get married. Besides, she had received all the training that Mama could have given her. Because of this, she was able to make a success of her marriage and could even look after us from a distance of seven miles.

The person, I think, adversely affected was Somhlophe, just thirteen at the time of Mama's death, no longer a child, but not yet a grown-up. There was no mother to tide her over this period of puberty, in spite of all the love and care Tata gave. She needed a mother to do it. Like the three of us, Somhlophe was strong, and in addition she had a charm that was infectious and exuded warmth. She was a gentle person. Because of these qualities she drew a large circle of all sorts of people as friends. And yet, for all these qualities, she tended to be less resourceful and leaned on Tata, Granny, Ntangashe and me, even though we two were younger than herself. Unfortunately, she married a very selfish man, a male chauvinist, who wanted to break her into what he thought a married woman should be. Upington Villie, her husband, would complain: 'Your father spoilt you and made you think you were white women.' Tata never taught us that. All he taught us was that we were the equals of everyone else and should never take second place to anybody, including men. Somhlophe could not handle this situation. She tried to meet the demands of her husband, but could not, for she was not brought up that way. So throughout her married life, she was not happy. Ntangashe, faced with such a situation, would have known what to do. I would have known too, I am sure.

Growing Up

But life must go on. We soon got back to the routine of school; chased butterflies as all children do; dug our wild turnips in the school paddock; swam in the deep pools of the Nqabarha behind the school.

Though I was much younger than most of my classmates, I soon made friends in school and earned respect because of my good grades. After a year in the sub-standards, three of us, all good friends – Vuyiswa Mbeki, Noma-Indiya Ntshanga and myself – were promoted to Standard 2, on condition that we kept our good grades and our good attendance.

A month after I had been promoted, I fell ill and had to be away from school. I cried and cried, fearing I would be sent back to Standard 1. It had been arranged that I should go to Colosa to my aunt Agnes, to be nursed. I refused, for if I went my attendance would be affected and Vuyiswa and Noma-Indiya would leave me behind. So an arrangement was made that as soon as I was better, I would attend school at Colosa and my attendance could be transferred. Only when I had been assured of this did I agree to go to Colosa. My aunt put her own condition: that while I was with her, Tata would not visit me, but would receive reports of my condition regularly. 'For if you come,' my aunt said, 'you know Phyllie will want to go home even if she is not well yet.'

Tata accepted these conditions. This was the trouble with us: we did not want to be away from Tata. Tata held out for two weeks. My sister Granny came to see me at the end of the first and second weeks. (Granny was now teaching in Old Idutywa in the same district.) On Friday of the third week, we had just come back from school, running in and out, putting away our slates and books, when I heard the neigh of Tata's horse even before he appeared. I ran out, shouting: 'There's Tata! There's Tata! There's Tata!' When he met my aunt he apologised, telling her the wait was too much for him. He missed me; the place was empty and Ntangashe was miserable without me. Because it was Friday and Granny would be home for the weekend, Tata spent that night at Colosa with us. We had a good time. I remained at Colosa one more week and then came home. Fortunately, the school term ended in April.

Looking back at my schooling, I see there was too much emphasis in our lessons on England, English culture and Europe. Hardly anything was said of Africa and very little about South Africa, except an excerpt in our Standard 3 reader on Sir George Grey, who was described as 'one of the wisest governors that ever came to South Africa'. Three things he set himself to do: to break the power of the Native chiefs, to stamp out superstition (to this end, Grey Hospital in King William's Town was established) and to eradicate ignorance and laziness among the Natives. I also recall 'A Post Office on Wheels' in our Standard 4 reader with pictures of the post coaches and the men hauling in the post or putting it into coaches. The text began: 'Imagine yourself at Euston Station. It is a foggy morning in London.' There was nothing about the 'talking drums' of Africa, used in conveying messages from person to person and from village to village. And while in the 'The Adventure with a Shark', we were shown Peterkin and his friend in the boat with a shark after them (and I can still hear Mzimkhulu Maphukatha read: 'Haul up the line, Peterkin! Quick! It's a shark!') we never learned that somewhere on the Zambezi, Lozi boys of the same age were paddling their dugouts, dodging crocodiles. All we knew of Africa were her big rivers, the Gold Coast and Egypt, which was somehow projected as part of Europe. We even recited 'The Loss of the Birkenhead', where one line reads 'our English hearts beat true'. With such brain-washing, it is a miracle we did not all become sell-outs and collaborators.

When I first started school, there were no trees around the premises. Those trees that form a wind-breaker on the north side were planted by us in the days of Rhodes Cakata, our principal teacher. We also started a school garden in groups of four students, except the little ones, each group managing a vegetable plot. Once a month there would be a feast for the schoolchildren and the teachers. The female teachers, Miss Dlova and Miss Ntshona, assisted by some of the mothers, would provide the baked goods. Mr Cakata and his assistant, Mr Bomela, both of whom came from families with a lot of sheep, would provide the meat. On such days, some mothers from the community would come to cook and feed the children. This was long before the days of school-feeding. My sister Granny, as wife of the principal teacher, was always there to supervise. She liked that role.

My happiest memories of school life are of that mission glebe on the bend of the Nqabarha River, playing rounders in front of the school gate or netball in the field near the big church bell; or going to concerts, when, after walking for miles to the venue of the concert, we would sing the whole night and would only feel the effects of the outing the next day. Those were the days of music competitions and eisteddfods. Even if we did not bring home the shield, our tears and sorrows were short-lived. We enjoyed the day in town, buying expensive sweets at Sparg's, or going to drink ginger-beer at Mrs Hill's by the river, or buying raisin buns at Vensky's bazaar.

Ntangashe and I were allowed to be involved in these concert-goings after Mama's death. She had never approved of concerts because they were all-night affairs. My sister Granny started going to concerts when she went to live with aunt Agnes at Colosa in Standards 5 and 6. Somhlophe was the backbone of the sopranos and the teacher could not afford not to have her at a concert. So weeks before the concert, the teacher and Tata would elicit a promise from Mama that Somhlophe would be allowed to attend. Even with that promise, Somhlophe would have to be on her best behaviour so as not to give Mama any excuse for gating her. Ntangashe and I never experienced that. Tata always came along to concerts and was proud, when he put his money on an encore from the choir from Duff, to mention that he had two daughters and a sister in that choir.

When I was barely six, I went to Umtata for the Prince of Wales's visit in 1925. Tata and my sister Granny thought I was too young to attend. But I felt I had to. A choir from our school was going and Ntangashe, though not in the choir, was also attending. Why should I not be allowed? I begged; I pleaded; I cried. In the end Tata gave permission. I do not even remember seeing any Prince of Wales, for whose sight I had shed such copious tears. All I remember is the train journey to Umtata; the children under the supervision of teachers from Duff, Thaleni, Colosa and Good Hope; sleeping on the train in Umtata; marching the next morning to some place with children in front and behind us; standing in the sun somewhere and then marching back to the train; and the journey home.

And yet my sisters and I were somewhat isolated, in that we only met and mixed with the other children at school. We never went to their homes to play; seldom did they come to our home to play, except when they accompanied their parents. The children we visited were those of the elite, when our parents went visiting.

But for all that, we could not be completely isolated from what was going on around us, for here was played out the whole drama of rural African life. In school we heard strange stories from the children of Bhongweni village. Stories of wild dogs that had been seen in the Colosa plantation; wild dogs that had attacked and killed people in these areas; or the story of the woman who ate people. She wore a red blouse, they told us, and appeared on foggy mornings or early evenings. This woman had already waylaid and attacked people in Gwadana and Qhorha villages and some had seen her in the Ngcingwane village, next door. And how scared we were of these wild dogs and this woman who ate people! We dreaded the months of February and March, for then thick fogs usually covered the valleys and the plains.

One autumn day, a day of thick fog, as Ntangashe and I were coming down the road through the ploughing fields, a head reared up. My sister called out, 'Phyllis! There's that wild dog!!' So saying, she grabbed me by the arm, and ran back with me. When we got to the top of the road, we stopped and looked behind us, only to see a young calf on its feet, beginning to stir itself and crop some grass. It must have been sleeping in the thick grass and our cries woke it up. We both exclaimed: *'Tyhini! Lithole!'* [It is but a calf!]

Here in school we learnt from the other children about the world they lived in after school, the world of young people's parties, called *iiTimiti* [tea meetings] and *imiBholorho* [parties for young people practising songs for a wedding and other occasions]. These songs were brought to school and sung during recess, away from the school house, down near the river. Good folk-dancers would dance to these, and now and again the boys would join in too, performing male dances. This was something to see! One popular song, sung at a *Timiti,* was of a young woman who had visited Qhakazana, a village about eight miles from us, where she met a handsome young man by the name of Jamangile. The song described what this dashing young man was wearing, the regalia of a country beau. Then the chorus would come in with:

> You are my hope, Jamangile,
> Your voice knows how to address a woman,
> Your smile is full of respect for a woman,
> Behold, here is a strapping young beau,
> Jamangile is his name.

To this day, this song brings to my mind the picture of the hunchback Nomtana Phukuza, singing it, eyes closed, her head gently swaying from side to side. She loved it and would sing it with that deep contralto voice of hers.

There is something very interesting about these country folksongs. From the words, all seem to have been composed by women, singing praises to a lover or appealing to him not to keep the beloved waiting. One such is where a young woman asks her young man:

> You rascal, how long are you going to keep me waiting?
> You rascal, do you realise it has been a long time?
> The sun is setting for me; the day is far spent.
> You wish to take me from my mother, a young maiden;
> Will you keep and treat me well?
> You wish to take me, young as I am;
> The question is: Will you look after me?
> You rascal, how long are you going to keep me waiting?
> The sun is setting for me; the day is far spent.

This was a wedding song which the bride's party sang, all of them voicing the bride's fears and her questions to the man she was marrying: 'Will you keep and look well after me?'

How could one not be touched by and be part of what was going on? It was in our church that weddings were performed, usually on Tuesdays. On these days, classes would be suspended for the morning and we would all assemble in the church at the back, with the two wedding parties, the groom's and the bride's, in front, one on each side. At the back we had a good view of the groom and the bride as they walked in and out of the church. How beautiful they looked, those brides, with head and eyes down, walking in on the arm of a father, brother or uncle. Then, half-way, the groom would come down to take his bride to the altar. I remember aunt Nomsisi Mathikinca, of all those beautiful brides, and her tall handsome groom, Berry Mrhasi, coming down the aisle to meet her. As they signed the register, the bride's party sang: *'Uz' ubhale kakuhle kwelo phepha lakho, kuba liya kude, phesheya ko lwandle.'* [Please write well on your paper for it is going far, far across the seas.] (The people thought the marriage register was not kept at the local office in Idutywa, but in some office overseas.)

After the ceremony, both parties rushed out, excited, ululating, declaiming about the bride and the groom. We schoolchildren were allowed out too, and with the two parties would stand in a semi-circle in front of the church door. In the meantime the groom's party would be singing: *'uYehov' ugqibile, uMfundisi uyalile aBangcikivi badanile; uxanase luphelile.'* [God's wish has been accomplished; the minister has advised and admonished. The envious and detractors have been foiled; all disputes have now been put to rest. Amen! Amen! It is all over. It is finished.] As aunt Nomsisi stepped out of the church door, aunt Ma-Miya, her uncle Isaiah's wife, stepped forward, throwing rice on them, ululating, inviting all to behold this gooseberry, smooth and shiny, just as a gooseberry coming out of its sheath, to behold this beautiful daughter of the No-Zulu, the Mbanguba, the Mpafane, they who came clad and adorned in fine regalia, looking fresh as the very treebuds in autumn. She spread her shawl for them to walk on. In competition, the groom's party was declaiming about their son, calling him 'the tall gum tree of the iBika forest'. To us schoolchildren, aunt Nomsisi looked just like that gooseberry. We never went to the house where the wedding party was going on. In fact, Tata's wedding was our first experience of a wedding at home.

In the villages of the red-blanket Africans, many of whom were our relatives, another drama of life was being played out. This was another world, a world of people stubbornly refusing to be touched by the new influences of school and church. This was a world of traditional ceremonies, of rites of passage for both boys and girls. Here were initiation schools for boys, hidden away in some valley or ridge-slope – settlements of grass-huts, cattle-folds, whose inhabitants painted their bodies white and wore sheep-skin karosses. The inhabitants were *abaKhwetha,* a common sight every three or four years in red villages in Transkei.

One initiation school site was on the ridge just below our ploughing fields. Now and again, when we were in the fields, we would have glimpses of these 'animals', the *abaKhwetha.* To us children, they did look like animals. It was hard to recognise them as the boys we knew. We were scared of them. Then some day at dusk, two or three of them (our relatives) would slip into our cattle-fold and start coughing to draw attention. Our herd-boys would run in to see who these were. Excited, they would run back to report to Tata that so-and-so were in the cattle-fold. Tata would then go out to meet them, exchange greetings and then walk to the sheep-fold, pick a harmel and ask the herd-boys to take it to the *abaKhwetha,* who would drive it to their settlement.

Our herd-boys never slept at home on such days, but at the school. In fact, the initiation school became a meeting-place for boys of the village, boys aged ten to sixteen. Here in the school there was always plenty of food – meat, milk, cooked food.

During harvest time, one could see the *abaKhwetha,* ten to fifteen of them, helping in the fields, bringing in the harvest. The rest of the reapers, especially women, would be confined to one side of the field for *abaKhwetha* may not be seen or meet their mothers or any women the age of their mothers. After the harvest was brought in, the people would relax, and this was the time for the great *imiDudo* and *imiTshilo* gatherings, when the *abaKhwetha* would entertain the community. I have watched them, clad in their short skirts of dry palm leaves, with coloured braid hanging from their knees to the ankles, and more braid from the upper arms, wearing their masks of dry palm leaves, passing on the road just outside our fence, going to dance next door at uncle Rhamba's place. The *iKhankatha* would be prancing and dancing in front of them as he led them into the courtyard. The women would already have started beating the ox-hide *(iNgqongqo)* and singing to its rhythm. Then the dance would begin and the whole place would be agog with excitement.

The women, all clad in their finest beads and bracelets, with large multi-coloured *doeks* on their heads, would have perhaps stopped at our house, to look at themselves in No-Might's tall mirror. They would come all excited: 'Woman, please let us look at ourselves in your big mirror.' Their faces would be painted with red clays, amber, beige and white, tastefully applied and not covering the whole face. Entering Mama's room, each would look at herself with her shawl on, then with her shawl off, turning around and around as a model does, her companions complimenting her. At the end of it all, one or two would dance for Mama, showing her what they were going to do and how they danced to the songs. I remember Nonginya, Gerber's mother, in her big voice, singing and dancing for Mama to her favourite song:

uNyawo lwe Gqwirha lub'emzini Hamba,
   Ngxwashul' ekhaya.
Lwagqith' enkundleni kwafa' amathole;
Hamba, Ngxwashul' ekhaya
[The tread of a wizard is a bad omen in a homestead;
When he passes through the courtyard, calves die.
Go, Big-foot, threatening the homes].

They would make sure before they came in that Tata was not home, for all feared and respected Sa-Mzolisa. So we would be posted at the door to see that Sa-Mzolisa was not coming.

Though the *Mtshilo* took place at uncle Rhamba's just fifty yards from our house, we were never allowed to go there. We would sit half-way between the two homesteads, satisfying ourselves with fleeting sights of what was going on. It was years later, when I was at Fort Hare, that I told Tata I had never seen an *uMtshilo* and would love to see one.

'You have never seen one?' he asked.

'Of course not. Have you forgotten that you never allowed us to go to such places?'

Fortunately, for me, there was an initiation school that year in one of the neighbouring villages, and by special request, one *Mtshilo* was staged for my benefit, even though the season had not yet started. When I saw it, I knew why these dances provoked so much excitement and why the good dancers from each school became famous for generations after.

Coming home one winter holiday, I found a lot of excitement among my red-blanket aunts and cousins. Preparations were afoot for my cousin Nomavila and my aunt Nongakubani to go through the adult rite of passage – *iNtonjane*. This is a rite that a girl experiences after she has had her menses, to prepare her for womanhood and marriage. Both girls and parents look forward to this with great excitement. For a month or so, the girl is secluded in a separate house, only going out early in the morning and at night, when there are not many people about. In the house where she is secluded, there gather at night her age group – boys and girls – under the watchful eye of two chaperons. During the whole month, the young people meet here to sing, dance and make love. They have a lot of fun.

The end of the rite would be marked by a big feast – the coming of the girl. On this day she is given presents by her parents, relatives and friends. It is during this period, too, that her parents know officially who her boyfriend is, for on an appointed day, while still in seclusion, the boyfriend sends her presents – a washing-basin, toilet soap, a towel, comb, mirror and other ornaments of brass and beads.

As senior member of the family, Tata had to give approval for every ceremony and ritual within the family. Protocol demanded this, though it was known he would not be there. Even uncle Joel Hleli had come to Tata because his ancestors were calling him (to become a diviner) and he could not answer that call until some ritual had been observed. This put Tata in a dilemma, for as a Christian it was one ritual he would not observe. Uncle Joel, fed up with Tata and his Christianity, left. But when he came years later, Tata referred him to one of my uncles, a non-Christian, who helped him out.

Tata always went to the ceremony to give the 'go-ahead' for the feast to begin. Sometimes we came along with him. Meeting some members of the family assembled there, he would find out from the senior man among them if everything was all right. After the report, he would delegate that man to take charge and to see that all procedures of protocol were observed. He would then ask for leave to go, and depart.

A very respectful people, these my red-ochred relatives! When they visited us they made a point of sitting in the kitchen or on the veranda, so as not to stain with their ochre the beautiful things of the 'school woman'. Even when they went into her room to look at themselves in the big, tall mirror, they walked in gingerly, making sure that their skirts did not touch anything.

They were excited about us and called each one of us by a nickname. Granny was Gleni (a corruption of Granny), Somhlophe was Cikicane or Chiki, Ntangashe was Rhinirhini, I was Nomfilazana or Filifili or Nogqaza, names I still love to this very day. They would hug and shower us with kisses when they came. Ntangashe did not quite like this. I understand that when she was a toddler, she would protest saying: *'Ndinonika ukusulelwa yimboka'* [I am afraid of getting stained with ochre], when they invited her for a kiss. 'Nonsense! What are you afraid of? Don't you know we are your red-ochred kinswomen?' they would say.

I would be all over them when they came. I could not wait for that aunt or cousin to unstrap her baby from her back and let me cradle it. Even at that age, I wanted to carry those babies on my back. Some of them allowed me to, making sure I did not walk about with the baby. By the end of the day, I would be ochre all over. Mama always said: 'My poor child! She loves babies so, but her mother does not have any.'

Ntangashe loved them too and knew they were our relatives. But they belonged to another world, a world she did not quite know or understand. It could not be otherwise with us, for if anyone at home used foul language or a word considered uncouth, he or she was told or threatened with *'Uyakubhek' emaqabeni'* [You will be sent away to live with the ochred non-school people]. To this very day, I find it difficult to use ordinary, clean Xhosa words, words I was taught euphemisms for. It is easier for me to say these words in English or Afrikaans than in Xhosa, for when I grew up these words were considered uncouth and vulgar.

And yet even in this world, the old ways of life were gone. The tall, big mirror in No-Might's room at which my aunts and grandmas came to look at themselves, the wash-basin, mirror and soap which the young lover gave to his girlfriend when she went into seclusion, the Venables shop from which they got their supplies and to which they sold their wool and produce, the magistrate's court in Idutywa, were all evidence that the old order no longer existed. A new culture, an amalgam of the old and new was emerging; a culture that is the dynamic reality through which people express their desire to make their life worth living. For had they not all, school and non-school people, been drawn into the economy of the West? Were some of them not already destined to leave these areas, never to return, but to live and die in the cities, mines and farms of South Africa, where they would be excluded from living any meaningful, fruitful life?

It is very interesting that the most vocal and persistent resistance to government measures against the rural Africans came mostly from the non-school people. They were the ones the progressive elite in the people's organisations could depend on in the rural areas, knowing that they would not sell out. Perhaps this should not surprise us if we remember they had resisted the missionaries and their message from the start, as well as the Bhunga system of councils set up by Cecil John Rhodes, which was, to them, suspect from the beginning, and none of them ever offered themselves as candidates.

Tata had always been a member of the Transkeian General

Council, the Bhunga as it was called. This body was set up under the Glen Grey Act of 1894, as a local administrative body in Transkei. Cecil John Rhodes, prime minister and father of the Council system, had created these bodies to give Africans the illusion that they were governing themselves. This is what Cecil John Rhodes said in support of his motion to establish the Council: 'They [Africans] are a very clever people, fond of argument and debate; so we must give them something to occupy their minds, for if we don't, within a hundred years, nay, I say fifty, they will be debating with us in these chambers.' Suspecting none of these motives, the educated of the Transkei took their Council system very seriously. They knew it was advisory, but they thought their advice would be taken seriously by the government, as it came from the majority of the people. So serious were they about it that on the opening day the councillors came in their morning suits – striped plain-bottom pants, tails and top hats – like members of other parliaments. This was theirs.

Through the Bhunga the Transkei accomplished a few good things, chief of which were the establishment of three agricultural colleges, the Fort Hare Scholarship Fund for their sons and daughters, and the Transkeian Bhunga contribution to Fort Hare.

The councillors came from all twenty-six districts of Transkei. Four were elected by the people in each district, two nominated by the magistrates, with the magistrates being *ex officio* members of the Council who had no vote in Council meetings. The members from the twenty-six districts then met once a year in Umtata as the General Council. Here were brought, debated and passed resolutions from the various districts. On going back home, the councillors called those who had elected them for a report-back meeting. In our area this report-back meeting was always held at our home. The men from the area came to hear the report and to ask their councillor questions pertaining to their lives.

On such days, Ntangashe and I would relocate our doll village to be within earshot of the men assembled by the side of the cattle-fold. We wanted to hear Tata give the report and answer questions and also to listen to the discussion that would follow. On one occasion, Tata told the people: 'No, my people, the government does not want to hear a thing about our children being trained in the use of arms. This is one resolution from the Bhunga they do not even refer to when they reply.' One red-blanket man, Gabiso, remarked: 'So, in all these years, the government does not trust us. Haven't we shown them over the years that we are willing to live with them? A white man is really difficult to understand!' Another one, Caley Gxoko, replied: 'No, Leta, it is not that they do not trust us; they know that the day we, too, have this stick [gun] whose sound makes men mess themselves up and we can shoot them back, that will be the end of their arrogance.'

Tata and Me

I not only look like him, I am his finished product. He raised me, nurtured me, moulded me and instilled in me values that I will treasure to the end of my days, values that made me socially conscious. I sensed Tata's wish and hope for me and I tried my best not to fall short of those expectations. We had always been close, even before Mama died – as in fact were all his children – and we drew closer after Mama's death. The only thing that is not Tata in me is that I am an extrovert – a Balfour trait – for Tata was somewhat reserved. This man was not only my parent, he was my teacher and best friend. The best moments of my life were with him. We would sit together chatting and discussing any and every topic that was within my understanding, with me asking him this and that question. He engaged in these conversations with all of us, his girls. With Tata, even shy, quiet Ethel would blossom. Even when Mama still lived, we missed Tata when he was not there. After we got married, we came home because we missed him.

At home I was with him everywhere – in the cattle-fold, at the stables, in the ploughing fields, on the veranda, talking, talking and asking questions. I knew they had hoped for a boy when I was born and the people around would say in my presence: 'Why didn't God make this one a boy? She is not as beautiful as the other girls.' So I made up my mind to be as much of a son as I could, doing those things that sons are supposed to do. And how Ntangashe and I prayed for that son! In our doll play, when we had church service, we never forgot to ask God 'to give this family a son'. Even though this prayer was for one of our doll families, it was in fact our parents we were praying for. That son was to come some eight years later, with the arrival of Mzukisi (Nqokothwana), my stepmother's first-born. That is why this child has such a special place in our hearts. We had prayed for him.

I was going to be the son Tata had hoped for! So when he came back from work, I was there holding the bridle of his horse as he alighted, helping him unsaddle the horse, and if the horse had to be watered, I would give it water. If he was mending a fence, a bench, or a gate, fixing a window, sealing a leaking trough, I was there to hold and hand him his tools. As a result, today there are very few do-it-yourself chores I cannot do around the house. As we had no boys and Tata depended on hired help, he worked with us in the fields, planting and cultivating, leading the team of oxen or the horse he used. It was joy working with him for he had a way with children, showering praises on those working with him. At the end of a work-day, he would stand in the kitchen door to remind those there that he would need a warm bath and would say: 'Please don't forget Phyllie.' How considerate! how wonderful! how beautiful!

The herd-boys could not always be relied upon. Sometimes they absconded, leaving the stock unattended in the pasture. On such occasions we had to fill in until a new herd-boy was hired. Or the herd-boys would leave at critical times – stock-dipping days – and we, the girls, had to take our cattle to the dipping tank. It was at these times that I witnessed bull fights. Our bull, Roland, was a champion fighter. The inspectors at the dipping tanks were always very kind to us. They would ask the other herders to stand down for us, so that our stock would go in first, and we would not wait long in the queue.

My first lessons in the history of the Wars of Dispossession were from Tata. Having been born at the end of these wars, he had learnt from those around him a lot about them and had grown to be a local historian of sorts. I would sometimes pick up something, or bits of a story in his conversation with another man, sitting on the veranda or under the trees. Then when we were alone I would ask him: 'Tell me what happened to Makana after he surprised the British at Grahamstown'.

Tata would then relate the whole incident and how the British never forgave Makana for their near-defeat at Grahamstown. And that was why they did not treat him with honour when he came to negotiate. They captured him and sent him to Robben Island, where he and others escaped one Christmas morning. He was drowned just a few miles off the shore of Cape Town, Tata told me. But the

Xhosa still believed that Makana would come back and lead them to victory, hence the Xhosa saying *'Ukuza kuka Nxele'.*

One day, Tata had been chatting with his good friend Oom Joel Nombewu of Chizele. I caught this bit from Oom Nombewu:

> *Kou! into ka Matiwane!*
> *Umsila gojela phantsi kwe Ntab'e Nqadu*
> *Usidl' imizila yamadoda;*
> *Udada ngesabhokhwe kuma Khumsha.*

Some days later, when we were alone, I asked Tata who this *'Dada ngesabhokhwe kuma Khumsha'* was. 'That is Mhlontlo, son of Matiwane, king of the Mpondomise. He was the centre of the so-called Mpondomise Rebellion.' After eluding the British forces for months, Mhlontlo fled to Lesotho, where he remained for some years until his capture, having been betrayed by Jonathan, son of Moshoeshoe, and the Roman Catholic priests. Tata told me that Mhlontlo was brought home a prisoner. Standing on the Nqadu mountain, he looked around and saw his land all fenced in. He cried like a child, saying: 'Where were the people? Where were the people that such a thing could happen?' It was years later, from my husband, that I was to hear the details of the killing of Hamilton Hope, magistrate of Qumbu, and the flight of Mhlontlo, how he hid for months among the Mpondo of Mqikela, who sheltered him until a place had been found for him in Lesotho.

We were sitting by the hedge at home one day when Tata told me the story of the flight of Sarhili and his people after the War of Ngcayechibi. And because the places mentioned in the story were places in Idutywa – Bende, Falakahla, Gwadana, Chizele, Ncihana, Mbashe – the story assumed a life of its own. He used to like describing how, after a night on the banks of Mbashe River, Sarhili himself, under cover of a thick fog, led his people across the river and not a beast was lost. Tata would say, 'The Gcaleka will tell you that the dusky son of Nomsa, after he had ordered all to wake up, pointed south, pointed north, pointed east and pointed west, and a thick fog enveloped them and he led his people across. If you were to say that it could not have been so, the Gcaleka would kill you.' And then he would laugh.

When he was a student at Zonnebloem in Cape Town, he had seen in the Cape Town Castle the cell where Cetywayo, king of the Zulu, had been kept, and also the cell where Langalibalele, king of the Hlubi, had been. I was to see these too when I came to live in

Cape Town.

In those days our Xhosa readers comprised a series from Standards 1 to 4, written by Candlish Koti, Mama's cousin, and published by Longmans Green and Company. In the Standard 3 book were the praise poems of some of the African monarchs of the period of resistance. I went through several of those poems with Tata; he explained to me the meanings and events surrounding the incidents mentioned. For example, Tata explained to me why the bard refers to Sigcawu Mqikela, king of the Mpondo, as

> *I-Nunw' emsil'ulurholokoqo*
> *uxab' ezindlini zabe Lungu*
> *kwezo Meje noMadonela.*
> [The huge snake whose long tail bars the entrance to the dwellings of the white men, even those of Major [Elliot] and McDonald].

According to Tata, when the British captured Sigcawu and locked him up in the jail in Kokstad, the Mpondo followed him to prison, refusing to have their king sleep there alone. There was no room for all the crowds who came, asking to be locked up with their king, and the British were forced to let Sigcawu out.

The praises of Sigcawu Mthikrakra contain these lines:

> *Ngumahob' azizantanta ngenxa yokhozi,*
> *Ma-Rhudulu! lozililela neliswel' amaphiko!*
> [He, in whose domain the doves are aflutter
>   for fear of the falcon.
> I swear by the Rhudulu, woe unto that one
>   that has no wings].

Sigcawu Mthikrakra, I was told, was a cruel king whose people deserted him and sought refuge with other kings.

Veldman Bikitsha's praises have the line:

> *Siyawubanga lomti ka Bhokolo.*
> [We claim this tree of Bowker].

This was explained to me as referring to a trader, Bowker, who had a store in the area when the British carved up Sarhili's country. They fixed this store as the boundary between the Xhosa and the belt of Mfengu whom the British had settled here as buffer. Veldman Bikitsha, a Mfengu, collaborated with the British throughout this period. As a reward he was given a farm in Nkondwane in the district of Centane.

Sarhili, the Xhosa king, is associated with the line:

Nguzwe lafa ngembiza zika Mbune.
[He whose land died on account of Mbune's beer-pots].
Here the bard castigates the king for allowing the country to go to war over a quarrel that started at a beer-party, when the people involved were already drunk. The bard could correct the king if he felt he was wrong, Tata told me, and that was why there were those lines in Sarhili's praise-song.

I do not remember getting any 'don'ts' from Tata in our growing up. We knew in a way what he wanted of us and what he expected us to be and not to be. Throughout our life we were guided by: What will Tata think? Will this hurt him? Will this please him? And throughout, we tried to do those things that would please him, things he could be proud of.

The Lean Years

In mid-January the schools opened and many people left our house. Granny was going to teach at Old Idutywa, eight miles away, and could only come home on weekends. Somhlophe had left for eMgwali Training School for Girls, near Dohne in the Stutterheim district. By the end of January, only Tata, Ntangashe, myself and the help were left at home. But aunt Daisy, still at Grandma's, took charge.

Even though Tata was working (he was clerk in the Land Office in Idutywa) and had to be in the office by nine in the morning, he saw to it that Ntangashe and I were fed before we left for school. He established a routine, whereby he would be in the kitchen fixing breakfast, while Ntangashe and I made the beds and got ourselves ready for school. Together we would have breakfast and then be off to school and he to work.

When we came back in the afternoon, there was always *amasi* (sour milk) in a jug for us. There were usually plenty of vegetables, and Ntangashe and I would pick some to cook for the evening meal. By the time Ntangashe was ten, meal preparation was in her hands more or less, with Tata pitching in now and then. Making the beds and tidying up were my chores and sometimes we would do these jointly, Ntangashe and I. Though we never said it to each other, we were determined to keep Mama's house as tidy as we had known it. Mrs Qavane (aunt Ma-Mlambo) came to do the washing every week and sometimes the ironing. But it was Tata who ironed our clothes regularly.

Granny came home on weekends, and would sit around reading papers, then go to Grandma's to chat with whoever was there. Tata would complain: 'Granny, when you are home, do give my children a rest.'

To which she always replied: 'These kids are big. They can do the work.'

Ntangashe and I wondered just what she would do when she got married; she was so lazy. She would be a disgrace, we told each other.

Early in April, a telegram came saying that Somhlophe was ill. Before Tata had decided what to do another one came: 'Very ill. Anything can happen.' Tata left immediately for eMgwali. The neighbours came every day to pray for him and my sister throughout the period he was away. That Sunday in church, the congregation said special prayers for Somhlophe. When all these people came home for the prayer meeting, aunt Daisy was there to receive them. In this she was assisted by aunt Ma-Miya, the same who comforted Somhlophe as we were leaving the graveyard on the day of Mama's funeral.

Tata sent a telegram from eMgwali: 'Crisis over. Coming home with Nonkululeko.' They came home amid the joys of everyone in the community. God had heard their prayers. Somhlophe was always a favourite of all the local people. With Somhlophe at home, the burden of work no longer lay so much on Ntangashe and me, and Tata was relieved of his kitchen duties. However, he never slackened in his ironing duties.

Gradually, our way of life was completely changed by aunt Daisy, who remained still at Grandma's and supervised at our house. We, who used to eat at the table, were now being taught to sit on the floor when we ate, eating from one basin. We, who never shared our clothes, even among ourselves, were now made to share them with her sister-in-law's daughter who was with her. Both Ntangashe and I resented this, and we reported to Tata. Tata stopped at once the sharing of our clothes. Aunt Daisy was always complaining too about Somhlophe and her friends. Somhlophe had not returned to eMgwali after her illness, so was home for that whole year. Here was a fourteen-year-old, at home, with very little to do! Aunt Daisy thought she was getting out of hand and had to be bridled. One day Somhlophe and Granny came back late from town. The sun had already set. Aunt Daisy was furious with them. She demanded to know who had been with them in town. Not satisfied with whatever answer they gave, she went to Tata to ask him to find out. Tata quietly said: 'Daisy, please don't cause trouble between me and my children. They know what I expect of them.' Aunt Daisy was furious. She could not understand it.

She had her good points, though. Now that she was here with us, we could wrap ourselves up in her shawls on cold days when we went to school. This was a privilege we had never enjoyed in Mama's days: we used to wear coats to school, and how Ntangashe hated that black coat of hers! As soon as she was out of Mama's sight, she would throw the coat over her shoulders as one wears a blanket. All the other children in school came wrapped up in mothers', aunts' or sisters' shawls, big and small. How I used to envy Fannie Guduza, wrapped in her Grandma's big woollen shawl. She looked so warm and comfortable in it. I think aunt Daisy even bought us little shawls to wear to school. With that all her sins were forgiven.

Aunt Daisy liked reading to us, and from the way she did so she must have been a good teacher. I remember the day she read us the book *Nomalizo* by Enoch Guma. When she opened the dialogue with *'Nomalizo! Nomalizo! Yiz'apha mntanam!'*, I thought she was calling her daughter Nomalizo. Another story aunt Daisy read well was 'Little Red Riding Hood', especially the dialogue between Little Red Riding Hood and the wolf.

Aunt Daisy had been a teacher before she married and continued to teach afterwards, because they could not find a qualified teacher where she was. She told us that her mother-in-law advised her to shorten her skirts because she was teaching. 'How will you manage with those long skirts, NoHohita [her married name] my child, when you take drill exercises with the schoolchildren?' So aunt Daisy wore her skirts mid-calf.

Life was rather rugged at home. Somhlophe had, the following year, gone back to school at Lovedale, and Granny was engaged to a young Idutywa man teaching at Healdtown. Tata was under pressure to get married. How could so big a household be without a wife to look after things and his children? people were saying.

In April of that year, Tata resigned his position as clerk in the Land Office. What precipitated his resignation was a case of bribery and fraud against the assistant magistrate and one of the clerks in the same office. Tata offered to give evidence against these two on behalf of a red-blanket man who had been cheated out of his piece of land. Because of the shortage of land, the Land Offices in the rural areas were as corrupt as the Pass Offices in the urban areas.

Tata was a terror to those assistant magistrates. He brooked no non-sense from them and would beat them up right in their offices if they were rude to him or showed any arrogance towards him; they always lost their jobs into the bargain.

Africans of Tata's age had joined the civil service when it still embodied the old British tradition of service to the people. The mag-istrates, even though white, and the white clerks knew they were there to serve and were seldom rude to the African members of the service with whom they worked. As these British-trained magistrates retired, they were replaced by South African whites, young and arro-gant, full of their whiteness. Tata took no nonsense from them and unfortunately for them, when they went to complain to the magis-trate – an older fellow who had worked with Tata – they were told: 'You must have provoked him. He is one of the finest gentlemen we have in these offices and would never assault you unless under extreme provocation.' After such an incident, the assistant magistrate would be told he was being transferred or his service was being ter-minated. The African policemen, Khweza and Jayiya, liked Tata for handling these rude assistants in this way and they would relate the stories with relish.

When Tata broke the news of his resignation to Granny, she asked: 'But how are you going to manage, with a child at boarding school and these two still to follow?'

Tata answered: 'I cannot bear to see the life of these two so rugged. I must be home to take care of them. I'll manage.' Then, pointing to the ploughing fields behind the home, he said: 'Do you see this land behind us? I'm going to till it and live on its produce. I'll raise, improve and increase my stock. I'll manage.'

And he did just that and saw us all through school – first the three of us from his first family and then the nine from his second.

Second Marriage

Tata came under pressure to find a wife to help him run his home. Friends and relatives were scouting around for a suitable girl, and suggestions were coming from all sides. I would not be surprised if some women offered themselves or that some mothers offered their daughters. At forty-two he was a very eligible widower and a man of means, who had almost everything that most women look for in a marriage – security and position.

Sis' Millie, Mama's niece, strongly recommended a young woman who was a teacher from All Saints, Engcobo, and from a well-known family. Sis' Millie even sent Tata a picture of the woman, a picture that hung on the wall in the room for some time. Sis' Millie knew Tata very well; she knew his likes and dislikes, having stayed with her aunt, my mother, before she got married. Her candidate was a good woman with a good background and would not only make a good wife, but would also be good to the children, Sis' Millie had written. Then there were three others – one in the Umtata district and the other two in the Butterworth and Centane districts.

The Qhushekas in eGoso, the people of Malume Menziwa's mother, also came with an open recommendation for a woman from among the Mgudlwa princesses at Qhumanco, a royal family of the Jumba house of the Thembu. Tata followed this lead. In all this he consulted with his daughter Granny and his cousin Agnes, because most of these women were about their ages and either had been to Lovedale or eMgwali and knew them or knew about them.

With his friend Oom Joel Nombewu, Tata headed in his Cape cart for Qhumanco to find himself a wife from among the Mgudlwa princesses. They asked to be directed to the royal house of the Mgudlwas, and were told that Theodore Hlathikhulu, son of Falo

Mgudlwa, was the one who held court here. To this court they went and made known the purpose of their visit. Yes, this house had a princess, unmarried, Edwina Thandiwe, second daughter and fourth child of Theodore Hlathikhulu Mgudlwa by his wife No-India, granddaughter of Maqoma, the warrior-king and first-born son of Ngqika. Here was a mother, a princess of royal birth! No girl could have better credentials. They were hooked and by the time they came back all the preliminaries had been finalised.

The Mgudlwas wanted for *lobola* (bridewealth) thirty head of cattle, fifty sheep and two horses, especially Tata's racing stallion Thembu, of which they had heard so much. Tata pleaded that he could not give them Thembu. He was prepared to give two horses instead of this one. This was accepted.

When Tata came home his kinsmen exclaimed: 'Thirty head of cattle! Are you crazy? What sort of princess is this one? That's *lobola* for three girls!' G.G. – as Tata was popularly known – was not to be moved; he had accepted the Mgudlwa challenge, and no one was going to make him withdraw. When both Granny and aunt Agnes, his cousin, heard which one of the Mgudlwa girls this was, they remarked: 'Why not Judith? She is tall and more beautiful. Or even the aunt, Nobengula, she is more comely!'

The day the thirty head of cattle were brought in from the cattle-post to be driven to Qhumanco, they filled our whole yard. As they were driven out, aunt Daisy cried: 'My father's cattle! My father's cattle!!' This is usually an exciting moment, with the women of the home ululating, calling in excitement: 'Bring her home! Bring her home!' I do not remember any of them doing that. They all stood in wonderment and quietly exclaiming: 'So many cattle!' Even those who wanted to ululate could not, with aunt Daisy crying: 'My father's cattle! My father's cattle!'

Yes, aunt Daisy was right, these cattle were her father's which were shared among the children when Govan, their father, died. What Tata had acquired during his first marriage he could not touch. The will he drew up did not allow it. All that property was to be divided among us, his four girls. He had usufruct rights to it for as long as it remained with him. Of his inheritance from his father's stock, with thirty head of cattle gone, perhaps he was left with only half.

They drove all that stock to Qhumanco. The third horse followed after the wedding. Tata and Edwina Thandiwe Mgudlwa were married early in December, the end of his second year of widowhood. It was a big wedding, both at Qhumanco and at home. Ntangashe and I did not go to Qhumanco. Only Granny and Somhlophe went. Aunt Colosa had come down weeks before to see to the smooth running of things. Mama's sisters, Annie, Queenie and Margaret, were there too; so were Mama's brothers, Menziwa and Colenso. Uncle Menziwa accompanied Tata to Qhumanco to fetch his bride.

On the wedding day, Sis' Ma-Zangwa, who had come back for the occasion, assisted by Mrs Phetheni and Mrs Tolbatt, excelled in their catering. My people had heard that the Mgudlwas were a sophisticated lot; *wath'umntu kuzakudlan'iintsimbi namhlanje*, we are going to show them what stuff we are made of.

When my red-blanket aunts saw the Mgudlwa women who had come down, accompanying their kinswoman, they said: 'The Mgudlwas cheated Sa-Mzolisa [Tata]. This woman is too short for him. Why didn't they give him this one, Judith, the cousin, or this one, Nobengula, the aunt?' This was the same remark Granny and aunt Agnes had made when they heard which of the Mgudlwa girls it was.

In the afternoon of the wedding day, aunt Colosa took Ntangashe and me to Tata in the room. He had not seen us for a week and in the excitement he did not know how we were doing. He was sitting on his bed, tie and jacket off, in his stockinged feet, resting. When we saw him, we both ran to him and he folded us in his arms, kissing us all over our faces. He asked us to sit at his feet and asked aunt Colosa to bring us food.

'They have already been fed, Bhuti,' Colosa said.

'No, I want to see them eat,' he responded.

We sat in the room there with him watching us eat. We did not have much to say to each other. People were going in and out of the room. Then it was time for him to go to supper with the bridal party. We had missed him. He had missed us too and must have been feeling guilty that in the excitement he had neglected us.

At the end of the wedding, the guests left. My aunts, Annie, Queenie and Margaret, and uncle Colenso stayed for a few more days to introduce themselves to their new 'sister'. They liked her and she liked them too. Uncle Menziwa stayed longer, and had nothing but praise for this princess so nobly born. Colosa stayed for two weeks more.

The first night we were alone as a family, with only aunt Daisy and aunt Colosa there, Tata read from the Bible the portion which says: 'You are all members of the same body. If one member is diseased, then the whole body is affected.' As our new life unfolded, I knew why he had read that.

Before she left, Colosa called Somhlophe, Ntangashe and myself and said to us: 'This is your mother. You are not to call her anything but Mama. If you accept her, she will accept you. Anything you want, you ask her; never go direct to your father now that she is here, nor complain to him about her. Remember always that your father can no longer devote the same attention to you as he did before. He has someone now to share his life with. Make no demands on him for his time. Edwina is his partner and she is your mother.'

It is amazing how such admonitions stick with one. To this day, I cannot speak of Edwina as my stepmother, but always as Mama. I remember years after, at Fort Hare, when Mrs Matthews, who had known Edwina at Lovedale, asked me how she could have such a big girl already, I could not for the life of me tell her that Edwina was my stepmother. I heard Colosa saying: 'Never call her anything but Mama.'

Colosa said goodbye and we were left alone with Tata and our new mother. My poor stepmother was a coddled princess who had never been trained for any position of responsibility, even the responsibility of providing for the basic needs (except sex) of the husband she would marry, let alone his children or the welfare of her own children when they came. What was worse, she had never been taught the art of good human relations. Plunged into a position of great responsibility, how could she cope? How was she to handle it successfully? And yet, if she had known the art of human relations, many would have served her with pleasure and compensated for all those shortcomings. But unfortunately, she thought that every young woman was there to seduce her husband. And people left, even those who tried to help.

How tragic that some parents, in bringing up their children this way, never think of the time when the children will be on their own in the world. When her son Mzukisi was a year old, my stepmother wanted him to be brought up by her people. Tata left the child there for only a year and had him brought home, saying: 'I can never have my child brought up by the Mgudlwas, people who do not know how to train children.' This was from what he saw of their daughter – the lack of social grace, the lack of responsibility.

Everything seemed all right at first. The old friends dropped in now and again. Preparations were afoot for Granny's wedding to the Healdtown teacher, now principal at Duff. Early in the year Somhlophe had gone back to Lovedale. Sis' Ma-Zangwa was itching to go, telling us that she was just waiting to cook the dinner for Granny's wedding during the Easter break. Again Malume Menziwa came for Granny's wedding and so did Colosa, to help Mama with all the work. They seemed to hit it off well with their new 'sister' and she liked both of them.

Colosa left soon after Granny's wedding. But before she left, she called Ntangashe and me aside and said to us: 'Now, Granny is gone, married; gone to join another family. She no longer belongs here. Things, unpleasant perhaps, are going to happen to you. I beg you, my sister's children, never run to Granny to report anything. I do not want her to come here to cause trouble between your father and his wife. As I said to you before, do not go to your father with any reports of what your mother is doing to you. If and when things are bad, your father will notice it. Keep everything between the two of you, comforting each other.' And didn't we heed that advice!

Granny never got any reports from us about our life at home, not even when, as the principal's wife, she came to the school. What reports she received were from neighbours who would plead with her to visit home now and again for our sake, because we were just fending for ourselves, our stepmother did not care for us, and most miserable was Ntangashe, whom she seemed not to like.

My stepmother never abused us – never beat us up or called us names. It was just a case of benign neglect. She knew no better. So it is difficult to blame her. Granny never came; we never went to her house. She saw us on those occasions she came to the school, sometimes delivering dresses she had made for us.

We soon noticed that while our stepmother was prepared to accept me, she did not quite accept Ntangashe, who was shy, quiet and reserved. Perhaps she thought that this child who took time to warm to people, did not accept her, and she could not handle that. She would give me things – a treat perhaps – and not give Ntangashe. I would ask, 'What about Ntangashe?', and if it was not forthcoming, I would not accept mine. At one time, my stepmother wanted to take me to Qhumanco with her to meet her people who had heard so much about me from Tata. I asked if Ntangashe was coming too. When she said 'no', I told her I would not go anywhere without Ntangashe.

Early one autumn, Ntangashe went down with a severe attack of bronchitis. She was very ill. Tata and I took turns nursing her. Tata would leave some broth with me to give to Ntangashe, even if it was just one spoonful, and also to give her the medicine. I remember pleading with Ntangashe to take just one spoonful of the broth, because she would die if she did not. When she fell asleep, I would run outside to play, only to run back shortly, and bend over her to find out if she was still breathing. I was scared. I was a child only nine years old. I cried and prayed to God to save my sister, not to let my Ntangashe die. I have never prayed for a life as I did on that occasion. I had not lost my faith.

Tata would come in the afternoon, sponge Ntangashe, give her the medicine, coax her to take some broth, make her comfortable, and when she fell asleep, he would go to the house. He would come back again to sit up with Ntangashe in the night. Not once during that whole period did my stepmother come into that rondavel where the child lay sick. She saw Ntangashe again when she was strong enough to drag herself to the kitchen.

During this period of Ntangashe's recovery, Tata, on coming home one evening, asked Edwina how Ntangashe was. They were in the room together and I was in the dining-room, getting teacups.

'Leave me alone!' shouted Edwina. 'I do not want your children!'

I can still hear the pain in Tata's voice when he asked: 'Just tell me, Edwina, why do you hate my children? What have they ever done to you? Please, please tell me!'

Now that I have children of my own, I know just how hurt Tata was when he heard that outburst, 'I do not want your children!', that afternoon in the room.

Aunt Colosa had told us to go to our stepmother for anything that we wanted. We did, telling her we needed this and that for school. But she never did anything about our requests. So on one occasion in desperation, we – Somhlophe, Ntangashe and I – sent a joint letter to Tata with the list of the things we wanted for school. We slipped the letter under his pillow, each one fearing to give it to him. When he saw it and read it, he came to us in our room to ask us why we had written him a letter.

'Because Colosa had told us never to come to you direct, but ask through Mama. We have done so. But nothing has happened and schools are opening soon,' said Somhlophe.

'I understand,' said Tata. 'But in future never write me letters. Come to me directly for anything you want.' The next day he took us to town with him to buy the things we needed. Granny made and sewed all our dresses. The materials would be sent to her or Tata would send her the money to buy the materials. Then she would come to our school to take our measurements, and when the dresses were done, she would bring them to school. It was not until we were in boarding school that we went to her place on such occasions, and remained with her for a few days.

At that early age, we learnt to close ranks, especially Ntangashe and I. Being older, she took me under her charge, protected me and established a routine for coping. We had learnt to work at a very early age, even before Mama died; we got some good training under aunt Daisy. We fed ourselves before and after school, made our beds, washed our clothes and Tata's, cleaned the kitchen and tidied the dining-room. Two children whom the Mgudlwas had sent to come and help their daughter, Mbikreni and Lezina, could not take it; they ran away. They had never been in a situation where children fended for themselves. Ntangashe and I did. We survived.

We were to do the same for Edwina's children when they came, for at eleven o'clock in the morning their mother was still sleeping, blissfully unaware perhaps that there were toddlers to be fed and schoolchildren to be fed before they went to school. As a result, her children, especially those who were born when we were still at home, became very close to us, in spite of what their mother was teaching them, that we were not their sisters. How in the world is anyone going to convince a three-year-old, a seven-year-old, a ten-year-old, that this person who feeds you, buys you nice clothes, washes you and dresses you, showers you with love, is not your sister, and you should give such a person a wide berth? It is well-nigh impossible, I think.

What my stepmother was teaching her children bore fruit when her third son, Zwelebhunga, got married. Or rather boomeranged. According to custom, there are lots of gift-exchanges between the groom's and bride's families. When the bride arrives, she brings gifts for her father-in-law, her mother-in-law, the husband's senior sister and other relatives within the family. Zwelebhunga's wife had observed this custom, bringing gifts for her senior sister-in-law. In our case, this was Granny, and everybody knew this. But my stepmother would not accept it. Zwelebhunga's senior sister was her daughter Nokhwezi. She did not raise the matter when the gifts were being distributed. But she did so sharply in the kitchen among the women. Granny was still there, busy helping feed the visitors. She never entered into the women's conversation. Then at breakfast Granny announced that she would like a meeting of the family as she had something to say before she left.

After breakfast, the family gathered in the dining-room, and in walked Granny with a basket still full of the presents that had been passed to her the day before as senior sister-in-law. 'I understand from the talk of Mama and the women in the kitchen that Mama is upset that these things were passed on to me. They belong to Nokhwezi, senior natural sister of Zwelebhunga, her son. Here then are Nokhwezi's gifts. But before I go home, I would like to take with me all the presents that our husbands gave to their mother-in-law, beginning with Rhodes, my husband, a warm winter shawl; from Upington Villie, Nonkululeko's husband, another warm winter shawl; from Mahoney Mda, Ethel's husband, a warm winter coat; and a car coat and handbag from A. C. Jordan, Phyllie's husband. All these I'll take to their rightful owner, the mother-in-law of all these men.' Even before Granny had finished recounting the gifts that our husbands had brought, everybody knew that Edwina had no case. She, as mother-in-law, had accepted all these presents. There was never a question that she was not our mother.

Tata in reply said: 'No, Lawukazi,* whoever questions your position in this family is wrong. You and you alone are the senior daughter of this house.' My poor stepmother! Had she forgotten, when she raised this, that Granny had given her brother Zwelebhunga two head of cattle to add to the *lobola* that was asked for, and that Ethel, Zwelebhunga's sister, had given him another head of cattle? My sisters had done this in recognition of Zwelebhunga as their brother. Had Edwina forgotten that?

There had never been any lessons from Tata to us on these mutual responsibilities and obligations. We sensed that this was what he wished and wanted, that we should know each other as sisters and brothers. That has always been and always will be our attitude towards those children.

* This is our clan name. My people, the Sukwini, are said to be a branch of one of the Khoi clans, *amaLawu* in Xhosa. These are some of the Khoi who, through marriage, were completely absorbed into the Xhosa group.

My stepmother! Bold and daring, with the kind of boldness that makes people do the unthinkable. When Somhlophe got married, Edwina went away a week before the wedding, locking everything away – linen, crockery, cutlery – the things that would be needed for the wedding guests. Granny came home on the weekend before the wedding, and had to go back and fetch things from her house. Where she had gone and why nobody knew, and Tata never asked her when she came back.

It is unfortunate that a second wife has to live in the same area, sometimes even in the same house, as the first wife. It is grossly unfair to the second woman, for people will talk, in many cases not meaning to hurt, but they will make comparisons. People were still talking about Mama when Edwina came and they continued to talk about her years after – how beautiful she was, how well she dressed and how she carried herself. Even to us, those who knew Mama would tell us straight to our faces: 'You are not as beautiful as she was nor will you ever dress as well.' These were not compliments to us. But we came to accept this as fact. Such talk made my step-mother very insecure and resentful of all those who were close to Mama. So all the people that we cared for and who cared for us she chased away from her place, one by one. In most cases her manner of doing so was not very pleasant.

She refused to go places with Tata, for fear of these comparisons. And yet she lived in constant fear of other women meeting Tata when she was away. It may be that Tata had mistresses. Who knows? Tata would go to Umtata, perhaps to the Central Show. Edwina would refuse to come along with him, and yet the following day she would board the next train, put up at some hotel in Umtata, to see what women her husband would be going around with. She failed to realise that with her there, no women would be buzzing around him.

My poor stepmother, whose parents sent her out into the world never having prepared her for life. She could have been a success, for there were times when she showed she could do things and do them well. But like all people with a weak sense of responsibility, there was no consistency. Throughout her life there were ebbs and flows when things were not done right or not done at all, and then chaos reigned. Children cannot be brought up in such an atmosphere. If Tata, Dabawo and all those other people who were present had not been there on and off, I shudder to think what could have happened to those children.

Once, after I had begun teaching in Kroonstad in the Orange Free State, I returned home on holiday. A few days after my arrival home, Somhlophe came, very much concerned about a strange story she had heard from aunt Margaret, Mama's youngest sister. Aunt Margaret had just come back from East London, and here was her story: In the streets of East London, one afternoon, aunt Margaret had met my stepmother, poorly dressed, going from house to house looking for a job. Edwina had wept as soon as she met aunt Margaret, telling her that Tata was not providing anything for her children, so she had decided to come to East London to work. Aunt Margaret had already written to Tata, shocked that something like that could have happened, pointing out to him that this was a shame and a disgrace. Somhlophe too had come to ask Tata why. What a disgrace, his wife working for white people in East London!

Tata calmly told us that he too was surprised. He had received the letter from aunt Margaret and was amazed, for as far as he knew Edwina was home in Qhumanco, where she had gone to visit her sick grandfather. A taxi had come to pick Edwina from the house, the day she left. But strange, Tata said, she had not written since she left, even to say how her grandfather was. 'You know,' Tata continued, 'a day after Edwina left, I met cousin Fred who told me he was on the morning train to East London with Edwina. I was sure he was making a mistake, that it must have been on the afternoon train. So Fred was right. Wow! That is Edwina, all right!'

He showed us the letter that aunt Margaret had written to him. The next day Tata sent a telegram to her uncle Harold Guleni Mgudlwa, asking him to find out if Edwina was in East London. Her uncle acted at once and sent word to another uncle in East London, with whom Edwina was staying. She went home to Qhumanco and came back to us just two weeks before I left for Kroonstad. That incident was to have a profound impact on me. It changed the course of my life.

Healdtown

Our principal teacher, Rhodes Cakata (now married to my sister Granny), strongly recommended that Tata send me to Healdtown, instead of Lovedale, when I passed my Standard 6. He had been trained at Healdtown and had taught there for some three years before taking up the principalship of our school. Healdtown was a good school, he said, better than Lovedale where class divisions were encouraged. At Lovedale students slept and ate according to their pockets. It was only in the classrooms that the students were thrown together irrespective of how much each paid. At Healdtown all students paid the same amount, slept in the same dorms and ate at the same tables. Moreover, the high school at Healdtown was small and at my age I would not be lost in that setting, which he feared would be the case if I went to Lovedale, where there were so many departments and students.

No one in my family had ever been to Healdtown and I doubt if I would have gone there if Mama was still alive. To her, Lovedale was the only school worth sending a child to. She had been born there and her forebear, Balfour, had been present at the founding of Lovedale.

I was just beginning my twelfth year when I first went to Healdtown. To this day I am still teased about how young I was and how the students would say when they saw me: *'Abanye abafazi balumlela kule Nxikhwebe ngoku'* [Some mothers think this institution is now a place for them to send their toddlers]. Fortunately for me, my cousin Linda Koti was also a student in the high school at Healdtown. Her father, Candlish Koti, cousin to Mama, had just taken up residence at our mission as the new minister. This meant that Linda would take charge of me at Healdtown and I would be starting the journey with her right from home. This must have been a great comfort to Tata.

My sister Ntangashe was by now away at boarding school too, at the Indaleni High School, near Richmond in Natal, so my departure meant even more to Tata. It was the one that I think he dreaded the most. Throughout the holidays he would tease me: 'Are you really going to leave me? Who is going to unsaddle my horse when I come home? Who is going to make me tea?'

'I'll write to you every month,' I always told him.

On the day I left, Somhlophe packed the provisions and we set off to the mission house to join Linda, and then proceeded together to the train station. Tata was already in town, waiting for our arrival. In town we met a lot of students bound for Healdtown from Colosa, eMgcwe, Hlobo, Fort Malan, and Gatyana – both boys and girls. Before we parted Tata gave me some money – one pound – and told me he was giving the rest – five pounds – to Linda for safe-keeping. This was to last me the whole term in school, and was meant for things like toiletries, shoe polish, shoe repairs, and so on. Generally there is not much that students need until they come home for the holidays, as everything is usually provided before a student leaves home. Tata then hugged and kissed me, saying he was not going to wait for the train, and left. Half an hour before the train arrived, Tata came back.

'I thought you had gone home,' Somhlophe exclaimed. 'Oh, Tata, you think I cannot manage?'

'I had to come back, just in case,' replied Tata.

We boarded the train, bade farewell again, and off I was to Healdtown.

There is nothing as exciting to young people as those train journeys to and from school. There is a lot of laughing, teasing and meeting of old friends after a long Christmas holiday. The new students are introduced to these friends, and with hope and apprehension they smile back and shake hands. How many times on that first train journey did I not hear my cousin Linda say to her friends: 'This is Phyllis, my cousin. She is my newcomer and nobody is going to touch her.'

The next day about two o'clock we were at Blaney where we had to change trains. Thereafter there was another two-hour stop at King William's Town where the train picked up more students. Here Linda introduced me to her friends, among whom was Muriel

Magamase Ntloko, a tall girl, broad-faced and with a quick smile. She came from Ngcongcolorha, Tsomo, in the Transkei. Linda and Gamase were in the same class and were good friends. 'Gamase, this is our newcomer, Phyllis, my cousin. Between us, nobody is going to touch her.' So saying, Linda left me with Gamase, to attend to other interests and other friends. That meeting between me and Gamase at King William's Town that Saturday afternoon was to be important for us for the rest of our lives. From the moment Linda left us, Gamase took charge of me and kept me by her side throughout the journey.

It was a summer afternoon, so most of the time we stood at the window, watching the scenery flash by and noting the difference between this part of the country and that from which I came. The homesteads here were not like those I had known in Transkei. They seemed to be poorly built, haphazard, with no fences around them. Above all, very few had any cattle-folds. The homes seemed deserted. There were no people visible – no women cooking or coming from the river with buckets of water on their heads, or men and boys leading a team of oxen from the ploughing fields, even though this was still a busy time of the year. All seemed desolate.

Where I came from, there was no mistaking a man's homestead, even if it did not have many imposing rondavels. There it stood with its three or four buildings, the courtyard, and beyond that, the cattle-fold. What had happened to the people here? was the question in my mind. My first letter to Tata, among other things, dealt with this desolation I had found in the Ciskei. The causes I was to understand later when I got to learn about the Wars of Dispossession and their consequences.

As the train approaches Mgqakhwebe, past the mimosa groves in and around King William's Town, one can see the Amathole Mountains with their highest peak, the Hogsback. Below them are the Hoho forests, in which is found the *iNtaba ka Ndoda,* the peak that has inspired Xhosa poets. S. E. K. Mqhayi called it the 'footstool of my gods'. It was from these mountains and in these forests that Hoho, the Khoikhoi queen,* carried on her guerilla warfare against

---

* Before the vanguard Xhosa, the Rharhabe, crossed the Kei River, this whole area was occupied by the Khoikhoi under their king, Hintsathi. After years of protracted guerilla war, the Xhosa offered the Khoi over a thousand head of cattle to allow them to settle here. Hoho, the widow of the king,

the Rharhabe. The Xhosa were to use these tactics against the British colonial forces a generation later, forcing the British to resort to scorched-earth warfare, burning the villages and the cornfields of the Xhosa.

These mountains are among the most beautiful in South Africa. Beyond the mountains are the amaLinde plains, where the combined Xhosa forces punished Ngqika for having abducted his uncle's wife, Thuthula the beautiful. After this defeat Ngqika invited the British to come and help him crush his uncle Ndlambe. This gave the British an excuse to involve themselves in the affairs of the Xhosa under the pretext of helping Ngqika. For having involved the British in Xhosa affairs, Ngqika is known as the first African quisling. Too late was Ngqika to realise what he had done when the British, no longer needing him, threw him out, an empty shard. It was then that he came to call the British *'OoQhina ka Qhonono, mayizal' imaz' enkomo, size kudl' isigqokro'* [Those who will tie up fast the pregnant cow, so that when it calves, they, and they alone, will have the milk curds].

As the train passed Ncerha (Alice), beyond which one saw the trees surrounding Lovedale, I could not but think that here my mother's forebear had given his life in the service of his people, that somewhere among those trees was the spot where Mama was born. Passing Alice, the train wound itself along the valley below the Gaga range and reached Fort Beaufort at six o' clock in the evening. All these scenes fascinated me, for I had heard them spoken of with nostalgia by Mama's people, the Balfours.

Healdtown lies at the end of a ravine in the Mankazana range of mountains. It is situated in one of those fertile valleys of the Kat River, with the Mankazana as backdrop. The Rev. John Ayliff of the Wesleyan Society was granted this land by the British government shortly after the War of 1834–35. To this mission station Ayliff, with the encouragement of the British, brought some of the Mfengu who had settled originally at Peddie. These Mfengu established themselves in three communities immediately around the mission station – Tyatyorha, Lamyeni, Ngwevu – and another, Nobhanda, some five miles away. They were placed here as a buffer between the colonists and the Xhosa whose land this once was, and were to be the eyes and the ears of the colonial government.

commanded the Khoi forces after the death of her husband. These forests are named after her.

What surprised me about these communities was that about three-quarters of all able-bodied adults worked for the whites at the mission station or walked the ten miles to Fort Beaufort to work for white people there. Their fertile fields for the most part were left uncultivated. Again I was to understand why later in life. This whole area had once belonged to the Xhosa. South of Mount Moxen was Tyhali's area – Tyhali, Ngqika's son by his favourite wife, Nonibe. North of Mount Moxen towards the Katberg range was Maqoma's area – Maqoma, warrior-king, first-born son of Ngqika. Maqoma held his court not very far from where the town of Fort Beaufort stands. It was in this area at Mthontsi near the Katberg that Maqoma once routed the British forces. The Xhosa were thereafter driven out of the area beyond the Tyhumie River, and the land they vacated was declared a 'ceded area' in which no settlement would be allowed.

When I got to Healdtown, the Mfengu community was agitated. These people had been allotted land on a quitrent system, which gave each family a piece of arable and residential land accompanied by a title-deed. A year before my arrival the government had demanded that the people surrender their title-deeds. The people refused and a court case ensued. Every Sunday – students and the community worshipped in the same church – special prayers were said for the case of 'the title-deeds' – *iTyala le Tayitile* – and a special collection was taken for the pending case. Fortunately for the people of Healdtown, after years of litigation the government withdrew its demand.

There was in those days no transport for students from Fort Beaufort station to Healdtown, a distance of ten miles. The institution sent lorries to pick up the students' luggage, which was all dumped in the dining-hall at the boys' school, where students collected it the next day. We had to walk those ten miles in the darkness, reaching the school at eleven o'clock or midnight, tired, dirty and hungry. Though walking or doing anything as a group can be great fun and though the distance was great, I did not feel it until I reached the school. Since we could not get our luggage until the following day, it meant carrying our provision baskets with us as there would be no food when we got there. I do not know who carried mine as I could not have carried it all that distance. I can only guess that Linda's or Gamase's friends helped me.

When at last we reached the school, we went to the bathrooms for a cold shower. Then according to area and friendship each group sat down in the dining-hall, opened the provision baskets and fell to. After this late supper, we were all sent off to bed. As there were as yet no mattresses we slept on the floor, making do with our travelling rugs and coats. After breakfast the following day, we were all marched to the boys' school to pick up our luggage. Even though it was Sunday there would be no services for us until the evening. So we lingered around the boys' school, with young sweethearts meeting after the long holiday, new hearts conquered or to be conquered, and just the excitement about being back. These are some of the good things about boarding-school life!

In the afternoon we lounged about, had supper from our baskets – who wants to eat institution food so soon? – then we were off to evening service and bed. By now we had our mattresses, for we had been given an hour in the afternoon to fill them with coir fibre.

Monday was my first day at school. There were only three departments at Healdtown in those days, namely the teacher-training school, the high school and the practising school. The teacher-training school comprised about three-quarters of the school population, with the high school and practising school sharing the remaining quarter of the boarding students. This quarter at the practising school was enlarged by the children who came from the surrounding communities.

It was indeed a small high school, with only six members of staff, including the principal, Mr Ball, a Welshman. The others were Messrs George Caley, son of the principal of the training school, Macpherson, son of a missionary, John Milton Zakade Noah, one of the first graduates from Fort Hare and son of the principal of the Buntingville mission school in the Transkei, Seth Mokitimi, who was to become the first black president of the Methodist Church in South Africa, and Frank Noble Black Lebentlele, who taught at Healdtown for thirty years, before taking up the principalship of Maseru High School in Lesotho. There was no woman staff member. But before I left more staff had joined the high school – black and white – including Weaver Mthuthuzeli Ncwana.

I must have been bored most of the time in class. I was so fidgety, talking, playing and pricking the other students with pins. They were forever telling me to be quiet. The teachers were very tolerant, except Mr Mokitimi who would send me to the office. I soon learnt to behave in his class.

The girls' school was about half a mile from the boys' school, at the top end of an avenue of jacaranda trees. Nothing was more important to the girls, especially on Sundays in their uniforms of black and white, marching to the rhythm of the school brass band, as coming down that avenue. By the time the girls proceeded down the avenue, the boys would have assembled four deep in the square next to the teacher-training school. Then the girls would arrive and stand at right angles to the line of boys. The Union Jack would be hoisted and, accompanied by the brass band, the school would sing 'God Save the King', after which the whole assembly would troop into the church for morning service. The community parishioners would already be inside the church.

In charge of the girls at the girls' school was a matron with an assistant. The African women teachers, who lived at the girls' school in our day, assisted with tasks at the boarding department, supervising evening studies or meals in the dining-hall, and helped in the general running of the school. In the kitchen were the cooks, women from the surrounding communities. The general cleaning-up was done by the students.

If there was anything the authorities at Healdtown feared, it was the free mixing of young people, boys and girls. To be seen talking to a boy, without the permission of the matron or the boarding master at the designated places, was an offence. Some children were expelled for infringing this regulation. Though Healdtown was a coeducational school, it was only in the high school that classes were conducted coeducationally. In the training school, the girls occupied one side of the block and the boys another. They were not supposed to talk to each other even if they met in the quadrangle. It was only in the senior teacher-training school – higher primary – that the boys and girls sat together in class. During my last year mixed dinners were introduced, which would become an important feature of Healdtown institutional life; some boys would come to eat dinner at the girls' school on Sunday and a corresponding number of girls would go to the boys' school for dinner there. Both girls and boys liked these occasions, for they were allowed to dress as they pleased. Then one saw the children who came from homes with money. They went to those dinners dressed to kill.

Healdtown! What a cultural desert! There was nothing to do but go to class and church, eat, sleep and play sport. I liked tenniquoits and soon became one of the star players. From junior netball, I graduated into the senior team, playing centre. I had played netball at Duff and could have gone into the senior team when I reached Healdtown, but for my age.

The teachers! I do not remember any that I can say inspired me, not even Mr Ncwana whom we all liked. In vain I looked for the history that I learnt from Tata in his classes. True, that sort of history was not in the history books, but sometimes teachers digress and connect what is in the textbooks with what is outside in the world. Not my teachers at Healdtown, however. They had no social consciousness. The first African graduates from Fort Hare were concerned more about proving that their degrees had put them a peg above the rest of the African people and nearer the whites. Even the few of them who went to the United States of America to further their studies and broaden their horizons came back excited about bridge parties, swimming pools and mixing freely with whites. They said very little about the position of blacks in the United States. If they had met Paul Robeson it was because he was a singer. Professor Z. K. Matthews, the first graduate from Fort Hare, was an exception in this regard.

What a racist place Healdtown was and continued to be until its demise in the aftermath of the 1976 students' protest! Outside their various departments there was no mixing between black and white teachers. At the girls' school, the two matrons – both white – ate alone in their dining-room, while the African women teachers ate with the students in the dining-hall. At the boys' school, the white unmarried teachers ate with other staff in the Governor's living quarters, while the African staff ate with the boys in the boys' dining-hall. Most of the staff played tennis, but they never played together. One white staff member, George Cook, son of the warden of Wesley House at Fort Hare, had to resign his teaching post at Healdtown because the other whites complained that he was fraternising too much with black staff, fellows he had known at Fort Hare when they were all students there.

At least at Lovedale there was some semblance of inter-racial living among the staff members. There were inter-racial mixed choirs of teachers and students, mixed social gatherings, staff teas and dinners at the principal's residence, and black and white here knew each other. Not at Healdtown! I could not wait to get out of that place!

Fort Hare

When I was fifteen I was awarded a Transkeian Bhunga Scholarship to Fort Hare. The Transkeian Bhunga was one of the four pillars that supported Fort Hare. The other three were the Presbyterian Church, the Methodist Church and the Anglican Church, or the Church of the Province as it is known in these parts. All their contributions to Fort Hare were financially matched on a pound-to-pound basis by the government. Apart from the Fort Hare Fund, the Transkeian Bhunga had set up a Merit Scholarship Fund for boys and girls from Transkei or with roots in Transkei to go to Fort Hare. It is these Bhunga scholarships that have given Transkei an edge over the other areas in the number of college graduates it can boast.

Fort Hare is named after Colonel Hare, one of the British officers in the so-called War of Maqoma. The fort he built here still exists and is now an historical monument. The college itself was the brain-child of Dr James Stewart, principal of Lovedale from 1872 to 1905, but the organisation and the plans were only set in motion after his death by church leaders and Africans who gathered at Lovedale for a commemoration service, where the idea of starting a college as a fitting memorial to Dr Stewart was embraced by all who came. The delegates were each instructed to preach the idea of a college for their sons and daughters to their own communities and to collect funds for its construction. All who were there did just that. At the inaugural meeting the question arose of admitting women. Without a dissenting voice, the delegates decided that women should be admitted from the start. When Fort Hare opened in April 1916, of the forty students four were women, two from Transkei.

The first members of staff were Dr Alexander Kerr, from Glasgow, and Professor Donald Davidson Jabavu, who was the only black member of staff until Professor Z. K. Matthews joined him during my last years there. There was another black family on campus in my time, Dr Max Yergan, his wife Susie and their children. Dr Yergan, a black American, had been sent to South Africa by the American Student Christian Association.

The Fort Hare women (I was no longer a girl now, I was a woman) were housed in makeshift cubicles attached to the Jabavu house on the banks of the Tyhumie River, just across the bridge from Alice. There were only nine women when I got there. Here again I met Nozipho Ntshona, who had shared with me her wild turnips at recess on my first day at school at Duff mission. She was completing her degree. Here also was Gamase Ntloko, who had taken charge of me at King William's Town on my first journey to Healdtown. Gamase had preceded me to Fort Hare and was finishing her matriculation. Except for Nozipho Ntshona, all the girls were from well-known Transkeian families – Soga, Mahlangeni, Ngozwana, Ndamase, another Soga, unrelated to the first, Ntloko, Madapuna and Kaoli.

Our warden was Florence Thandiswa Jabavu, wife of Professor Jabavu and daughter of the Rev. Elijah Makiwane, an intellectual giant among Africans and one of the best brains that ever came out of Lovedale. Of all his children that I know, his daughter Florence Thandiswa was the one who inherited his depth and breadth of intellect and outlook: a woman in a man's world! But as warden, she was a complete failure. She had no interest in us, her wards, nor in our welfare, and no faith in what she and her husband were doing at Fort Hare. Mrs Jabavu told us many times that we should not even imagine ourselves in the position she was in. She, too, had been fortunate to have a father-in-law who had had the foresight to send his son for education overseas.

While we would be invited for teas or dinner by Mrs Cook, wife of the warden of Wesley House, or by Miss Smyth, sister to Bishop Smyth, when they were still there, we never had any such invitations from Mrs Jabavu. She was not even there when some of the girls got bad news from home – the death of a mother, father, sister, or brother – and she would only become aware of it when she saw the girl in black and would ask: 'Mahlangeni, why is so-and-so in black?' The girls looked after each other, comforted each other and loved each other. Here was another case of benign neglect.

The other black family on campus, the Yergans, Afro-Americans, puzzled us too. They had no contact whatsoever with the black students on campus. No students and few black staff were ever invited to their place. When the Yergan children were due to go to school, the parents tried to enrol them in the white school in Alice and not at the Lovedale practising school, where the children of African staff and some of the white staff at Lovedale went. Rather than sending her children to this school, Mrs Yergan undertook to run classes for them at home. The Yergans stayed in South Africa for twenty-two years, eighteen of which were spent at Fort Hare. I wonder if by the time they left they could say 'Good morning' in Xhosa. Dr Yergan was supposed to be working among the people, but he never learnt their language. Puzzled, we would ask each other: 'Why did America send the Yergans here? For what purpose?' In the end we concluded it was to show us, blacks and whites in South Africa, that a black American can live as a white person.

The Yergans left South Africa on a year's sabbatical to get their children into schools in America. For part of his sabbatical Dr Yergan travelled to the Soviet Union and came back to Fort Hare as an avowed communist. Only then did they start to show an interest in the students, inviting to their house those who would go. It was too late. The American Student Association that had sent him called him home. When we came to the United States in the early sixties, Dr Max Yergan was one of the lobbyists for South Africa in Washington, D.C. At the time of the Congo trouble, he wrote a most stinging article on the backwardness of the African. He knew them, he said. He had lived there for over twenty years. No wonder white South Africa loved Dr Yergan.

As soon as Beda Hall was completed for the men students, we – the women – were moved to the old farmhouse that had housed the men. As warden we had Mrs Graves, whose husband was a general overseer of the whole institution. What a difference! We were made to feel at home, which was never the case at the Jabavus. The Graveses were a very musical couple and when they discovered that we knew many of the English choruses and madrigals, music evenings were organised in their living-room, and we all sang and had great fun. The Graveses were good to us and we enjoyed them.

Even as we started the year with the Graveses, we were told that they were only a stop-gap, for our warden would be coming in six months. She was going to combine the duties of warden with those of librarian. True enough, when we came back after the June holidays, Miss McCall, our new warden, was already installed. She too came from Glasgow and had been a classmate and friend of Mrs Kerr. A kinder, more loving person we could not wish for. Here was someone interested in our welfare, our studies, our families and our boyfriends. We were in and out of her kitchen. We went out on long walks with her, and there were feasts and teas for us over some weekends. Miss McCall was just wonderful to us.

But we soon noticed that while she was so nice to us, she was not to aunt Nonke, her maid, in the kitchen and to Oom Charlie, the old yardman. Whenever Miss McCall saw Oom Charlie resting and smoking his pipe, she accused him of stealing *her time.* Aunt Nonke in the kitchen was accused of stealing *her food,* when she preferred to take her plate of food home rather than eat it at her place of work. We discussed this among ourselves and decided to boycott Miss McCall's teas and accept no more favours from her. After prayers one evening we told her why. But Miss McCall continued to display her lavish spread of cakes and tea on Sundays. The girls would not take any. The boycott held firm for a few months. Then one Sunday, Nobantu Kabane was visited by her brother, Mr Kabane, a teacher at Lovedale, and his wife. Of course Miss McCall served Nobantu's guests tea. Nobantu sat with them and had the tea. This was enough for some girls who were waiting for some excuse to eat the cakes. One by one they went back to Miss McCall's tea and cakes, until only three of us held out to the end. I do not know if Clarissa Mzoneli went back after Lulu William and I left Fort Hare. I suppose it was expecting too much to hope students would resist Miss McCall's spread of all those goodies on Sunday.

I enjoyed all my classes with Professor Jabavu, who was not only a good teacher but an entertainer as well. Above all, he loved young people. Professor Jabavu took us for Latin. Miss Beatrice Dorothy Tooke, our English teacher, loved literature and she made it live. I remember, after reading *A Tale of Two Cities* with her, how the events that led to the French Revolution became so real and hit home. Every one of the characters in the novel was to me a real person and I identified with them. In vain did I look for Madame Defarge, The Vengeance, Miss Pross and Monsieur, when I studied the French Revolution in my History I class with Professor Chapman. When I did not find Dickens's characters in the history text, I wondered if the historian had all his facts right. Years after, when I was in France, I had to go to Saint Antoine to find the wine shop where

Monsieur Defarge and his wife had run their business. I felt the same urge when I got to London to visit Westminster Bridge, early in the morning, to capture the mood Wordsworth had expressed in his sonnet 'Earth has not anything to show more fair'. We stood there one morning with Nandi, my daughter, reciting the whole poem.

Fort Hare is a beautiful campus, a good and healthy place for young people. The campus is situated in a fertile valley on one of the bends of the Tyhumie River, about three miles east of Lovedale. All around are sparsely wooded mimosa groves and other tall trees and brush, which extend to the banks of the Tyhumie. Along the river are the most romantic foot-trails, leading sometimes to a ford in the river, sometimes stopping just at the water's edge and other times continuing endlessly along the banks. Walking along these foot-trails, one can hear the *swish-swish* of the water as it washes over the rocks, or the *whoosh-whoosh* murmur of the water in the deep pools as it glides along. Above are the noises of the tree-dwellers – the twittering of birds or the *bang, bang* of the wood-pecker, just ahead of one.

How I enjoyed following those foot-trails on a weekend afternoon with a friend, male or female! I was young; life was good. I was a young lady, beautiful, elegant, hotly sought after by the young men at the college. Having been brought up by a man, I like men. I am, in fact, more comfortable with men than I am with women. At Fort Hare I liked the attention that so many men paid me. While I discouraged some, there were a few that I kept around me, played with them as a cat plays with a mouse, kept a leash on them, with each one of them hoping that some day he would carry home the prize. Measuring the distance, I always made sure that I was in command of the situation all the time. I do not think I did this because I wanted to hurt anybody. I kept these men around me because I liked their company. I did not mean to be cruel to them. To me it was just a game. I am grateful that none of them hates me for this. Many have remained friends with me since our Fort Hare days.

When my future husband, A.C., first showed interest in me, I was shocked. Such an old man! Did he think I was meant for an old man? I wasted no time. I told him to forget it. He left me alone. He was much older; had been out in the field, teaching; had come back to further his education and he was one of the serious senior students at Fort Hare. I was only seventeen and a freshman. This was early in the year.

After the Completers' social at the end of the year, A.C. escorted me home. How this came about I do not understand, for ordinarily my boyfriend or one of our set should have escorted me. As we parted at the gate, he asked for a date on the last day of my examinations. It was agreed upon – five o' clock on such-and-such a day. I told my boyfriend the next day and we both laughed. 'He still is keen on you, Miss Phyl,' my boyfriend said and we laughed.

I completely forgot about the date with Mr Jordan, remembering it only when I saw him going towards Stewart Hall, apparently from our hostel. Mrs Jabavu told me that Mr Jordan had been to see me. I had been in Alice the whole day to see off my friends from Lovedale. I was busy with my own packing and preparing to leave the next day, when Mrs Jabavu came to the rooms: 'Phyllis, Phyllis, here's Jordan to see you. Comb your hair and tidy yourself up a little.' I did not even have a decent dress out to put on. I grabbed Gamase's and went in to meet him. We met in Mrs Jabavu's pantry; this was the only private place, as the Jabavus had guests and the house was full. Mr Jordan brought up the subject again. I made it quite clear again that it was 'no'. I was polite, civil and dignified. Parting, he said: 'If I ever bring up this subject again, don't blame me.'

I laughed inside, thinking: Poor fellow, where in this wide world is he ever going to meet me? He was going to his part of the world and I was going to mine. Where was he ever going to meet me again? Poor fellow!

'Are you continuing with Latin, next year?' he asked.

'I think so.'

'You may find this useful,' (handing me a key to *Pro Milone* which was going to be one of the Latin textbooks the following year).

'Thank you!' And we parted.

My boyfriend and I left for home the next day, made an overnight stay in King William's Town and continued the journey the next day. On this train was Mr Jordan with other Fort Hare students going home.

After playing these cruel games with men with very little remorse, I decided to go steady at seventeen. I realised that the game I was playing, though not cruel in my eyes, was dangerous; I would not always be in command. If things got out of my control I could be hurt. I settled on a handsome, tall fellow, elegant, charming, warm, generous, patient, a romantic whose tastes suited mine to a T. He had been very popular among student music groups at Lovedale and was so even now at Fort Hare. At Lovedale, he had been one of the famous Palladium Big Four of those days, and here at Fort Hare he was a hot number for duets, many of which he sang with A.C. This was Halley Oyama Mgudlwa, cousin to my stepmother, brother to the Judith whom most of my folks had wished Tata had married. His father, Harold Guleni Mgudlwa, and Tata had become great friends since Tata married his niece.

Halley was already at Fort Hare when I got there. He had been an uncle in every way, pampering me as uncles would. Having been doted upon by Tata and others, I simply liked and enjoyed this. He had watched me develop, blossom into a charming, elegant young woman, and his closeness had contributed to that development. As the years went by we became very friendly and drew closer to each other. I do not think either of us realised what was developing between us. It was the kind of relationship that starts in mutual trust and respect and over the years blossoms into love.

Halley was the man who stayed and anchored me, who taught me that life was not a game, that love was the most beautiful thing that any two people could share. Like Tata he never lectured me on this. Like Tata again, his generosity, his attitude, his actions, his unselfish concern about me, spelt all this out to me. With him I was happy, relaxed, secure, comfortable, as I had been with Tata. As he told me one evening while we stood outside our hostel gate, over the years at Fort Hare I had become part of him as buds on the branch of a tree. I knew it was so. I knew I had permeated his whole being, for had he not too become a part of me? I had found a place for myself and a place in my heart for a man other than Tata. I was crazy about this man. So crazy I was that when he said to me, 'Miss Phyl, good wine needs no bush,' I stopped wearing make-up and jewellery. If my perfume was rather heavy, he would complain: 'Miss Phyl, people are going to think I am wearing perfume. I do not like it.' And yet this was the same fellow who had a rose for me every morning before we went to class, who sent me flowers even after he had left Fort Hare, whose letters to me were full of lines from love poems. I was just crazy about him!

My 'Prince Hal', how hurt he was when I left him to marry another! How he agonised and grieved and wondered what had gone wrong! How could it have happened? It took him a long time to accept the fact that I was gone and he could not get me back. He never got over it, even though he accepted that life must go on. I wept and grieved too. I too could not understand how it could have happened this way.

We were a fine pair on that Fort Hare campus and we knew it. One had to see us on that dance floor doing the waltz or the tango, or walking up the 'two-twenty' track between the dining-hall and Stewart Hall. The other Fort Hare students were kind enough to compliment us after they had got over the shock of a love affair between uncle and niece. A cartoon once went up on the bulletin board in the tuition block. On a cricket pitch stood dimpled Phyl, in high heels, in front of the wickets. On the other side, glowering down the mat, was Prince Hal, who delivered a devastating ball that sent all three stumps flying. With bat over her head, dimpled Phyl cried: 'Oh, uncle!!' And still with that look on his face, Prince Hal challenged: 'What uncle?' Halley was hurt when he heard about that cartoon. He never saw it, for his friend took it down before he could. He came to see me as soon as was possible between classes, fearing he would find me in tears. I laughed as soon as I saw him and we both laughed and forgot about the cartoon.

Halley had four sisters at Lovedale, three younger than himself and the other, Mrs Kabane, just before him; a younger brother, Sonto, was there too. With them were my stepmother's younger sister, Sheila, and many other cousins. They were all crazy about me, as I was about them. My sisters, especially Granny, thought this was the nicest boy I had ever brought home. Tata, though he never knew officially, watched the whole affair with warm interest. It is one of the ironies of life that while my stepmother was so mean to us (and her people knew this) her whole family loved and accepted us as nieces and grandchildren. To this very day I speak of the Mgudlwas as Mama's people, and I mean this. It is only when there is mention of the Balfours that I explain that the Mgudlwas are, in fact, my stepmother's people. When we visit any of them we are extended the same favours and privileges enjoyed by nieces anywhere in our part of the world.

Halley did not come back to Fort Hare the following year and the year after. He had to go and work, as now his younger brother, Sonto, was at Fort Hare. But nothing would shake me. Men were buzzing around me, trying their luck. I hoofed and kicked them with a vengeance and in the end only the most daring came anywhere near me.

Fort Hare is a difficult place for young women, even these days. There is always a shortage of women. It was worse in our day, when there were only thirty women to over two hundred men. Though there are women at the Macvicar Hospital – staff and student nurses – and women staff and students at Lovedale, Fort Hare men would rather go out with Fort Hare women if they can. So the most eligible women at Fort Hare have a rough time keeping men at bay. In such instances it helps to be haughty. Halley's brother, Sonto, and K. D. Matanzima, his nephew, now students at Fort Hare, were watching me with interest and were glad to note that I could handle all these suitors.

After Halley left we could only meet during vacation. For my last six months of my final year at Fort Hare, he was with his sister, Mrs Kabane, at Lovedale. He had an examination to write and had come up to prepare. It was a good thing he was around, because the marriage of Ntangashe in September that year had upset me. Not that I did not know Ntangashe's wedding was pending. I knew. She had been engaged for over a year. All the same, the fact that she would not be there when I got home was none too pleasant for me. Halley helped me over this difficult period.

Sometimes I think it is just as well that Halley and I did not end up together. There was a lot of excitement and many expectations on both sides of the family. To the Jordans I was a total stranger and so were they to me and my family. With them there could never be: How could so-and-so, of whom we expected so much, whom we thought we knew, do this and that? No, not with them. Perhaps by reflecting in this way I am able to ease my guilt, guilt that has stayed with me for years. On occasions when there was a lot of misunderstanding between me and my husband, the thought that it was not myself and Halley always comforted me and I could get over the whole thing and forget it. Strange!

Halley and I never met again except once in King William's Town in 1959. We were both married and had children. I was on my way to Cape Town and had made a stop at Fort Hare to visit an old student from Kroonstad. While there I heard that he was still in the civil service in King William's Town, and I visited him in his office. When I told him it was a friend who had informed me he was in King William's Town, he simply said: 'How strange that you should not even know where I am and you should be told by someone! How strange!' He still called me 'Miss Phyl'.

Any regrets? I do not think so, for my married life was good and fruitful. Through my marriage to A.C., I was able to grow and develop intellectually. I have had the advantage of living in a wider world – Cape Town, Europe and now the United States of America. In all these places I have rubbed shoulders with intellectuals, of different outlooks and views. This has helped me develop and mature into the person I am today.

Life with A.C. was an intellectual life and he involved me in his intellectual pursuits. As colleague and friend, he encouraged me, stimulated me and, as he grew, I grew with him. In the end we were not just husband and wife but intellectual friends and colleagues. For this I'll forever be grateful. It would not have happened had I married Halley, much as I loved him and he loved me. Maybe this is what the gods had in store for me from the day aunt Ma-Mpethwana saved me with her herbal brew. I'll forever be sorry that I hurt the man who loved me so. This sense of guilt I carry with me always.

Kroonstad

TELEGRAM: REPLY PREPAID.
To: Phyllis Ntantala, Duff, Idutywa.
Offering High School teaching post, immediately.
From: Reginald Cingo, Principal, Bantu High School,
    Kroonstad, O.F.S.

It was a Tuesday afternoon, early in February. Uncle Nonono had brought the telegram.

'Any bad news?' he asked.

'No, it is an offer of a teaching post,' I replied.

'Where?'

'Kroonstad.'

'Kroonstad! That side of Bloemfontein! Too far!!'

We spoke about other things. In the meantime I had shown Mama the telegram. (She was in one of her good moods.) Tata was in town and I could not wait for him to come home. When he came uncle Nonono told him. 'Phyllie has been offered a teaching post in Kroonstad. No, it is too far, Mkhuluwa. It is too far!'

Tata read the telegram and put it aside. After some time, when he had had a cup of tea, he asked: 'Who is this Cingo?'

I told him.

'Oh! He must be the son of Walter Cingo of eMfundisweni, one of our good men in the Bhunga. Does he know you?'

'Hardly,' was my reply. 'But there are two teachers on his staff who know me – Miss Soga, daughter of your friend T.B., and Mr Jordan. They were my seniors at Fort Hare.'

'How would they know you were going out to teach and not going back to Fort Hare?'

'That I would not know – but. . . .'

We left it at that.

The question of my going out to teach or returning to Fort Hare had been discussed a lot by Tata and me during the Christmas holidays. I feared going back. I would be lonely without my two friends, Lulu William and Pitise Jukuda, who were going out to teach. Halley would not be there either and I shuddered to think what life would be without these good friends. Moreover, I had reached a plateau in my education and did not quite know what I really wanted to become. I thought being away from Fort Hare for a year at least would give me time to sort myself out. I had taken my college teaching diploma so I was qualified to teach high school, even though I had not completed my degree. Tata could not quite accept these reasons. I had to go back to finish my degree. I did not have to follow any particular field, he argued, but to be at college, reading around certain subjects which I thought I liked, sorting myself out; by the end of the year I would know what I wanted to do. He had hoped I would go in for medicine, and when I told him I was not interested, he had suggested law.

The two of us reached a compromise. If I could get a teaching post, then I would go and teach for a year, after which I would return to Fort Hare to finish my degree. If this did not happen, then I would go back to Fort Hare. It seemed fair to both of us. Now this unexpected offer from Mr Cingo solved my problem and, reluctant though he was, Tata was bound by the decision the two of us had made.

The message said *'immediately'*, for schools all over the country had opened in mid-January and it was now February. This meant I had to leave that same week – that Friday, in fact. The following day, Wednesday, we sent the message: 'Accepting offer. Arriving Sunday. Phyllis Ntantala.' In the meantime I rode to my sister Granny's to tell her I was leaving on Friday. The next day she and I met in town to buy a few things I might need. Mama pitched in too, preparing and packing my provision basket. It was hectic up to the time the taxi came to fetch me to take me to the train station. In town I sent this telegram to Halley: 'Leaving for Kroonstad, O.F.S. to teach. Will meet in Queenstown in June. Love, Miss Phyl.'

Tata came to the station to see me off. He waited there with me until the train steamed in. He was very apprehensive and was greatly relieved to see that a family friend, Mrs Ntlabathi, was on the

train. It turned out that her ticket took her only as far as Queenstown, where she was hoping to raise the rest of the fare from relatives who lived there. 'I did not want to tell Bhuti George that I was
only going as far as Queenstown for now. That would have upset
him. He is anxious about you, Phyllie. But don't worry, there will be
people in the train who can take care of you and will continue the
journey with you.'

True enough, when Sis' Ma-Rhadebe got off the train in Queenstown, another lady got on, a comely, motherly lady in her fifties. She
was Mrs Magumane, going back to Sophiatown, Johannesburg,
where she lived. Mrs Ntlabathi told her about me, stressing my background and my youth, and asking her to please take care of me, tell
me where to get off, as this was my first journey alone so far from
home. I was now under the charge of Mrs Magumane. Mrs
Magumane was a kind, motherly woman. In her prayer in the com-
partment, she asked God to look after and guide this young child,
going alone to a far-off place, to live among strangers. 'Keep her,
good God. Be her guide, O Lord, I pray you.'

Even though Sis' Ma-Rhadebe had told her that I was going to
Kroonstad to teach, Mrs Magumane had doubts. She would ask, talking to herself: 'O God, I wonder if her mother knows that her child
is on this train.' And then she would ask me: 'Are you telling me the
truth? Does your mother know that you are here?'

To which I would reply: 'Look at my suitcase and this provision
basket. How could I have left home without my mother knowing
that?'

'I guess you are right. It is just that one never knows what you
young people will do.'

As the train sped through the Orange Free State, she told me
about all the sights. 'Once we pass Bloemfontein, we are not far
from Kroonstad. There's just one big stop, Brandfort, in between,
then mimosa groves all the way to Kroonstad.' (Kroonstad is known
as Maokeng – 'at the place of the mimosa groves' – by the Sotho,
whose land once this was.)

'Do you know anybody in this Kroonstad?' she asked.

'Hardly any. But there are two teachers I know from college,' I
replied.

'Will they be at the station to meet you?'

'I guess the principal will send someone to meet me.'

'But there are always taxis at the station. I'll get one of them to take you to the principal's. What did you say his name was?'

'Cingo.'

'Yes! Cingo. I have heard that name before. Please, dear God, look after this child, keep her and guide her, dear Lord. Now we are pulling into the station. Come stand here with me at the window to see if any of the teachers you say you know are here to meet you.'

I went up to the window and looked out. As the train was pulling to a halt by the platform, I spotted A.C. and told Mrs Magumane, pointing out which one it was.

As soon as she saw him, she called out, beckoning: 'Come here! Come here! Look at me! What's your name? I am Mrs Magumane of Sophiatown.'

'Jordan is my name, Mama.'

'Please, look after this child for me. Look after her. Do you hear me?'

'No harm will come to her,' said A.C.

He helped me with my luggage, put me in a taxi and we drove to where I was to live. Late in the afternoon A.C. and Miss Soga took me to the principal's, to meet him and his family. When Miss Soga and I met, we hugged and kissed.

A.C. remarked: 'Phyllis, you did not do that when you met me. Why are you so partial?'

On the train Mrs Magumane had given me her address in Sophiatown and invited me to visit her should I go up to Johannesburg. I wrote to her during my first year in Kroonstad, but never went to visit her. After we were married A.C. often said how he wished to meet her to tell her that he was still keeping his promise to her that afternoon at the Kroonstad train station, making sure that no harm came to me. When the rest of my family heard that I had gone to Kroonstad to teach, a place beyond Bloemfontein, they questioned Tata's wisdom in allowing me to go that far. Tata always told them: 'She will be all right. She knows what I expect of her.'

But how did Cingo know of me and that I was looking for a teaching post? – a question Tata had asked. I was to get the answer from A.C. a month after my arrival in Kroonstad. 'You know, coming back to Kroonstad, I met Nosithe on the train,' he said. 'In fact it was from her that I got to know you would not be going back to Fort Hare, if you got a teaching post. A strange coincidence!' he remarked. 'I was to have taken the second train out of Umtata. But I took the first train – a bad connection for me at Blaney – because I wanted more time with my friend Robert Tutshana, who teaches in Port Elizabeth. On that train was Nosithe going to Healdtown. What a coincidence!' he said again. '"Where's Phyllis? What is she doing? When does she go back to Fort Hare?" I asked Nosithe.

'"She is home," Nosithe had replied. "About going back to Fort Hare, I do not know. She does not want to go back. I am sure she won't go back if she gets a teaching post. She and my brother are still arguing about that," Nosithe told me. Strange! So when we got here and one of our lady teachers had not returned, I thought of what Nosithe had told me and that perhaps you might accept our offer of a post here. I went to Cingo and told him about you. He was delighted and asked me to send you that telegram. To our relief you accepted. As you have already noticed, there is too much work here. We need more teachers, in fact. Strange, I do not know what made me take that first train out of Umtata. Actually it meant waiting for two hours at Blaney for the train up.'

How he knew my address, he never said. Maybe he got it from Nosithe or he may have known it from his days at Lovedale with Somhlophe. Who knows?

The majority of the people in Kroonstad location were Southern Sotho-speaking, with a good number of both Rolong and Kgatla Tswana, a sprinkling of Xhosa and a few *Orlaams mense,* a totally deculturated group of Africans who knew no African language or claimed they did not. About three-quarters of the people were Afrikaans-speaking, having grown up on the farms of the Orange Free State and moved to the city for better opportunities and wages. Among themselves the people spoke Afrikaans most of the time. Easily more than half were illiterate. My landlady, for example, a modern woman in appearance, could not read or write, something that amazed me, coming as I did from a place where those who could not read or write were the red-blanket people. More than three-quarters commuted to town where they worked in menial jobs. This they did five days in the week, and some of them six. The only day families were home was Sunday. Every morning father and mother left early to go to work, leaving the children to look after themselves before and after school. After school the children were in the streets until the parents came back in the late afternoon. For most of these children breakfast was dry bread and tea, for others there was not even that. The only full hot meal was on Sunday, when there would be meat, potatoes and stiff porridge, which they preferred to rice and vegetables.

The Xhosa were a closely knit group and among the few who had education up to Standard 6 at least. Some of them had come to the Orange Free State as teachers, being unable to get teaching posts in the Cape Province because they were not fully qualified. They had taken up posts in the farm schools and then moved to the cities. These Xhosa in Kroonstad prided themselves on this and on the fact that the principal of the school was Xhosa with a college degree.

Kroonstad had been one of the active centres in the Orange Free State in the heyday of the Industrial and Commercial Workers' Union. Here was the home of Keable Mote, Lion of the Orange Free State. Here lived some of the men who worked with him in the ICU, organising Africans on the farms and in the towns of the province, confronting the Boers and the police, exposing themselves to death and danger – men like Henderson Binda, Robert Sello and others. The ANC had once had its strongest branch in the Orange Free State here in Kroonstad. It was in the Kroonstad jail, among others, that women protesting against passes had been held during the First World War. So the people were politically conscious. Their community meetings in the community hall on civic matters were not only interesting but very educational. On community affairs they tended to act together regardless of ethnic and language differences.

I boarded with Mrs Monyake in B Location. Her house was a wood-and-iron bungalow and was one of the better homes in this section of the location. Most were flat-roofed mud houses with three or four rooms. Mrs Monyake's house was one of the few that had a coal stove; the rest used open braziers outside in the yard. None of the houses had running water or an inside toilet. At strategic points at the end of streets were communal water-taps. Fortunately each house had to have its own individual outhouse. I was greatly relieved to know that I would, at least, have a place that I could call a 'house' and could point it out to my friends.

Poor as the people were, most of them were standholders; that is, they had bought the lots from the municipality and built their houses. This was the pattern for most of the Orange Free State, and because of this one did not find in this province the ugly slums which are a feature of African urban living. In most cases, as soon as the economic situation improves, the people tear down the mud houses and build themselves better homes. Unfortunately, they never own these houses as the ground on which they stand belongs to the municipality.

All around was poverty, poverty, poverty! I was to see more of it among the students I had come to teach. Not that I had never seen poverty in the rural areas where I came from. I had. There was Nomentyi, Lolo's mother, with but one cow, ten sheep and a few chickens. She had to depend on others to till her fields and usually they were not ploughed on time. City poverty, however, is more stark than rural poverty. Here, if one does not have a cent in one's pocket, one goes without food; here people who have no houses sleep out in the streets, under bridges, in the gutter. What I saw frightened me.

The school, from Sub A to Junior Certificate, was a huge establishment of over a thousand students and with a staff of over sixty teachers, all under one head, Reginald Ndumiso Cingo, a graduate from Fort Hare whose home was at eMfundisweni, Pondoland, Transkei, where his father, Walter Cingo, had been principal of the primary school. The high school was young, only five years old and was the second day high school for Africans in the whole country. (The first was in Bloemfontein location, also in the Orange Free State.) There were seven teachers on the high-school staff – five men and two women. Of these seven, four were from Transkei, including the only two college graduates on the staff. I had come to fill in the place of a female teacher who had failed to report for duty when the schools opened.

These high schools had started as continuation classes beyond Standard 6, an idea of the then Chief Inspector of Native Education, Mr Kuschke. Mr Kuschke had been appalled by the number of African children still of school-going age who had to leave school after Standard 6, because their parents did not have the money to send them to fee-paying schools. Mr Kuschke had then come up with the idea of continuation classes, where students could be prepared for the Junior Certificate examinations. In Kroonstad these classes started under Joe Kokozela, one-time teacher of Z. K. Matthews in Kimberley. Mr Cingo had succeeded Mr Kokozela when he left.

Mr Kuschke had got the African churches – the Methodist, the Presbyterian and the Anglican – to pool their resources and merge their schools into one 'Bantu United School'. When this had been done, the municipalities were committed to putting up the buildings and buying the furnishings, while the Provincial Department of Education (Native Section) paid the teachers' salaries. In the Orange Free State, one found these large schools – 'Bantu United Schools' as they were called – with lovely buildings somewhere on the edge of the locations.

A school committee of elected members from the three churches ran the schools. They chose the chairman in rotation from among the members of the school committee. The principal of the school was an *ex officio* member of the school committee, though he had no vote. He could make recommendations about teacher appointments and selection.

The African response to this arrangement was tremendous, and great progress in education took place in a province whose people, in city, town and farm, were among the poorest in the whole country in those days. By the time I left Kroonstad, the Bantu High School had a staff of twelve, with only three lacking college degrees but well qualified to teach at high-school level. Matriculation classes had been started, and Standards 5 and 6, which at first had been part of the high school, had become part of a middle school. But all this was still under one principal, Mr Cingo.

The high-school students paid fees of two pounds a year, bought their books and school supplies, and wore uniforms – black and white for girls and grey and blue-black for boys. Boys could wear khaki in summer. Though the fees were low, many of the students could not afford to pay. In order to keep them in school, more than three-quarters had to be exempted from fees. I have yet to see children as hungry for education as those African children I taught in Kroonstad. They liked school, liked their school work, and became lovers of books, literature and everything that stimulated the mind. And yet many of them came from illiterate and semi-literate homes, where the parents did not even read a newspaper, let alone a book.

When I first came there, I could not understand how students who could not pay fees – only two pounds a year – could afford to have bicycles. I soon learnt that these bicycles were not for pleasure. They were used for carting Mama's loads of washing to and from the white homes in town and the suburbs. All able-bodied adults, men and women, apart from wives of ministers, teachers and business people, either worked in town or took in loads of washing. In the afternoon after school, the boys would cycle to town with a bundle of washed and ironed laundry, and come home with another bundle to be washed.

Kroonstad is a place of transit. Travelling salesmen to and from the Cape, Natal, and Transvaal make stops here. The hotels are always full on weekends with these men. They always need to have their cars washed before proceeding on their journeys. The boys from our school would be there on Saturday mornings to wash the cars and earn money for themselves. After washing the cars, they would go to the golf course to caddy. The money they earned would be used to buy books and clothes and add to the family finances. During the long summer holidays, some of them would go to Johannesburg, where the wages were better; they would come back with money for fees and books and continue their education. Working this way, many of them paid their way to teacher-training colleges and universities, all after graduating from Kroonstad Bantu High School.

Discipline and truancy problems were negligible. Because they were day students who came from homes where conditions were not conducive to good study, our students had to return for two hours in the afternoon from three to five o'clock. School was dismissed at one thirty to allow students to go home and eat. At three o'clock they had to be back for study. The teachers supervised for a week in rotation. In most cases, all that a supervising teacher had to do was to be there at three, see the children settle down to their work and come back at five to dismiss them. The class prefects were able to maintain discipline, and the other students responded.

By the time I left Kroonstad, the school had become the centre of their lives. On weekends, after running errands at home, they would go back to the school library for books, or to the game-room for indoor games. In summer they would be sitting under the trees, reading, or in the game-room, playing indoor games. All that the teacher–librarian had to do was to leave the key with one of the library helpers, ask him or her to check out books and check in the returns. The teacher would check the record upon returning on Monday. I know it sounds incredible. But it was so. I could not believe what I later saw in the North American schools, the misuse and abuse of books, books thrown on the floor, slashed with razors, pages torn out; the waste and destruction of school materials – paper, pencils, pens, maps, charts, you name it.

These Kroonstad students did not behave this way because they had been repressed or crushed. Not at all. They were like other children, active, lively, energetic, inquisitive. The difference is that they appreciated what they were getting at school and they wanted to make something of themselves. And they did. Some of them are holding positions of responsibility in South Africa and abroad: many of them are in the organisations struggling for the liberation of their country. Each one of them is playing his or her role to improve the lot of mankind. I loved those students and they loved me in return. To each one of them I was *'Mistress oaka'* – 'My teacher' – instead of *'Mistress oa rona',* 'Our teacher'. Nothing flattered me more than that, whenever I went back and met some of them, they would tell me they had named their daughters 'Phyllis' after me. Vanity?

It was in Kroonstad that I learned Southern Sotho, whose idiom is so very much like that of Xhosa. I was fascinated by the parallels in idiomatic expressions in Southern Sotho and Xhosa and would now and again surprise my students by saying a Southern Sotho expression. The students liked this and, excitedly, they would say: 'She knows Sotho! She knows Sotho!' When Nandi came and started speaking, my Sotho improved for she began with Sotho before Xhosa. Her nanny spoke Sotho and knew no Xhosa or English. Nandi would proudly tell people: *'Ke Mo-Sotho nna! Ake mo-Qhosa!'* (I am Sotho; I am not Xhosa!)

The beauty of Southern Sotho had impressed me on my first day in the school. At parade, Don Matsepe's choir sang *'Chu-chu makhala nto ya ma-Kgooa'.* It was beautifully sung and from the rhythm I knew it was something about the train. As if Don knew I had been impressed by his choir's singing, the next day they sang *'Morija'.* Both of these are compositions by that master of song, Pulumo Mohapeloa. I knew I had to learn Sotho. I am glad I did, for I was able to read Mofolo's *Chaka* in Sotho, and experienced the poetry of that master of the Sotho language.

There was not much social life for young people in Kroonstad in those days, apart from concerts and dances every week in the community hall. Even before I left Fort Hare, some of us had stopped going to concerts in Ntselamanzi Hall, because they drew all and sundry. We felt that, as the elite, we simply could not mix and dance with *anybody.* I brought these attitudes with me to Kroonstad, and avoided the dances and concerts at the community hall, unless they were special. There was also the choral group, a teachers' choir which staged concerts now and again and was active in the second half of the year, preparing for the music competition at the annual conference of the Free State African Teachers' Association. A popular troupe like Griffiths Motsieloa's Dark-town Strutters would stop in Kroonstad on their tour of the country and give concerts which the elite of the location attended. A.C. and Miss Soga were present at most of these functions, as dance partners.

Most of the time was spent in school, at home and on occasional walks in and around Kroonstad, with Miss Soga and A.C. showing me about. I was soon to learn that even these walks were not very safe in certain areas, for example along the Walsh River, on which the town is situated, for a sporty white fellow might try his marksmanship if you were black. In the Orange Free State, *what is not white is black,* irrespective.

Mr Brent, the location superintendent, and his wife would sometimes invite some teachers to their house for a musical evening. Mr Brent had grown up in Peddie in the Cape Province and spoke Xhosa like a Native. As a location superintendent, he was one of the most liberal. They do not produce that breed any more.

Miss Soga (Ngcude), A.C. and I were always together, during school and on the weekends. Fort Hareans always have a lot to say to each other. Not that we did not socialise with the other teachers; we did in school. But three were married and the other, a bachelor, had his own circle of friends in the location. In school Miss Soga, A.C. and I would sit together or have tea by ourselves at recess, either under the trees or on the veranda. At weekends, the two would come for me and take me out round the town. They did the same when there was an entertainment that I allowed myself to be dragged to; after the entertainment they would see me home. So we became very friendly. Never once did A.C. refer to the subject close to his heart for three-quarters of that first year. It was only sometime towards the end of the year, as we were sitting under the trees at school, waiting for Miss Soga to join us, that he said:

'Do you remember my parting words three years ago at Mrs Jabavu's?'

'I told you, Joe, to forget it.'

'But it is not easy to forget,' he replied.

'You can try,' was my response.

The subject was dropped when Miss Soga joined us.

As a colleague, A.C. was wonderful. He was always there to help

me, a new teacher, with any problems I might have. He was like this
with the other teachers too. He was an excellent teacher, patient,
thorough, painstaking, giving his best and demanding the same from
his students. Though he was strict the students liked him, for he was
fair and just. We were teaching the same subject, English. The students I taught in the first year of high school would pass on to him
for the second and third years. This meant a lot of co-ordination and
co-operation in our work. I learnt much from A.C. about what
makes a good teacher, and what co-operation and co-ordination can
do in the classroom. I was an apt pupil and in that first year I knew
teaching was my calling and that I was going to make a good
teacher.

Working closely with him, I began to see the good qualities in him
– warm though never demonstrative, kind, patient. Concerned about
others, he demonstrated humility in his concern for those students
who could not always pay even the low fees. A.C. was a scholar
whose breadth and depth amaze me even to this day, an intellectual
whose pursuits were limitless. I had been a budding intellectual at
Fort Hare and had noticed these things in him, but in those days he
was far away from me, part of the 'Establishment' for which I did
not care. It was because he was seen as part of the Establishment
that the students at Iona House nicknamed him 'The Big Philistine'.
Working closer with him I began to see him for the person that he
was. Even his respect for tradition, for which I did not care, began
to make sense; and his male chauvinism was the chauvinism I saw
in most men around me. I had always looked at men from the point
of view of Tata, compared them with him – he who had shed all the
male chauvinism he ever had, long before I got to know him.

When I went home for the June holidays, A.C. followed too. I was
to know this when I arrived at the train station in Idutywa on my
way back to Kroonstad. As soon as I stepped into the waiting-room,
I thought I heard his raspy cough outside. Soon he came in. He saw
me and smiled.

'My goodness! What are you doing here? I thought you were going
to Johannesburg to your brother?' I said.

'Ugh! It was so empty and lonely in Kroonstad and I did not think
Johannesburg would be any better. So after a few days, I decided
home was best.'

'When did you arrive in Idutywa, then?'

'I came up by train this morning.'

'You mean to tell me you have been in Idutywa this whole day?'

'Yes, I was even tempted to take a taxi to Nqabarha. (He never referred to my place as Duff.) On second thoughts I changed my mind for fear you might set your dogs on me. But I did follow, for about three miles, the road that goes there.'

'Oh, Joe! Set dogs on you! Who would do that?'

'Not the other people for they don't know me. But I feared you might.'

'Do you think I am that bad then?'

'How am I to know?'

We travelled back together. On getting to Kroonstad, I found I would have no place to stay as my landlady was going to Alexandra, in Johannesburg, to join her husband. A.C. was very much concerned. In three days, he found me a place with Mr and Mrs Henderson Kwayani Binda in D Location. Mrs Binda had, as a table-boarder, a medicine man, known throughout the location and its environs as Dr Rhadebe. Dr Rhadebe was in great demand among the blacks in the location and among whites in the city and on the farms. Every Friday evening a line of cars could be seen along the fence, bordering the open space in front of the row of houses in this part of D Location. These belonged to whites who had come to consult Dr Rhadebe. Once or twice a week, he would announce at table that he was going out to such-and-such a farm and the farmer would be coming to pick him up. In the mornings after such trips, he would come in, all smiles, and take out of his briefcase a wad of notes, money he had received the previous night, anything from 300 to 500 pounds sterling. 'You see, Miss Binda, what I get from one Boer? He pay me good. I does a good job too for him. His calves will not die any more, or his *nooi* will now gets a child. They be married for six years. They's can't make a child. She will get it this time. I give her good medicine, Miss Binda, good medicine.' (Dr Rhadebe did not know the difference between 'Miss' and 'Mrs'.)

On those days when he had been to the house of a teacher, nurse or priest, he made a point of telling us about the visits. I suppose it was his way of informing me that my colleagues were his clients too. Dr Rhadebe was also famous for his 'divining bones', unlike any that people in this part of the country had ever seen. Curious, I asked him if he could let me see them. He showed me. Laughing, I said: 'Is this all?'

'Do you know them, Mistress?' he asked, rather shaken.

'Of course I do. These are ordinary sea shells. *iNgqoqo,* we call them. There are lots of them along the sea-shore where I come from. People make beautiful necklaces, earrings and bracelets with them.'

'Don't tell them, Mistress,' he begged. 'The peoples here don't know. Please don't tell them.'

'No, I won't Dr Rhadebe. I'll bring lots more when I go home in December, all sizes,' I promised. I was really amused, and even though I had promised not to tell anyone, I could not help sharing this secret with Mrs Binda.

This was a completely new experience for me – whites and educated people going to consult medicine men! Where I came from, only the red-blanket people engaged in such practices. For a long time, I could not figure out why it was so. Then it dawned upon me that as the rationale for witchcraft is competition and jealousy among kinsmen and kinswomen, here in the city, where people are thrown into one melting pot, competing for the same things – jobs, favours from the boss – the whole social process goes beyond one's kinsfolk to strangers, who normally would not envy one for anything. In such a situation, one has to be protected even against the stranger.

In Kroonstad, I found more superstition among the educated than I had ever known among the red-blanket people of the countryside. This was to be my experience, too, in Langa location in Cape Town. When I talked about this with Ntangashe at one time, she advised: 'Just listen; don't even try to argue with them for they will not believe you. If anything, they will think you are pretending.'

It was in the Binda house in the evenings that I heard of the escapades and adventures of the men in the ICU in its heyday in the Orange Free State. I listened fascinated as Ntate Binda related these stories. There would also be tales from African history as well – the attack on Thaba Bosiu by Mpangazitha and his Hlubi, and how the Basotho hurled boulders at them and repelled them; the flight of Mpangazitha and his men and their last stand on the banks of the Caledon, where the Hlubi general fell. I heard the Sotho version from Keable Mote, great friend of Ntate Binda, and the Hlubi version from A.C., as told him by his father. Both versions were substantially the same. It turned out that this was another area where I shared an interest with A.C.

We journeyed together again in December when school broke up for the Christmas holidays. At home, I was to be hit by the story of Mama's sojourn in East London. This story shocked us: we felt ashamed and scandalised. Tata was hurt though he never said so.

As soon as Mama arrived, I went to Coffee Bay to visit Ntangashe. From here I was to go to meet Halley in Umtata. I really did not know whether I wanted to meet him or not. I felt so ashamed. How could I look him in the face after what had happened? Tata's wife, going from door to door, looking for work from white people in East London! Did he believe this story? If he did, what did he think about us? After all, Edwina was his cousin. Perhaps they sympathised with her.

Even as I got off the bus at Viedgesville, I was not sure what I was going to do. When the East London train pulled in at five o'clock, I jumped aboard. I was going home; I would write to Halley and explain and apologise. I was feeling too hurt and ashamed to meet him. On the train I met Nzwanenkulu Finca, a friend.

'Mntuwakusasa, why here? I thought you would be in Umtata.'

'Schools are opening in a week. I have to be home,' I said.

'No! Fort Hare is not due for a month. You mean to tell me you're not going back? Wow!' he laughed.

'I don't know. I think I like teaching. Moreover, we have to discuss the whole matter with Tata,' I told him.

We parted in Idutywa, he going home to Colosa, I to Duff.

'I thought you'd be in Umtata,' remarked Tata when he saw me.

'I thought I should come home so we can discuss the question of my going back to Kroonstad.'

'That was decided before you went to Kroonstad, that you would be away for just one year and then go back to Fort Hare. No, Phyllie, you have to go back and finish your degree. I won't have you leave in the middle. You have to complete that degree.'

'I understand all that. But this was only my first year of teaching, a year of trial and error, learning how to teach. Now I think I know what I want to be; I think I know what it is to be a teacher and I'd like to go back and teach.'

'Well, I don't know, my child.' A pause. 'What about your studies?'

'Tata, I'll complete my degree, I promise you. Actually, I think I'll do it privately.'

'And how you know how to argue your case! If that's what you want, then go ahead. Get yourself ready. When do they open in

Kroonstad, by the way?'

'Next Tuesday,' I replied.

'You have only three days then before you leave! You'd better get your things together,' he advised.

That Friday, I was on the train back to Kroonstad. I did finish my degree as promised, but after I got married, while teaching and raising my children.

My second year of teaching was a very bad year for me. I was hurt, hurt, hurt. Alone in my room at night, I would cry. Even on that bus and train journey from Coffee Bay, after abruptly cancelling my appointment with Halley, I had felt miserable and rotten inside. Why did I do it? How could I do such a thing? He would be there, hanging around, waiting for me to show up. What a horrible thing to do! I felt bad and hated myself. The presence of Nzwanenkulu in the train helped a lot; we had grown up together and were good friends. Back in Kroonstad, things were terrible. I wanted to hide myself. It was the students that kept me going and helped me keep my sanity.

I wrote to Halley as soon as I got home, apologising, telling him that I had decided to go back to teaching, that I had had to cut short my visit at home. I pleaded with him to forgive my thoughtlessness. He wrote back to tell me that when I had not turned up on the second day, he had reckoned I was not coming and had left. He understood, and I was forgiven. But my sisters, especially Granny and Ntangashe, were furious with me for having behaved this way. It was cruel and thoughtless, they said. Somhlophe was not as harsh, even though she too reprimanded me for my action.

I was feeling horrible. Even the manner I assumed did not always hide how I felt. Around Easter, A.C. started to make advances. Again I told him to leave me alone. This made me more miserable. I no longer wanted to go out with him and Miss Soga. I would always have an excuse when they invited me out to join them. A.C., noticing that I was not my usual self, backed off. He was very good to me during this period and understood I was going through some crisis. In school we continued to work as if nothing was amiss.

I did not come home that June. A.C. attended a vacation course at Fort Hare on African languages run by Professors G. P. Lestrade and C. M. Doke of the universities of Cape Town and the Witwatersrand. A touring Fort Hare soccer team stopped in Kroonstad. In the team were friends from my Fort Hare days. We had lots of fun together, for when they were not playing, the team spent most of its time at our high school. Halley and I still continued our hot correspondence and his letters proved a tonic.

School opened and our work resumed. One day in September, after discussing some aspect of our work, A.C. said: 'You know, I'd like to settle down. I am getting old; but you rebuff me every time.'

'Please, Joe, I thought this was settled between us for all time. Do not bring it up again.'

'And who is the lucky fellow? Halley?'

I was annoyed and my voice conveyed it. 'There's no lucky fellow. Perhaps not even he. I don't think I'll ever get married.'

'Goodness me! What a pity!'

I said nothing and we continued our work.

Before the end of the year, he teasingly said one day: 'I think my father might just visit yours this coming holiday.'

'What for?' I laughed. 'My father is rather a hard nut to crack, you know!'

'Not that we could not try,' he said.

'You just try.'

This was the nearest thing to a 'yes' that A.C. ever got from me. Schools closed and we all came back home to the Cape to our various homes. I think it was on that trip that we met some chiefs from Lesotho, going to East London. One of them thought I would make a nice wife for his son. Believing A.C. was my brother, the chief asked him about my age and enquired after 'our' father's address. When we parted at Blaney, the chief said to A.C.: 'Now don't forget to tell your old man that I am interested in your sister for my son.' This is how things are done sometimes in our part of the world.

Somhlophe came home for the holidays. Within a few days of her arrival, Tata received a letter from A.C.'s father, announcing his intended visit to my father. (I suppose what the Lesotho chief said made him move fast.) Tata showed the letter to Somhlophe and asked her: 'Do you know this Jordan in Kroonstad?'

'Yes, we were together at Lovedale as students.'

'I thought he was married and a family man,' Tata said.

'Not that I know of,' replied Somhlophe.

'But I thought there, there, eh, eh …,' Tata hemmed and hawed.

Somhlophe, understanding what he wanted to say, helped him out. 'You know, Phyllie never got over what happened last

December. She was very hurt and still is.'

'My poor Phyllie!'

Silence.

Tata always knew the boys interested in us, even though he was never told officially. African parents do not discuss such topics with their children. As Tata was the only parent we had, we talked a lot about our friends to him, including boyfriends. He could always guess who were our favourites. When I first came home from Kroonstad, and later in my letters home, I had told him how Mr Jordan, one of the teachers, had assisted me to find a place to stay, how he helped me with my work and how good he had been generally. From this, Tata had drawn the idea that Mr Jordan must be a responsible family man.

When Jordan senior, his younger brother, the Rev. Julius Jordan, and A.C.'s maternal uncle, Willie Mehlo, came to our home, my menfolk were there to meet them. They had all been told that Tata was expecting such guests. Mama was in her best mood, and she welcomed and received her guests with all the warmth they deserved. She could be very gracious when she chose.

The Jordans were not a known family in our part of the country. Only one person by that name had been heard of; this was John Jordan, A.C.'s uncle, who had been in the civil service in Idutywa. Tata knew him and had wondered, as he was talking to Somhlophe, if this Jordan in Kroonstad was not perhaps the son of John Nel, the name by which they knew John Jordan. So, before any discussions could be entered into, the question of 'Who are you?' had to be cleared. This question is asked of anyone who seeks a marriage relationship with a family. He has to give his credentials to establish his status, either on account of birth or service to the community. Even a man of lowly birth who has given noble service to his community can marry into the nobility. In our case, too, after the introductions, the question of 'Who are you, what are your roots?' was asked.

A.C.'s father answered the question and, as one of the younger uncles later related, he was in his element. 'I am Elijah Jordan, son of Nelani, son of Jordan, whose real name was Ndimangele. I am a Hlubi by birth, a citizen of the Mpondomise kingdom. Ndimangele, who later assumed the name Jordan, was a courtier of Maqoma at Ncgwazi. I was born at Ncgwazi in Maqoma's court. After the arrest of Maqoma and the dispersal of those around his court, Ndimangele, like many others, went to work for a white man, who gave him the

name Jordan. Nelani, my father, used his father's name as his sur-
name when, in fact, he should have used Nobhadula, the name of
his forebear.'

At the mention of Maqoma's court, my people realised these
Jordans were no upstarts; they were a family with a place of honour
among the people. It was interesting how later, both before and
after I got married, Tata would, in telling people about the man who
had married his youngest daughter, drop Maqoma's name, thus letting his listeners know it was no upstart family that his daughter was
married into. Another thing that impressed my relatives was Jordan's
claim to Mpondomise citizenship, thus showing he was no collaborating Mfengu. Such things are still important in the world we come
from.

With the families having thus placed themselves, negotiations
could now begin between my people and the Jordans. In the meantime, one of my uncles had been sent inside to find out from me if I
knew these people. I was so embarrassed that in reply I said, 'Yes
and no.' Yes, in that I knew who had sent them; no, in that I never
gave him permission. My uncle did not wait for anything more. This
was a good answer, and guided by it and their assessment of the
character of the Jordans, my people could make their decision. They
decided that this was a family they could marry one of their daughters into. After all matters pertinent and relevant to the question
were discussed and agreed upon, they talked together and feasted.

It turned out that like Tata, A.C.'s father was the local historian of
Mpondomise history and his people, the Hlubi. What an interesting
time these two had, recounting episodes from their history during
the visit. After three days the Jordans left. By the time I went back to
Kroonstad, I was engaged to A.C. He stopped in Idutywa on his way
to Kroonstad to meet my people and we made the journey together.

Still I was not certain if this was the right thing to do. Why did I
allow it to happen? How was I going to get myself out of this mess?
And a mess it was. I had allowed it to happen because during my
soul-searching and agony the previous year, I had often felt that perhaps marriage between me and Halley was not the best thing for the
two of us. If I was to marry, I would have to find myself a good
man. A.C. seemed to fit the bill.

Though the atmosphere at home had very much improved, I was
not happy; I was lonely now that Ntangashe had gone. True, Nosithe was there; we did things and went to places together, but she

could not fill Ntangashe's place in my life. Moreover, I was ready to settle down. I went to Umtata for a day after the Jordan visit and heard while there that Halley was expected. I left town immediately and we missed each other by just an hour. After a long period of uncertainty and hesitation, I eventually summoned up courage to write to him when I got back to Kroonstad, telling him I was engaged to be married. 'Guess to whom? The Big Philistine.' Anxiously I waited for his letter and his reaction. After what seemed like eternity the letter finally came. In it he told me that he had already got the news from his father, to whom Tata had written. He ended the letter: 'I am sorry, Miss Phyl. I suppose I waited too long.' I never asked Tata why he had written to his father with this news.

There was a lot of excitement in Kroonstad when we got back. Many had expected the engagement to happen. Sol Thlapane, in congratulating A.C., said: 'I understand now why you never invited any of us to the train station, the day she arrived.' Apparently, whenever a new lady teacher was arriving, the bachelor teachers would all go to the train station to see if she was worth a shot at. When the news reached Fort Hare, the reaction was: 'What? He got her? How did he do it?' They all decided it was teaching together that did it. And how true! It was just that!

My sister Granny was not too pleased. At this time she was corresponding a lot with Halley, of whom she was very fond. When she heard that I was engaged to A.C., she wrote to him in Kroonstad to congratulate him and ended her letter, saying, 'I hope Mama's baby will not be the meat, with you being the cat.' That was my sister Granny all right.

Even though Tata had now met A.C., he too was not comfortable. He wrote to a cousin of mine teaching at the Roman Catholic school in Kroonstad, informing him that I was engaged to A.C. and asked him to keep an eye on A.C. and see that he did not play around with me.

Now that we were engaged, A.C. took me out alone more often. We did things together and got to know each other better. We both went to Johannesburg for the winter holidays, he to his brother in Modder East, while I went to my cousins, the Mdingis, in Orlando East. A.C. came up to Orlando East one weekend to see me and meet my folks there. My cousins liked him, especially cousin Frank's wife, who thought he looked a reliable fellow. On the day I left for the beginning of the new term in Kroonstad, A.C. brought his two brothers and their wives to make themselves known to my folks in Johannesburg and to meet me. His eldest sister, Nombuyiselo, met us at Germiston train station. We spent an hour with her there before we proceeded to Kroonstad.

We planned to get married in December or early in January, and preparations were under way. A.C. had bought a house in Ngoanabase Street in B Location, had it torn down and rebuilt it into a five-roomed modern house. He moved in as soon as it was completed. So from October of that year, he was living in his own house, with someone coming in to clean and cook for him. I was boarding with Mrs Mochumi, a teacher at the Roman Catholic school.

Then lo and behold, early in the spring, a new correspondence between me and Halley flared up. It was thick; it was hot; it was romantic. I wrote to him every week and received his letters every Friday, letters in which were enclosed rose petals, and lines from romantic love poems. It was as if there was no A.C., had never been. We made plans to meet in December. Where? Right in my home town, Idutywa. *Omnium conspectu!*

Schools closed. A.C. came home to Duff mission with me and spent a day with us. I could not wait for him to leave so that I could finalise my plans for my meeting with Halley. Any definite plans? Not exactly; we just wanted to have our final fling together. I was excited. Alone in my room I waited with fear and trepidation. But I was not crying. I was too buoyed and excited to cry. In the midst of all this, my folks were excitedly anticipating the wedding in January. They were busy with preparations; invitations were being sent out; relatives were arriving; Mama had bought new curtains and a carpet for the dining-room, all for this occasion.

In an African setting where a marriage involves so many people, things reach a stage where they acquire their own momentum. It takes real courage to call a halt to proceedings. It suddenly struck me to ask myself the question: 'What will not happen if Halley and I meet?' All these people, who were now so involved, would be stunned. The thought of Tata hurt by me weighed heavily. Why didn't I tell him? He, who had been so generous and understanding, would have understood. My grand old man! How could I hurt him? I felt sorry for A.C. too. I could see him, frown on his face, reading my message, 'Married Halley', less than a week before he was due to have married me. How would he return to Kroonstad and look in the face all those who had wished him well and were looking forward to congratulate him, coming back with me, his bride? Would he be able to take it? O my God! I felt hemmed in. Then I cried, realising that I could not go through with it. I cried that whole Thursday night, and on 15 December I sent Halley this message: 'Regret, cannot go through with it.' This was just five days before we were due to meet. It was cruel; it was devastating. I had raised his hopes (and mine) to fever pitch, only to dash them to the ground.

A.C. was coming to be with us the weekend before the wedding. There were some documents to sign. I still had all the letters that Halley had written to me while I was in Kroonstad, as well as all his pictures. The Wednesday before A.C. arrived, I gathered all those letters, closed the door of my room and went through them one by one. The following day, I took an open tin, a box of matches and the letters to the far end of the garden behind the trees and, one by one, I threw them into the fire, pictures and all. I cried while doing this, for I felt destroyed in that fire was part of me. Then I came home, went into my room, closed the door, cried that whole afternoon, evening and night, and would not be comforted. Those who came into the room, trying to comfort me, thought it was anxiety about the pending wedding. It is usual for a girl to be in tears during this period. But little did they know why I was crying.

The next day, Friday, I went to town to meet A.C., my fiancé. He was glad and excited to see me. He never suspected anything. I wore my mask well. We came home together in the afternoon. By now, there was excitement in the whole place; women were moving about briskly, ululating; guests were arriving and everyone was looking forward to Tuesday. I, too, was swept up and looked forward to the big day.

That Tuesday must really have been a big day and I must have looked gorgeous. My baby sister, Nokhwezi, three years old and one of the flower girls, asked everyone who came into our kitchen the next day: 'Did you see me and Sis' Nogqaza getting married yesterday? We were so beautiful, I tell you!' And while Nokhwezi was saying this, Mama was proudly telling people: 'Phyllie looked so lovely; you would not think she was the same person who was with us at the breakfast table yesterday morning.' The last of the birds from Tata's first nest was gone.

Farewell, Gqubeni!

The day after a wedding in the country is usually very busy. The wedding guests start leaving for their homes; the groom's party is leaving for home, too, excited, carrying away their prize, the bride; the bride's family is busy packing what the bride must take with her – her own personal belongings, the many presents for the groom's family. It is a day of joy on the part of the groom's party; a day of tears for the family of the bride, crying because they are losing a loved member of the family. It is a day of admonitions and requests, of promises and thanks, a day of speeches.

In the afternoon, all the parties gathered in the dining-room, with A.C. and me sitting at the table, the centre of the whole affair. Oom Joel Nombewu, Tata's good friend, addressing himself to the Jordans, said: 'Here, then, is the vessel you came to ask for. It is beautiful, untarnished, untainted and we hope you will keep it that way. Should you at any time tire of it, please bring it back, for it always will have a place among our beautiful vessels.'

Two of my uncles' wives had admonished me to keep and carry myself well, as befitting my family, doing nothing to tarnish the good name of the home I came from; to uphold the Jordan name too, for now I had joined that family. Tata could not finish what he wanted to say. He began: 'When a married woman is accused by her in-laws of being a sorceress, they always say it was her mother who taught her the art. Should you ever accuse this one of that art, know that I —' and he broke down. I broke down too and so did everybody else – my sisters, uncles, aunts, cousins and friends.

Malume Menziwa, who too had wept at this point, soon collected himself and said he knew I would bear myself well, remembering the stock I came from, Mama's people, the Balfours, and my people, the Ntantalas. His sister Ida had held aloft the Balfour name to her grave. If she had not, he, Menziwa, son of Makhaphela, would not have been there to see me getting married. Then, addressing himself to A.C., Malume said this: 'Now, son of Jordan, I would like to remind you that at Fort Hare, you learnt a lot of things to give you wisdom; you learnt your ethics, your jurisprudence, your logic. But there is one course you never took and that is Wife Psychology, a strange course whose scope and content are not well-defined. One discovers these as one goes along. Now that you are married, you are going to take that course – Wife Psychology. Going through it means patience, understanding and endurance. You will not find any experts to help you along, for each case is unique.'

The Jordans responded, first thanking my people for what they had done, establishing a link that they so very much desired through this marriage of their son to their daughter. They promised to treat this precious vessel well and were sure they would never tire of it. The ceremony over, they left for Tsolo.

Usually both parties leave together. But on this occasion, it had been decided that there would be no party of my family going to Tsolo because of the distance. Only about six people would accompany me. There was going to be no dress-up parade at Mbokothwana, as is usually the case. My people would leave with me the following day and A.C. would leave with us as well. In spite of this, Granny suggested that at least the bridesmaids and my best man should go, lest the people at Mbokothwana should want a dress parade. 'You never know what Africans will do. They will want to see their son in his wedding outfit when we get there,' she said. And how correct she was. No one remembered any agreements made before the wedding when our party got to Mbokothwana.

We left home shortly after breakfast on Thursday, in a party of twelve, including the drivers. Mama, Tata, Somhlophe and other members of my family were on the veranda to bid us farewell. Ntangashe had slipped out of the house before this moment to avoid the farewell. I was glad: there were never any farewells between us. A.C. was to tell me later that when Tata took his hand, he held it for some time, looked him up and down, sizing him up, then looked him straight in the eye before he dropped that hand.

'I knew what responsibility I had,' said A.C. 'If I ever messed around with you, your father would have killed me.'

We stopped at Umtata where Granny bought bouquets, one for

the bride and two for the bridesmaids, and a buttonhole for the best man. At about one o'clock we arrived at Mbokothwana. As our cars drove into A.C.'s home, women came out, chanting: *'Siza kudl' umkhupha! Siza kudl' ijiki! Siza kudl' ijiki!'* [We are going to eat stone-ground corn bread; we are going to drink home-brewed beer.]

Other women were engaged in a mock performance of hoeing, sweeping, plastering, grinding corn and all the other tasks that women are involved in around the home. This was a new experience for us; we had never seen it before. We did not even know what *mkhupha* was, and it was only during our stay there that we learnt it was stone-ground corn bread. In a neighbour's rondavel where we were housed, the grindstone was built into the floor. As things were beginning to acquire meaning, Malume Menziwa, in his humorous way, said: 'Hey! They do grind corn here! The grindstone is part of the floor, not something that a woman brings in when she has corn to grind. Hey! Hey! I wonder if my sister's child will be equal to the tasks here. I swear by my sister Ellen, daughter of Makhaphela!' He was really concerned and so were all the others. The women outside had not ceased their mock performance. Now and again, they would appear and continue with it. This was something!

An hour after our arrival, word came that we should dress for the wedding parade. Said Granny: 'Did I not tell you, Malume? I knew they would want us to dress up, and that was why I insisted that the bridesmaids and best man should come with us. There is not even a question of whether we are prepared or not. They assume we are. Africans!'

So we dressed up; first it was the wedding dress, and we paraded in that. We had lunch at A.C.'s and then returned to our quarters. In the late afternoon, we changed into the second dress and paraded in that. I wore a knee-length two-piece.

In the evening it was the same hand-over ceremony again, with speeches and exhortations, now mostly from A.C.'s people to their son and to me as a new member of the family. In his speech, A.C.'s father warned me not to drive a wedge between A.C. and his mother. 'Damfie is his mother's son; no one is as important to Damfie as his mother. I hope you will not wean Damfie away from his mother. To us here, you will be known as *"No-Tuis"*, which was Jordan's wife's name – Nokhaya in Xhosa.'

As if in reply to what A.C.'s father had said, his uncle Willie Mehlo responded: 'Gxukumfana [a name he always used], you have been a good son, reliable and dependable. I hope you will honour and respect your wife and listen to her advice. If you look around and count the number of men who have made something of themselves, you will find it is only those who heeded their wife's advice. Those who never did are nothing in the community.'

Then an old man, a Madikiza, kinsman of the Jordans, got up to add his piece. 'I am glad to be here. I was looking forward to the wedding of this young man for we are all proud of him. He has brought honour to this house of Nobhadula and made our name known among nations. But to you, young woman, I must say this: to me you have disgraced yourself, parading in short skirts while you are a married woman.'

Behind us, I could hear the remarks of the women sitting there, in complete agreement with the old man. 'He is right! He is right! Yhu! Does fashion mean this? Did you see her? She did not even close her eyes! They were wide open! She saw everything! Yhu! It is too much!'

My folks were offended. But they did not say anything in that gathering. As A.C. was taking me and my sister Granny back to our quarters, my sister remarked to him: 'Well, Sbali, I do not know. It seems your people are already finding fault with my sister even before they have known her. We thought you were an educated man, a college graduate, who wanted a modern woman befitting his status. That is why we brought with us a modern woman. But it seems we were wrong. If your people pick on this child now, even before we leave, what will they not do when we are gone? I shudder to think of it.'

A.C. left us at the door and went back. Inside our quarters my folks were talking about the remarks of the old man with great concern and also about the performance of the women outside during the day. 'Will Phyllie manage here?' was the question on everyone's mind. Because of their concern, they had already persuaded aunt Nosithe to remain with me to help me with all these tasks I would be required to do, some of which we had never done before. Perhaps between the two of us, we could manage. Poor Nosithe was so concerned. Like Ntangashe, she never wanted anything to hurt me.

Just as we were getting ready to sleep, A.C.'s father and his brother Fottie came to apologise for the remarks of the old man.

'Please forgive us,' said A.C.'s father. 'That was an old man's talk, not shared by anybody in the family. Have no fears; your child will be treated well by all of us. We are good people. We know how to treat our women. Have no fears.'

Malume Menziwa responded: 'Thou educationist of the days of Langham Dale,* I am glad you came. We were concerned, fearing for our daughter, thinking that perhaps we had made a mistake by marrying her into this family, a family not well known in our part of the country. We know now we made no mistake for in you, thou educationist of the days of Langham Dale, I see a man who moves with the times, a progressive man. We are grateful you came and we thank you for allaying our fears.'

After this speechifying, all were pleased and these two left. We did not sleep much for my folks were leaving early the next day. So after leaving me and aunt Nosithe at A.C.'s, they went.

Months later, I was to laugh at Malume Menziwa for remarking about my short skirts. He had come up to Kroonstad after Nandi was born to see the baby. I was excited and buzzing all around him. Looking at me, he said: 'Phyllie, these skirts are rather too short. I hope you let them down when you visit the old people in the country.'

I laughed. 'That cannot come from you, Malume. When they complained about my short skirts, you were the first to defend me and demand an apology. No, not from you, Malume!'

'No, it was not that we did not appreciate their point. We did. What we were objecting to was to be told to our face about our faults. That is not the way to treat people. You speak behind their backs about faults you think they have, especially if there is nothing you can do about them. You don't tell people to their face. No, that is not the way. That was our objection.'

We had taken Malume to the school on this visit, where he addressed the teachers and the students. This was one feature of Kroonstad High School. A number of people, mostly Africans, were attracted by the experiment and would, on passing through Kroonstad, stop at the school to see for themselves. Cingo always invited them to address the teachers and students. Tata had done the same too when he came up to visit us in the winter before Nandi was born. Malume came back impressed – so did many of them –

* Sir Langham Dale was Superintendent General of Education in the Cape Colony in the days when Malume and A.C.'s father qualified as teachers.

by this huge establishment of over ninety teachers and over two thousand students. What pleased Malume was that it all operated under the principalship of the son of his friend in the Transkeian Bhunga, Walter Cingo, father of Reginald Cingo, our head.

Archibald Campbell Mzolisa

Archibald Campbell Mzolisa was the third and youngest son of Elijah Jordan by his wife Fanny Makhosazana, daughter of Twana Mehlo of Mbokothwana, Tsolo, in Transkei. Among his friends he was popularly known as Joe or A.C. To most of those who grew up with him and those who watched him grow, he was fondly known as Damfie. To the workers from his home area, he was known as Thiyane, the Ambusher. This is his clan name, or *isiDuko*.

As a young man Elijah Jordan had come to Mbokothwana to be principal of the higher primary school there. Fanny, who was to become his wife, was a pupil in the school at the time. Elijah and Fanny had eight children, five girls and three boys. After Fanny died during the influenza epidemic of 1918, when A.C. was twelve years old, Elijah married a cousin of Fanny, Lele Sothomela, one of the teachers on his staff. This woman gave birth to two sons, Monde and Bantwini. The Jordan family is a family of teachers. All the aunts and uncles, sisters, brothers, and cousins have been teachers.

It was not easy for the older children to accept life under a stepmother, so the eldest sister and the two brothers, all teachers, left home and went to Johannesburg to try their luck. After a short stint teaching, the brothers found work in the mines as clerks, where they remained until they retired. The sister taught on and off until she established herself as a businesswoman in Benoni location. The second sister married a local teacher. A.C. was at home with the younger sisters throughout the years of their growing up, and thus at an early age he was thrust into the position of protector.

A.C. was an excellent student from the day he started school, showing an interest in literature even in those early years. His father was not only a choirmaster but a poet and music composer as well, and a keen sportsman. Cricket was his love. All three of his boys grew to be cricketers, A.C. developing into a good batsman and his older brother Bingie a devastating bowler. A.C., brought up in a home of poetry and music composition, was to become a poet, music composer and choirmaster as well.

Having come to Mpondomiseland at the time of British penetration, Elijah developed an interest in the history of the people among whom he lived. He became the local expert on the history of the Mpondomise and their neighbours, the Mpondo, Bhaca and Xhesibe. A.C. was to develop that interest too when he grew up, an interest that led to his becoming one of the few experts on oral African history, told from the point of view of the African people, the history that one seldom finds in books written by the historians of the conquerors. By the time of his death, he was keenly sought after by students of African history, in South Africa, Europe and in the United States of America.

The family's origins were at Ngcwazi in the court of Maqoma, warrior-king, where their forebear Ndimangele was courtier. Elijah, son of Nelani, son of Ndimangele – now known as Jordan – was born at Ngcwazi. The whole area where Ngcwazi is situated is the home of the Xhosa language; here Xhosa was first reduced to writing. Hearing good Xhosa spoken made Nelani, Elijah and later A.C. very sensitive to the beauty of the language, written or spoken. Elijah made it his duty to instil in all his children, growing up in an area where one seldom heard good Xhosa, a love of the language. Unfortunately, only A.C. seems to have captured this from his father; the other children speak the dialect of the local people.

Mbokothwana was an outpost of St Cuthbert's mission at Ngcolosi, and there was much interaction between the two. The missionaries at St Cuthbert's had a tremendous influence on all the Jordan children, especially A.C. and the sister just after him, Nontsikelelo, who at the age of seventeen joined the Order of St John the Baptist for African nuns. Contact with the fathers at St Cuthbert's, some of whom were scholars from Oxford, opened new vistas for A.C. and made him look beyond his immediate horizon.

After completing his primary schooling at Mbokothwana and then St Cuthbert's, he went to St John's College in Umtata where he qualified as a teacher. He taught at St Cuthbert's for a year, where he excelled as choirmaster, the second best in the whole district of Tsolo after Diniwe Madala, now principal of Mbokothwana after the retirement of Elijah Jordan. A.C. then went to Lovedale on an Andrew Smith Bursary. It was while he was a student here that A.C. met my sister Somhlophe; they moved in the same circle of friends. In fact, the character Nomvuyo in his novel *iNgqumbo ye miNyanya* is modelled on her. It was during this period, too, that I met him for the first time. I was twelve. Every time we came home on holiday, I had to leave the train full of Healdtown students and join the Lovedale train at Alice to travel with my sister, who would take charge of me.

From Lovedale, A.C. proceeded to Fort Hare to study for the B.A. degree. By the time he completed it he had developed an interest not only in English literature but also in Classical literature and history. It was during his Fort Hare days, too, that he was introduced to the world of classical music by Professor Jabavu. This was to become one of his loves. By now he was writing poetry for the college student magazine and later for an African newspaper, *uMthetheli wa Bantu*. His poem on the invasion of Abyssinia by Mussolini, written in Xhosa, became very popular among the students at Fort Hare and among the politically minded in the country.

A.C. was not just a bookworm. He loved sport, especially cricket, which he had played as a youngster at Mbokothwana, with his father as coach. He later played for the college first cricket team and at one time won the Principal's Bat for being best batsman of the year. Back home he played for the Transkei cricket first team, which competed with other teams in the Cape Province and Natal. When he came to Cape Town, he was keenly sought after by cricket clubs there. But being the patriot he was, he chose to play for the Transkei club, Thembu United. This made the Thembu so popular that even players who belonged to other clubs, whose homes were in Transkei, came to join it.

Later in life he was to broaden his interests to include African languages and literature. It galled him that the authorities in African languages were whites, sons of missionaries, who had grown up speaking the languages and had developed an academic interest in them. Professors Lestrade, Doke and Malcolm, and Inspector Bennie were in the forefront of this work, while Professors Kirby and Hugh Tracey led the field in African folk music. To A.C. this was not right. Africans should be there as well, in the forefront of this field of study.

Though he could have written in English as well as in Xhosa, he wrote his first novel, *iNgqumbo ye miNyanya,* in his native tongue, addressing himself to an African readership, a readership that was already in existence, for Africans had been writing for other Africans since the middle of the nineteenth century. *iNgqumbo ye miNyanya* was an instant hit and was acclaimed as the best novel ever written in the Xhosa language. It is a novel for all time, showing the African at the crossroads. It treats African culture in a dignified and wholesome way, showing its qualities and beauty. Yet at the same time, the author is very much aware of the new forces at work among the people, depicting the new man who is beginning to look critically at the new ways and trying to forge for himself a course that will perhaps serve his interests better. No wonder the book was such a hit with both young and old.

A.C., a humble man of simple and frugal tastes, a loyal and faithful lieutenant, warm but never demonstrative, was kind, gentle, patient, tolerant, compassionate. He was one of only three people I know who would go all out to help others. These other two are Tata and Gladstone Mxolisi Ntlabathi. A.C. was very understanding, trusting and conservative, a respecter of custom and tradition, a man who always had his feet on the ground. He had a tremendous intellect of staggering breadth and depth; a scholar who followed each pursuit with an analytic mind, searching for the essence. And yet for all that he never lost the human touch, the respect for the common man.

His last name, Mzolisa, is that of my brother, the brother I never knew. Often after we were married Tata would say, in his dignified way, when he heard of a milestone in A.C.'s life: 'I wonder if there is not something in that name "Mzolisa". These are the things I had hoped for in my own boy.' Talking of names, his older brother is Theophilus *Ndabakayise,* the only person other than Tata to have that name. His eldest sister is Theodora Nombuyiselo, Theodora being my sister Granny's first name.

This was the man I had married. He never was a lover, but a husband. Because he was not demonstrative, there were very few romantic scenes between us even during the period of our engagement. He was excited in his own way, though I never experienced that romantic excitement I had known with Halley. He loved and respected me and this grew over the years.

I do not know that I could say I ever fell in love with him. I had matured and was thus able to look for other things in a relationship with a man. One thing I know, though, is that as I got to know him better, I developed a great respect for him and I knew I would never do anything that would undermine his love, trust and respect for me. On this determination I built my marriage.

A.C. never once asked me if I had terminated my relationship with Halley. He left it to me to be honourable enough to do it. Friends came to our house, some of whom knew me though not him, and some of whom were still interested in me. A.C. welcomed them and never once said he disapproved. There was one young teacher in Kroonstad, Sipho Nyembezi, a great friend from our Fort Hare days. Sipho and I used to go out cycling for miles on weekends before and after I was married. A.C. never complained. Sipho remarked one day: 'You know, Joe is a wonderful fellow, not to have stopped our cycling together. Another fellow would have.' I suppose A.C. was secure enough not to fear anything. The burden was on me to be faithful to him and deal with him honourably. Most times, because he was busy with his university work, I would go to conferences and meetings alone, where I would meet all sorts of people. A.C. never said 'no'. The only condition was: Would I pay for the trip with my own money? After he died and people asked me why I did not find myself another man, I thought: Where in the world would I get another one like A.C., with all the qualities he had? There are not many like him.

And yet, as in all marriages, there were times when things seemed to be heading for the cliff. I am sure it was A.C.'s maturity and tolerance that saved the day. I can be very obstinate and unless I am presented with a good case, it is very difficult to move me. I seldom do things for sentimental reasons. There must be logic and reason for what I have to do. One such occasion was the question of my confirmation as a member of the Anglican Church. I was born Presbyterian and had become a full member of the church even before I left Fort Hare. But in my last years at Fort Hare I had cooled a great deal towards the church. All the same I resented the arrogance of the Anglican and Roman Catholic churches maintaining that they and they alone were the true churches and whoever comes to them must be re-admitted. To add insult to injury, as far as I was concerned, I had to be re-confirmed as if I had not been a full member of my church. A.C., on the other hand, was a blue-blooded Anglican, steeped in the rituals and traditions of his church, and loving them. He could not conceive of his wife not being a member of his church. Unfortunately we had not discussed this aspect of our future life. It was assumed, I guess, that as I was going to drop my name and assume his this was going to be the case even as regards church.

After putting my views to him, I told him that I would compromise and go for the confirmation, but would attend no classes. On this I was not prepared to budge. A.C. came up with all the arguments: the two things went together; I had to know the whole ritual of confirmation, and the classes prepared one for that. I would not budge. He called in Father Martin, his priest, to come and talk to me. I told Father Martin I was not going, reminding him that I had never wanted to be an Anglican in the first place; *they* wanted me – and it had to take place on their own terms. This I was not prepared to do.

Whatever rules and regulations govern this aspect of confirmation in the Anglican Church had to be waived. Father Martin sent me books to read about this rite and I was confirmed. A.C. had been hurt. He tried everything to make me see and accept his point of view and that of his church. I would not budge. It took him time to get over this, poor fellow. But he did. However, he never referred to it throughout those years of our married life.

The other major disagreement between A.C. and myself took place after the birth of our son Pallo. He was six months old and his sister Nandi was twenty-six months. A.C. wanted us to take his son home to see his grandfather. I suggested that I would send the grandfather a train ticket to come and see the child in Kroonstad, as this would be more convenient for me and the children. No: Pallo, as the boy, had to be taken to his ancestral home, A.C. insisted.

'Do you mean to tell me I have to inconvenience myself and the children for the sake of having Pallo sleep at the Jordan home in Mbokothwana?' I asked.

That was what they, the Jordans, had always done. This was what was to be done with his son too, he insisted.

I was not just obstinate for no good reason. After Nandi was born, at three months, I had taken her to Mbokothwana to see her grandparents. We had the most terrible time. The stepmother said goodbye three days after our arrival to visit her sister, leaving us to fend for ourselves in a strange home and strange place. I had been to A.C.'s for only two weeks, after the wedding. So this was a strange place to me. I was a total stranger there.

Mbokothwana, that barren patch between the Xhokonxa and the

Tsitsa rivers! The Jordans were by no means poor. After all, as a teacher's family, they were among the elite in the whole district. But they led a very frugal life, living on just the bare essentials with no extras. I came from a simple rural home too. But we had a few extras that made life a little easier and more comfortable. For example, at home we always had a barrel of water for cooking, besides the water in the tanks which was used for drinking. One went to fetch water from the river only when the barrel was empty and the boys were not there to refill it. Here at Mbokothwana one had to fetch water from the river for cooking, and in my case it meant water for the baby's diapers as well. I was on my feet going to and from the river. Again, at home, Nkomo, our general factotum, chopped and split the logs for firewood before he did anything else. We chopped and split logs only when Nkomo's pile was finished. At Mbokothwana, this was women's work since they were the ones responsible for cooking. I told A.C. that this I was not prepared to do and, further, that to me it was scandalous that his sister Nomaza should be splitting logs while he and his younger brother Monde were there. A day or so after I had told him this, I saw Monde chopping and splitting wood before going on to the pasture. A.C. helped, too, now and again.

It had been a terrible time. Because of the strain and exhaustion, my milk dried up and my baby cried all the time. I thought A.C. understood that things were rough for me. Apparently he had not, or understanding, he thought I should be put through it again. I asked myself again and again: Did he not understand? He was there and saw it all. Was observing a Jordan custom more important to him than the comfort of his wife and children? I was angry, hurt and bitter, and I am afraid that bitterness never left me.

On leaving Mbokothwana that first time with Nandi, I made up my mind that I would not again subject myself to such conditions. If the parents wanted to see us, I would send them tickets to come to Kroonstad. But now, here was my husband insisting that I go there with a baby and a toddler. I told him I was not going. We had reached an impasse.

A.C. wrote to my sister Granny, telling her I was refusing to take his son to his home in Mbokothwana, because I felt it was not good enough for me. But humble though it was, it was his home and he was proud of it. My sister wrote me a long letter, ending it: 'You foolish child, do you not know that the Mfengu are a people of custom? Do you think they are like you, an iLawu* that observes no custom? Your baby is Jordan's son and if he wants certain rituals performed on his son, and those can only be done at his home, let it be so. Whether you think that is rational or not is beside the point. Pallo's father wants it that way. Period.'

That was my sister Granny all right. I was hurt. I was furious. I thought of telling Tata. On second thoughts I decided not to. I had never told him about the rough time I had had when I had taken Nandi there.

'All right, you can take your children to Mbokothwana. But I will not be there to see them suffer. Take them. They are your children. Take your son to Mbokothwana to observe your family customs and tradition. But I am not going.'

He must have thought better of it for when he went to buy the train tickets, only his went to Tsolo, his home. Mine was for Idutywa, my home. At the end of the holidays, he joined us in Idutywa and together we proceeded to Kroonstad. Pallo's grand-father came up to see his grandson in the autumn. This was good for him and he liked it. I had sent him the train ticket as I had said I would.

I did eventually take A.C.'s sons to Mbokothwana. Pallo was three and Lindi six months. It was an overnight visit. So the shades did spread their spirit over them and gathered them in their arms. They now rest in peace.

As years went by I soon noticed that clashes like these affected Nandi, our daughter, who would get very ill when the relations between us were not normal. It was our concern for her that would bring us together. Nandi was the barometer of our relations. When things were good between us, Nandi was in the pink of health. I was also maturing and learnt to avoid confrontations with A.C.

A.C. was growing too. He was becoming less conservative, thanks to our moving to Cape Town. It was here that he was to shed a lot of his conservative ways. This was thanks also to his best friend, I. B. Tabata, an advocate of women's rights, who helped A.C. embrace the new ways and attitudes.

How does one reconcile the tastes of two people – one expensive, the other simple and frugal? I always laugh when I read A.C.'s description of the room of the teachers at Ngcolosi, in his book

* Derogatory expression used for anybody who behaves in a way strange to the African people.

iNgqumbo ye miNyanya, for that is exactly A.C.'s idea of what furniture should be found in a room – a bed, a table to work on and a suitcase for one's clothes. The only addition he would have was a bookcase, record-player and music records. It is very difficult to reconcile tastes that are so different. Sometimes it is better not to try at all. Realising that ours were so different, I decided early in our life that I would always work, so as to have my own account and use my money to buy the things I wanted, and let him pay the house bills. I never asked him for permission to do that. I just told him this was how I was going to do it. I had seen this done by my red-blanket aunts back home, wives of men of means. Whenever these women went out to earn money, it was known by their husbands that such earnings were for their personal use, to buy themselves beads and other ornaments they wanted. Their husbands had no say in such earnings.

Tata had never indulged us. But he always bought the best that his money could buy. So with my money I dressed myself and my children, furnished my house with the best within my means, and gave the children money to buy books and albums they wanted and other things that growing children want. This worked well for all of us. If I had the money, I could go anywhere I wanted. In this respect, I was a free and emancipated woman. But I emancipated myself, and fortunately for me A.C. made no fuss about it.

However, on one occasion in Cape Town, I bought new sitting-room furniture. A.C. was not sure if this account was in his name and, anxious, he never said anything about the furniture, whether he liked it or not. He was greatly relieved when the sales papers came in the mail and they were not in his name. Only then did he say he liked the pieces I had bought. The children and I laughed, for by now they too had come to know just how frugal their father was.

On another occasion, when the bill from our chemist came and it was rather high, A.C. was angry – he paid for all such – and came asking: 'Why is this bill so high? There are three kinds of toothpaste here. Why?' I explained that two of the kids liked one kind while the other two liked another, and the third one was for the two of us.

'No, no! The children must use ash to clean their teeth.' (This was what children used in the country in his days of growing up.) He had forgotten that his children were town children who had never even seen people use ash for cleaning their teeth. Besides, where was I to get the ash in Cape Town? I was not using a coal stove, but an electric stove. I did not say anything at the time, for he was annoyed. Days after, I asked him where I would get the ash for the children to use. Did he want me to contract for ash with Mrs Mduli or Maria and Gertie, down the road, the only people I knew who used coal stoves in our area? He never said anything. But I think he understood that his children were growing up in a world completely different from the one he had grown up in.

So when his daughter Nandi started smoking at fourteen, he learnt to accept that such things would happen. But great was his embarrassment when any of our African friends came and saw his children not behaving like African children, not even like those in town. I had to say to him: 'Look, A.C., our African friends have to accept that our children are not growing up in an African environment, but in a mixed neighbourhood, mostly Coloured. They are not going to be any different from the children they are growing up with. If our African friends cannot understand that and accept the children as they are, hard lines.'

Awakening

I often tell people that it was my experience in the Orange Free State that really roused to anger my social consciousness. As I looked at my class of forty or forty-five students, knowing that of these only about ten could say for certain that they would go beyond what our school gave, I often asked myself: 'Why? But why?' I had been brought up in a home where the destitute always came for help. So I was sensitive to my pupils' needs and situation.

At Healdtown, Lovedale and Fort Hare, the students with me, except for a few, had known from primary school that they were headed for these places. Most of our students in Kroonstad did not see any future for themselves beyond their school. They remained in school because it was a good place, better than life in the location. I knew that something was wrong somewhere. What it was I had not figured out.

In my last years at Fort Hare, a number of us began to question some of the things we were being taught. We came out with the slogan 'South African history is a lie'. We did not have all the facts to prove our statement, but we knew South African history was like the story of an animal hunt that glorified only the actions of the hunters and said nothing or very little about the heroism and strategies of the hunted. The early history I learned from Tata told me that the African people had been cheated and robbed. The reasons for this wholesale robbery had not been clear to me. They were to be made clear in Kroonstad, during my years as a teacher there.

When I came home in 1936, I found Tata and many others getting ready to go to Bloemfontein to hear the reply of the government to their 'no' to the Hertzog Bills, which proposed to take away their vote. Qualified African males in the Cape Province had exercised the right to vote long before the Union of South Africa. This was a right they were proud of. One of their number, Dr W. B. Rubusana, had represented them in the Cape Provincial Council from 1910 to 1914. Now the government was proposing to take away this right. No wonder there was so much agitation among the Africans of the Cape Province. Those who had titles to their lands feared that it was the vote today and would be their titles tomorrow.

The African males in the Cape lost their vote in 1936. A new Act proposed the representation of Africans, in both the Senate and the House of Assembly, by four white persons in each chamber, and representation by whites on the Provincial Councils. In addition, they would be entitled to elect members to a Natives Representative Council, a body that would advise the government on all things affecting the African people. Some argued that, after all, it was only in the Cape Province that Africans had the vote; in the other three provinces Africans did not have this right. And it was more land that the Africans really needed; had not the loss of the vote been compensated for by the release of more land? The white liberals, who were already offering themselves as candidates for the new institutions, were telling the African people that half a loaf was better than none. The Africans, though sceptical, decided to try these new structures. Out of their conference in Bloemfontein in 1936 came the All-African Convention, a federal body to which were affiliated all organisations of the African people and which would be their mouthpiece.

The first round of elections under the new law came and went, and it was now the second round. Africans felt that perhaps the fault was with the team they had sent to parliament the first time, and that was why nothing had changed in their condition. Maybe the team had not fought hard enough. If, with this second round, they sent to parliament fighting men, things would change.

In the Orange Free State and Transvaal, the outgoing Senator Rheinallt-Jones was seeking a second term. Opposing him was a brilliant lawyer from Johannesburg, Hyman Basner. Most of the young people in both provinces were for change and for Basner, arguing that the Rheinallt-Jones team had been in parliament for four years and the lot of the African people had not changed one iota. Though I was not actively involved in the campaigning, I too was for Basner. The candidates scheduled meetings in Kroonstad. When Basner came, the municipal hall was filled to overflowing; his organisers had done their part and people were excited.

It was the beginning of June. My baby, Pallo, was only three weeks old, but I was determined to go to the Basner meeting. I did not tell A.C. this. I arranged with my help, Joanna, to baby-sit for me that evening. As A.C. was going to be one of the interpreters, he left immediately after supper to give himself time to meet the candidate and speaker. As soon as Joanna arrived, I followed to the municipal hall. There was excitement all round; the air was charged. In his opening remarks, Ntate Ntanga, as chairman of the meeting, said enough to make it known who his candidate was. Then Basner, tall, impressive with a big head and powerful voice, started:

> I am not here seeking your votes to send me to parliament as your representative, because I think there is anything I can do there for you. Nobody can do that for you. You and you alone will do that, the day you have the right to go into that parliament and speak for yourselves. I am seeking your votes so that I can, as your representative, go around these farms, factories and mines of the Orange Free State and Transvaal, telling the African people why they are in the position they are in; tell them why they and their children are starving in a land of plenty; tell them why they are so poor in so rich a land; tell them that they are the creators of the wealth of this country; tell them that it is their labour on the farms, the factories, the mines, that has made this country rich. But the fruits of their labour are for the benefit of others, the big farmers, the factory owners, the mine magnates, and that is why they, the producers of this wealth, are poor, hungry and riddled with disease. As a private citizen I cannot go around, telling people this. The laws of the land forbid any citizen to do that. But as your representative, I can.
>
> I will go round these farms, factories and mines, telling the African people, my constituency, that they and they alone can right this wrong against them; that united as a body of workers, the creators of the wealth of South Africa, they can grind to a halt the economic machinery of South Africa, that they can bring down the whole system. I will go around telling the Africans why. And when we speak together in one big voice, when we act together, we will make their farms tremble and their mines will quake and a cold shiver will run through their

factories, for they will know that the oppressed, exploited African worker has now discovered the great power he has in his hands, the power to withhold his labour and bring this country down. Nobody will ever do that for you. I cannot do it. But I can show you how together you can do it.

Basner was eloquent, inspired and fiery. The interpretations into Xhosa by A.C. and into Sotho by A. T. Sello were as inspired, simultaneous and brilliant; speaker and interpreters were on the same wavelength. There was no pause at all. One would have thought that Basner was speaking in these languages. Now and again when the speaker's voice rose in a crescendo, there were shouts of *'Bua, Ngoana Basner! Babolelle!'* [Speak, child of Basner. Tell them.] His audience followed every nuance of his speech and was with him to the very end. And Basner knew it.

After the meeting I hurried home. A.C. came home shortly, all excitement. But before he could make his report, I quoted him excerpts from Basner's speech.

'You were there?' he asked, excited.

'Of course I was there. Did you think I would miss this meeting about which everybody I know is so excited?

'Just like you, Phyllie!' He hugged and kissed me.

In school the following day, all talk was about the meeting of the night before. The teachers commended both A.C. and Sello on their interpretation, and those who knew both Sotho and Xhosa said: 'At some point, I did not know which language I was listening to. I heard all three simultaneously.'

Basner won the Orange Free State–Transvaal Senate seat. He was still in parliament when we got to Cape Town in 1946, though he was becoming disillusioned and confessed that he had not done half as much as he had hoped to do in those four years. Legislation coming out of the South African parliament was making it difficult even for those representing Africans to advocate strike action by Africans. When the mineworkers, 70 000 strong, struck on 14 August 1946, mining was brought to a standstill on the Reef, for a whole week. But the striking workers were sent down the mine shafts at gunpoint, with nine killed and many injured.

Basner's candidacy awakened even the teachers in the Orange Free State and the Transvaal, two provinces where the teacher was not treated as a professional. The Orange Free State African

Teachers' Association and the Transvaal African Teachers' Association started looking critically at their contracts and their conditions of service. In the Orange Free State, teachers organised branches in city, town and dorp, with some farm teachers (at great risk to their lives and jobs) joining the local branch of OFSATA in the nearest town or city. In March 1943, the Bloemfontein teachers staged one of the biggest demonstrations ever held in the city by Africans, protesting against the new service contract that had just been drawn up. I had gone to Bloemfontein to write a supplementary examination the day before the demonstration, hoping to give myself a day of rest before the exam. Swept into the tide of the demonstration, I marched with the teachers to the offices of the Secretary of Education. When we got there his assistant came out, with the new service contract, trying to tell the teachers that this was the best ever in the whole country. Joey Jacobs grabbed it out of his hand, tore it to pieces and threw the pieces into his face. I wrote the examination the following day still full of the excitement of the day before. It was good I had been there for I could report first-hand to A.C., who was now president of OFSATA, on the mood of the teachers in Bloemfontein and its environs.

During the two years of A.C.'s presidency, new branches of the organisation sprang up in the most unlikely places in the Orange Free State – Clocolan, Wepener, Steynsrust, and other little places that one hardly ever heard of. The teachers' involvement in the Basner campaign had shown them that there was something they could do about their lot. It was an exciting time.

Plans to liaise and co-ordinate with the Transvaal African Teachers' Association were initiated. By 1945 this body and OFSATA were the most militant in the whole country. Who would have thought then that OFSATA would be the first African teachers' organisation to welcome Bantu Education? The old stalwarts left the province on retirement, transfer, promotion or death, and new men took over the organisation – quislings and collaborators. While in the Cape Province and the Transvaal the government had to create new African teachers' organisations to promote Bantu Education, in the Orange Free State the once-militant OFSATA would promote it for them.

That night in June 1942 at the Basner meeting, I obtained the answers to some of my questions. I knew where my place would be in the South African set-up. I understood even the slight racism of places like the Cape Province, Lovedale and Fort Hare, which I had thought were free from racial attitudes. I understood some of the reasons behind promoting an elite among the African people and why the first graduates of Fort Hare were so elitist in their attitudes. Though born and brought up in that milieu, I would try to shed those attitudes and involve myself in the struggles of my people.

Back to Fort Hare

In August 1944, A.C. was offered a post at Fort Hare. Professor Jabavu was retiring and his position was offered to A.C. Friends wrote urging him to accept the offer. We were all excited, even our little Nandi. She told all who passed by our gate that 'We are going back to the Cape. We will not be coming back.' Nandi was just three-and-a-half years old.

I had not been to Fort Hare since my student days. A.C. had been there twice – once for the vacation course and again for his M.A. graduation. But now we were going back permanently to our Fort Hare. If, in the years in the field, we had grown this much, how much further could we grow in an intellectual centre like Fort Hare?

There are places in this world which are not of this world, little islands where the inhabitants live a life of their own, completely unaware of what is going on in the world around them. Institutions of higher learning are just such places; even in the colonial world, these institutions carry on this tradition, where the colonial elite have nothing or very little to do with their fellow men. This was what we found at Fort Hare when we arrived there.

There are three institutions at Alice, all connected – Lovedale, Macvicar Hospital and Fort Hare – all within a three-mile radius of one another. All three have multi-racial staff, with a predominance of whites at Fort Hare and Lovedale. The few Africans who taught on the staff at Fort Hare were the most frightened people I ever had the misfortune to meet. They were not happy about the discrimination there, but they spoke of it in whispers, for fear of losing their jobs. Racism was rampant in the staff lounge. A number of Afrikaners had joined the faculty, and in the staff lounge they sat in groups around a certain strong man – Mr Meiring, an Afrikaner from

Bloemfontein. In another corner was the Fort Hare old guard, who seemed somewhat lost in this atmosphere; and in yet another corner, the small group of African staff, looking timid and lost. Professor Z. K. Matthews seemed to be the only one who moved from group to group with ease, now cracking jokes with the Afrikaners, now with his white liberal friends and now with his African brethren. The whole atmosphere stank. And what did they talk about? Nothing much – the weather, the war (without any depth), their work – all the things that intellectuals in their ivory towers talk about. Weekends were for movies, irrespective of the kind of movie showing. Beyond that, it was parties, and the talk of the staff revolved around who was invited or not invited to so-and-so's house party. There was a lot of animosity between the administration and the student body. The same was to be found at Lovedale and the Hospital, though here it was not as pronounced as at Fort Hare.

And what about the student body? They were a reflection of the staff. Their interests were movies, women, sports and getting their degrees. In our days, there had been a collective Fort Hare spirit; students had been proud of Fort Hare and of doing (or not doing) things in the name of their college. No, now it was 'my hostel' first. This had engendered a very unhealthy competition between the hostels, particularly in sport. Another thing that surprised us was the regionalism of the student body – up-country and down country; Transvaal and Orange Free State as against the Cape and Natal; town and rural area. This was ingrown and unhealthy.

As we came from the Orange Free State, students from this area and the Transvaal claimed us as home-people and visited our house in Alice. Those from the Cape, especially Transkei, claimed us too and were frequent visitors to our home. Many of them started talking to each other for the first time at our house, and from then on the barriers were broken. But there were others, like Diliza Mji, who would never condescend to talk to a 'stupid' up-country fellow, whose only interest was women and the movies. When Diliza came to the house (which he often did) and found any of these up-country 'fools', he would go and play with the children for a few minutes and walk back to Wesley House, returning some other time.

Among the students there was a group that was politically aware and had seen through the politics of Fort Hare and the role of men such as Z. K. Matthews and the other African staff. These soon found a place in our house where they could meet and discuss with grown-ups matters that were relevant to their lives as Africans at Fort Hare and in the world outside. Our life in the Orange Free State had brought home to us the disabilities of the African people, and both A.C. and I had chosen to be part of that section of our people that was struggling for liberation. Though merely paid-up members of the ANC, which was the only organisation we could join in Kroonstad, we had played a role in OFSATA and as teachers were very much interested in what the profession could do. So there was a lot that the political students at Fort Hare could share with us. Though not rabid Youth Leaguers, with their slogan 'Africa for the Africans', the Fort Hare student of the day was not quite clear about the role of the South African white in all this. None of them ever talked of 'driving the white man into the sea' as some Youth League zealots were advocating. My ideas on the question of whites were not clear either at the time. They would become so for me in Cape Town, where I gained a true analysis of the South African situation.

In May, A.C. gave his first Wednesday address to staff and students in the Christian Union Hall. This was a Fort Hare tradition, according to which every staff member or visitor would address the whole college on a topic of his choice. A.C. chose as his subject 'The Ethics of War of the Bantu'. He took certain episodes from South African history, the clashes between the Africans and the colonial power, and interpreted each episode from the point of view of the Africans – the lions, this time, telling their own story. A.C. was by all accounts terrific and made an indelible impression on the students. I had not gone to the meeting as I was in my eighth month of pregnancy. But even before he came home for lunch, groups of students stopped by, excited, telling me that for the first time, they had an African who was not afraid to interpret African history as it should be. Right through the day, students dropped by to congratulate him and to ask more questions. From that day on, A.C.'s place among Fort Hare students was assured. While the students were excited, his African colleagues were, however, embarrassed. As he was going out of the meeting, one of them, very close to him, came up to him and asked: 'Joe, how could you do that?'

'What have I done?' he asked.

The Fort Hare old guard, the white liberals, were shocked. They had never expected this from him. They had thought that he too would be one of their good boys. We heard later that one of them complained that the Orange Free State had embittered him. For this change of attitude, those white liberals never forgave A.C.

Some of the African staff at Fort Hare also shunned us and only saw us when it was necessary. But more and more students came and found pleasure in our company. The impact of A.C.'s talk was felt even at Lovedale. Now and again the most senior Lovedale students stopped at our house in Alice when they were in town. 'Rebels' like Sipho Makhalima, a teacher at Lovedale, loved by the students but feared by the authorities both at Lovedale and Fort Hare, were pleased. Sipho had submitted, for his Master's thesis, an African interpretation of the Nongqawuse episode, but no South African university would accept his thesis, which gave a totally different view of this tragedy from the version of the white liberal historians.

When we left the Orange Free State, we had hoped to join the local branch of the Cape African Teachers' Association. In my condition, I could not. But A.C. came back from each meeting thoroughly disgusted. How different things were with the teachers here in the Cape. Their meetings were still social gatherings. A.C. missed the militancy of the Orange Free State teachers. I did not join the Victoria East branch of CATA after hearing these reports, though I was to join CATA in Cape Town in 1947.

The Cape teachers were scared stiff of politics in their organisation. In 1945, those who had attended the annual conference of the Association in Port Elizabeth came back complaining that fellows like W. M. Tsotsi, principal of Freemantle School for Boys, and C. M. Kobus, a teacher at St John's College, Umtata, were trying to bring politics into the organisation: they had had the nerve to ask conference to allow I. B. Tabata, an avowed politician from Cape Town, to address them. Conference had refused this request, for the teachers knew that Tabata would speak nothing but politics. They were a professional organisation and they wanted to remain that way.

I had never been away from work for such a long time before. The longest period had been for six months – three months before my babies arrived and three months afterwards. Here in Alice, I had been away for more than eight months and I was itching to go back to work. Fortunately for me, Miss Trieste Tsewu, a teacher at Lovedale High School, decided to take up the position of librarian at Fort Hare and I was asked to fill in for her at Lovedale. I jumped at the offer. All the wives of the teachers at Lovedale and Fort Hare were shocked. Wives of teachers and other professionals in the Cape Province did not go out to work in those days. They stayed home, to look after their homes, husbands and children. Home-making was a respected calling. Why go out to work, as if one's husband could not maintain one? In the Orange Free State, because of a shortage of qualified teachers, women worked after marriage and only took leave of absence before and after the birth of a baby. And here I was breaking a Cape tradition. The other women were shocked. My baby was only three months old when I went back to teaching. I remember meeting some of the wives of teachers coming from school; they always made a point of telling me that, as they passed the house, they heard my baby crying. As if the baby would not cry when I was there! Mrs Matthews was shocked too, even though she never said it in so many words. She once gave me a ride on my way from school. As she was dropping me in front of the house, she remarked: 'And I do not know why one would leave a three-month-old baby at home and go out to work. Really I do not know.' I did not say anything. I thanked her and went inside.

It turned out these women were all waiting for someone to break this unwritten rule. After I had left Alice, many of them took jobs in and around Lovedale. Many others have now accepted the idea of women working after marriage. Nobody thinks it strange any more.

I enjoyed my teaching at Lovedale. The students were different from those I had in Kroonstad, and we enjoyed each other. The senior matriculation class was a tightly knit group, who called themselves 'The Board' from their set book, *Oliver Twist*. One of them, Louis Mtshizana, wrote an article on class activities for the student magazine, *The Emblem*. This the authorities at Lovedale did not like and a storm in a teacup followed, with Mtshizana called before the school discipline committee. Because of the article and the investigation that followed, all the boys except one in that class of twenty-five students were debarred from going to Fort Hare.

At the Completers' social at the end of the year, Mxhaka Sihlali delivered the farewell speech. In it he accused the Lovedale authorities of having broken their promise to the African people. Lovedale, he said, was not the Lovedale that had pledged at its inception to work for the welfare of the African people. It was now one of the imperialist forces in South Africa. Needless to say, Mxhaka did not get a recommendation to go to Fort Hare. There was an agreement in those days that whosoever was blacklisted at Lovedale, Healdtown, St Matthews or Fort Hare could not be admitted in the other three institutions, either as a teacher or as a student.

Throughout the following year there was a lot of unrest at Lovedale and in August 1946 the students went out on strike. The name of Jordan came up, with some of the authorities saying the students used to hold meetings at our house in Alice. This was not true. No Lovedale students ever held meetings at our house in Alice. Not even Fort Hare students had done so. All students were welcome at our house and we discussed a whole range of topics, including politics in these institutions and in South Africa at large.

In November 1945, A.C. received an appointment as Lecturer in African Languages at the University of Cape Town. He was going to be the first African to hold a full staff position in a predominantly white university. To this very day, the University of Cape Town prides itself for having taken this bold step. The University of the Witwatersrand had African people on its staff, but not as full staff members; they were all Teaching Assistants. Many Africans criticised A.C. for taking up the position at UCT. His reasoning was that UCT belongs to all people in South Africa, not only to the whites. He was going there to keep that door ajar, so that many others could come in, for only then could UCT pride itself as an institution of higher learning, free from the prejudices of South Africa.

We left Fort Hare at the end of 1945.

Cape Town

After rounding the Cape of Good Hope the pirate Francis Drake wrote: 'This Cape is a most stately thing, and the fairest Cape we saw in the whole circumference of the earth.' He was right. The city, built along the contours of Table Bay, snuggles up against the slopes of Table Mountain. Watch its sunsets in summer or winter – with Apollo's ball, a flaming red, slowly dropping into the Atlantic Ocean beyond Camps Bay. Or of a morning, stand at Rhodes Memorial above the University of Cape Town and look east and see a carpet of fog lying over the Cape Flats and beyond, as far as the Boland mountains. As the sun lifts from the eastern horizon, watch this carpet roll slowly back, revealing Tygerberg, then the Strand, then Bellville, Strandfontein, the Cape Flats, then Rondebosch and then Newlands, right under your feet. This is a beautiful city, and no matter from which end you see it, its majesty dazzles the mind. My soul found a resting place here and I knew I would make Cape Town my home.

A.C. had preceded us to Cape Town to find accommodation before I and the children came down. He found a place to stay in Langa, an African location twelve miles from the city centre. The place gets its name from Langalibalele, the Hlubi king who, after being imprisoned for some years on Robben Island, had been released on the Cape Flats where a settlement was built for him and his wives. I had hated living in the location at Kroonstad; I hated it even more here. At least in Kroonstad my house was not like the one next to it, and that made some difference; it had its own stamp and individuality. Here in Langa, the people are reduced to the same common denominator. What sets your house apart from the ones next to it is the colour of the paint on the door and the colour of the curtains in the windows. Though supposedly living in town, the people were more conservative than most I knew in the country. I could not imagine my children growing up in that atmosphere.

'What about all these other people?' A.C. would ask when I complained.

'Joe, I am not the other people, have never been and I am not going to begin now,' I would tell him.

It was brought home to me then what a location really was, why it was created in the first place – locate 'them' there, away from 'us', and let them stew together in their wretchedness. And if they give trouble, we can surround them and put them under siege. This is the sinister motive behind it all. I hate a location; it confines one not only physically but also mentally. And yet among the people living there I made a lot of friends, found many who understood exactly why they were confined to the locations, because they were reservoirs of labour for the city. These were the people involved in political work in Langa and elsewhere, and with them we fought many a political battle in Cape Town.

Because I did not want to live in the location, we started looking for a place outside, in the suburbs of Cape Town. And what a search! The Western Cape has always been regarded as the home of the Coloured people. Even though Africans have been present since the beginnings of the city, they have never been regarded as belonging there. I think they, too, did not regard Cape Town as a place where they could settle and make a home. As a result very few Africans in Cape Town had property, this in a city and a province where they could have bought property in any of the suburbs. And because of the preference given to Coloureds for jobs, many Africans had crossed over the colour line and were living as Coloureds. Coloured persons in South Africa range in colour from the blondest blonde to the blackest black. What determined whether one is Coloured or not was where one lived, and one's language: Afrikaans is regarded as the language of the Coloured people. All this was to affect profoundly our search for a place to rent or buy in the suburbs of Cape Town.

A clause in the 1936 Land Act had restricted further the right of Africans to buy land anywhere, stipulating that Africans could only buy land or property from other Africans. If from whites, Coloureds, or Indians, they had to have the permission of the Governor-General-in-Council. Quite early in our search, we had given up on the question of renting. The only people who seemed to have houses to rent were Jews, and the few we approached told us quite bluntly they had decided never to rent to Africans because they usually turned their property into a slum, taking in other families into a small house.

On weekends we were out house-hunting. We would be told of an African, Ndlovu, in Athlone who had houses for sale. When we got there, we invariably found Mr Ndlovu was no longer Ndlovu, an African, but Mr Oliphant, a Coloured person. We would go to a Mrs Siphondo, who we were told was African, widow of the Rev. Siphondo, minister of some African church in Athlone, only to find that Mrs Siphondo was now Mrs Spawn, a Coloured person. The Mthimkhulus had changed their names to Grootboom, Coloured people. Segalo had dropped the *o* in his name and made it into the Jewish *Segal* and he was now a Coloured person. It was a frustrating but educational search. We understood why people had to do such things. On it depended not only where one could live, but also what kinds of jobs one could get, and how much one could be paid. It was a matter of survival, 'beating the system' as they say in the United States of America.

It was on these house-hunting trips that A.C. and I got to know the large African and Coloured communities living behind the sand-dunes of the Cape Peninsula, hidden among the Port Jackson groves. Perhaps a friend would have come to take us to someone who knew a Jew who could rent us a place in Wynberg, Claremont or Lansdowne. This friend lived in Grassy Park, Steenberg or South Peninsula, we would be told. We went to one such place by train, got off at the station near Grassy Park, followed a hard road for about half a mile, and after that it was a sand trail into the bushes for anything from four to five miles or more. On our way we met some chickens pecking in the sand, and ahead of us came the sound of an organ playing; it was a little off-key, but one could recognise the tune for it was a familiar church hymn. Then, all of a sudden, we came upon a huge settlement of makeshift lean-to's, with a sprinkling of well-constructed wood-and-iron bungalows. There was no smell of urine and faeces here as was usually the case in Windermere or Kensington. There was a lot of activity: some women were cooking in their braziers outside; others were coming in with baskets on their heads, from the shop five miles away near the train station.

We went into the bungalow where the music came from. Sitting in front of the organ was an old man, Mr Bhinase, who was about my father's age. He was using an old fire-extinguisher with a cushion on top as an organ stool. Mrs Bhinase, his wife, was here, pottering around, keeping her husband company. As soon as we came in, the music stopped and Mrs Bhinase, addressing herself to our guide, said: 'Yho! Bhele, you are here already! Is this the young man who has such a big name, teaching white people? And this his wife?' Shaking hands, she said: 'The Good Lord be praised! Who ever knew that our sons would be teaching white people in their own schools? God is great!'

The Bhinases had been in Cape Town since after the influenza epidemic. It was that epidemic, in fact, which had made them leave home. All three of their children had died – a young man, just starting teaching, a girl starting at boarding school, and their youngest about fifteen years old. 'He was a brilliant boy, the teacher. And the hymn I was playing was his favourite,' said the father.

They had been teachers, too, back home in Tsomo, Transkei. When they first came to Cape Town, they lived in Ndabeni. But, when the Africans were moved from Ndabeni to Langa, they had gone to Claremont and then to this bungalow in Grassy Park.

'Go live in a location? Kraaled in like cattle? No, not me!' said the old man. 'I am glad you are looking for a place outside a location. That is no place to bring up children,' he added.

This was the attitude I found in all these settlements. Africans moved to these places to avoid living in the segregated locations.

In Parkwood, Mr Ngo, another teacher in his time, said to us: 'What a pity you come to Cape Town these days when Cape Town is no longer Cape Town. This used to be a place of culture, when people – white, Coloured, African – used to live together, with none of this segregation of the Boers. Now they send us, Africans, to the location, so we should not know these other people and they should not know us too.'

Mr Ngo still had his bookcase, with a few books, mainly English literature and works on Native Administration. He was an avid reader of the *Torch* and the *Guardian*, progressive newspapers in Cape Town. As we were leaving, he invited A.C. to come back and browse through his papers on the Industrial and Commercial Workers' Union in its early days in Cape Town. Unfortunately, the settlement the Ngos lived in, Parkwood, was destroyed by those fires so common in Cape Town during the months of September and October, and we lost contact with Mr Ngo. I often wonder if any of the old man's books and papers were saved.

These settlements were not just haphazard, they were properly run, with committees that saw to the welfare of the people, and that were responsible to the people who elected them.

'Life is good here,' Mr Bhinase had told us. 'We allow no illicit brewing here. People can brew, but not for business. Shebeens are things of the location. We don't want them here. Crime? Hardly any. Even the skollies [gangsters] know that they can't just come here. Our young men would beat the hell out of them.'

It was in Parkwood that I met Esther Bangani, one of the Lovedaleans who used to come home for dinner on the Sunday of the Lovedaleans in the days of my sister Granny. Together with another teacher, she had started a kindergarten for the children of their neighbours who were too young to walk the distance to the nearest school in Retreat. Another woman, a worker, Dora Tamana, had opened a similar kindergarten just beyond the vlei in Retreat. Were these women being paid by the Education Department for their services? No. Theirs were voluntary services. Those parents who could paid a small fee, but most did not and their little ones were never turned away.

I learnt a lot during the trips to these settlements in the woods. I got to know just how resilient Africans were and realised that no matter what the circumstances, the future was with them. None of them doubted that. To them all it was just a question of time. In these settlements in the bush, we met Africans who knew the value of the vote which they had lost; who understood that all these structures of government that were being set up were just mere gimmicks to delay the day of liberation.

In 1954, all these communities were moved, under the Slum Clearance Regulations of the Cape Divisional Council, and as 'black spots' under the Group Areas Act of 1950, to emergency camps, one west of Nyanga East, called Brown's Farm, and the other east, which later became known as Gugulethu (Our Pride), a name bestowed upon this monstrosity by Mr Rogers, the superintendent of Langa location. Brought to the east camp were African communities from Elsies River, Vasco, Bellville, Goodwood, Tiervlei, Windermere, Kensington and Eureka. Together they formed the huge location complex, fourteen miles east of Cape Town. When this all happened

I thought of the Bhinases and the Ngos who had resisted being kraaled in like animals.

We finally gave up trying to find a place to rent or buy without working through the prescribed channels. So we decided to apply for the Governor-General's permission. A land developer, one Guttman, had just opened an office on Lawrence Road in Athlone. We went to him. He laughed, saying: 'No, man, they will never give you that permission; you are a Native. I had a fine fellow here the other day and I was quite willing to sell to him. But he never got that permission to buy from me, a white man. They are very strict, you know. Personally I do not care to whom I sell. After all, I want money.'

A.C. asked him all the same to give us the particulars about the lot – its size, the area in Lincoln Estate, the street and the price. One had to supply all this information when applying for permission.

'You seem confident,' said Mr Guttman. 'All right, I'll reserve for you a corner lot and I'll wait until you receive a reply from the Governor-General. Even if it takes you two years to get that reply, I'll wait.' So saying, he gave us the information we needed.

The letter of application that a 'Native' must submit in order to buy from a 'non-Native' has to be sent to the following offices: the office of the Governor-General-in-Council, the office of the local Chief Native Commissioner and the office of the local town clerk for consideration by the Town Council. When we got home, A.C. wrote and sent off all three letters. And we waited. This was about October 1946. Then about the end of November, we heard that the City Council had approved the application and were going to make a strong recommendation that A.C. be allowed to buy the lot from Guttman. On the City Council the progressives were in the majority; there were three councillors who were Coloured and would support A.C.'s application. At least one hurdle had been cleared. Then in March, Dr H. J. Simons, a friend of A.C. on the staff of UCT and an expert on Native Administration, advised A.C. that perhaps it might be a good thing for him to meet the Chief Native Commissioner in Salt River so that he should know just what sort of Native A.C. was. That very same day, A.C. called the office of the Chief Native Commissioner and a date was set up.

When A.C. arrived, he found that the Chief Native Commissioner was a Mr Brownlee, grandson of the first Secretary for Native Affairs of the Cape Colony, Charles Brownlee. So the proceedings began on a very amicable note, with both of them talking about the older Brownlee, his writings and his observations on Native life in South Africa.

'Are you by any chance the son of John Jordan? I worked with him in Idutywa when I was magistrate there,' asked Mr Brownlee.

'No, he is my uncle, my father's younger brother. My father, Elijah Jordan, was a teacher at Mbokothwana, Tsolo,' replied A.C.

'Oh, yes! I know Mbokothwana. I once went to Tsolo as a Relieving Magistrate. A clever man, that John Jordan. What ever happened to him?'

A.C. told Mr Brownlee about the wanderings of his uncle and his death in the early forties.

'And by the way, your application for permission to buy from this Guttman. I don't know when they will make the decision. But it should not take long now. When did you hope to build?' asked Mr Brownlee.

'Before the winter rains, if possible.'

'You are right. They can be a nuisance here in Cape Town, I know,' remarked Mr Brownlee.

At lunchtime they parted with bows and 'a pleasure to have met you' on both sides. Within a month of this meeting, A.C. received the following communication from Salt River, the office of the Chief Native Commissioner:

> To: Mr Archibald Campbell Jordan
> School of African Studies
> University of Cape Town
> Rondebosch, Cape Town
>
> Dear Sir,
>   It pleases the office of the Governor-General-in-Council, in Pretoria, to grant permission to one Archibald Campbell Jordan, a Native, to buy lot 83, Fleur Street, Lincoln Estate, a sub-section of Crawford, from one Guttman, a European, etc., etc.
>   In your service,
>
> Brownlee, Chief Native Commissioner, Salt River, C.T.
> pp: Governor-General-in-Council

It turned out that in fact these decisions, though supposed to be made in Pretoria, are taken by the local City Council and the office of the Chief Native Commissioner.

A.C. was so excited when he came home that afternoon that as soon as he had had something to eat we rushed to Guttman's office. Guttman could not believe it. 'You are the first Native to have got this permission.'

In May 1947 work on the construction of our house started. We could not wait. After the walls were up, A.C. went by every day on his way home from UCT. The winter rains came and held up work for three weeks, but then the weather improved and work continued. In August 1947, our house was finished, and we moved into it in the middle of the month. We named it 'Thabisano', a place of mutual rejoicing, where we hoped to make each other happy. This was the home of our four children, the place in which they were nurtured, cultivated and groomed. In this house we all grew and matured intellectually; in this house, A.C. and I watched with pride the development of our four children. Thabisano!

Lincoln Estate

Lincoln Estate was a mixed community of working people, mostly Coloured, a good number of whites and one black family, the Jordans. Just below us, but not in Lincoln Estate, was another black family, the Mdulis, who were one of the few African families who had bought property in Cape Town. The people living in Lincoln Estate were young families with four or five children, many of whom were the ages of my children. Most of the Coloured and white men were discharged soldiers and this was how they had used their discharge benefits. Our children played together in the sand – there were no roads yet – and in the bushes around. Through our children we, the parents, soon got to know each other and some of us became close friends. It was a beautiful setting. Because of our books and my daughter Nandi, who loved children, my house soon became the place where the neighbours' children came to read and be read to. We all loved it.

We registered our children at St Mark's English Church school in Athlone. As Natives they should have gone to the African schools in Langa or the local African school in Athlone. Because this was a Methodist institution we used that as an excuse and sent them to the Anglican school, as we were Anglican. Though this was before the days of Bantu Education, the trend was already evident that children should go to the schools of their own ethnic group. The Teachers' League of South Africa, the most progressive Coloured teachers' association, was resisting this tendency and had instructed all member principals not to turn away African children from their neighbouring schools, especially children in mixed neighbourhoods of Coloured and African, just because of government pressure. So we could bank on support from the TLSA. The principal, Mr Abrahams, though a little uneasy, could not very well go against the directive of his organisation.

There were many other black children in this school, as was the case in most of the mixed neighbourhoods. The difference was that all these had registered as Coloured and ours were coming as African. In school they suffered no discrimination either from the teachers or from other children. They were happy at St Mark's and they all did well. But at the end of every year, Mr Abrahams made a point of telling A.C. that the inspector had asked how long our children were going to attend. Apparently he told the inspector that he had allowed our children at St Mark's because they were too young to take the bus to Langa. He was more than relieved when the first three passed Standard 4 (St Mark's had classes only up to this Standard). Mr Abrahams could not wait until our youngest, Lindi, passed Standard 4 at St Mark's, but asked A.C. to transfer him. Lindi still tells people that Mr Abrahams expelled him from St Mark's, an expulsion he did not regret, for it meant joining his brother and sisters at Rosmead in Claremont and going there by bus and train.

From Rosmead they all went to Livingstone High School in Claremont. But the atmosphere had changed drastically at Livingstone. There was a lot of friction among the teachers, which affected the students as well. After their Junior Certificate, they transferred to Athlone High in Athlone, which we had avoided because the principal was a member of TEPA, the conservative Coloured teachers' association, which was launched after the progressives gained control of the TLSA in 1942. Here the atmosphere was congenial among teachers and throughout the school. They were very happy here, and when Lindi left for England in the middle of his second year of high school, everybody missed him.

For the first five years of my life in Cape Town I remained at home, raising the children and settling in. But I was never impatient to get out and work as I had been in Alice. Though at home, I was busy with political work and in the Cape African Teachers' Association. This period gave me an opportunity to be at home and enjoy my children and for them to feel secure, knowing that when they came back from school Mama would be there. As soon as they came in, each one of them would go through the house, looking for me – 'Good afternoon!' – and only then would they put away their school books. After that, afternoon activities would begin. They were always with me, in the kitchen, in the living-room, in their bedroom, out in the yard, doing things together. Today there is not a house chore they cannot handle, from painting to cooking an eight-course meal. This goes for all four of them. Since they were fourteen years old, I have done very few house chores. I only do enough to give my children a rest.

We did a lot together – reading, discussing matters, distributing leaflets and going to political rallies, for how could they stay away from the rallies when they had been distributing leaflets and talking to those who took them? Strange that even though there was always a possibility the police would come and break up a meeting, I never thought of what I would do with four young kids with me, none of them older than seven years. At home, once every two weeks, they would put on an evening recital, showing us what they were doing in school. Now and again, A.C. and I would be asked for an item. A.C. always played *'Thina Mbokothwana'*, a school song he used to sing back home when he was a kid. My favourite was a portion from *King Solomon's Mines,* 'Dawn in the Desert'. I can still see the children huddled together, drawing up the programme for the evening. I do not remember any rehearsals. I suppose these were held in school.

Once a month, A.C. would put on a programme of music. This we always presented on Sundays after dinner. There the children would be, with one or two sprawling on the floor, another on the piano stool, another in a chair, and A.C., master of ceremonies, putting on the show, as serious as ever. There were very few cultural events that we did not take them to – concerts by the Cape Town Orchestra in the City Hall, shows and plays at the Little Theatre, ballets and open-air shows at Maynardville in Wynberg. No wonder A.C. could not understand, when they were teenagers, how children who had been exposed to such 'good' music could ever listen to jazz. To A.C. jazz was just noise, until we came to Madison, Wisconsin, where our son Lindi became a jazz expert and taught his father the nuances of jazz. For four hours they sat together in the living-room, with Lindi playing from his collection. After Lindi left, A.C. said: 'I am pleased. I did not know that Lindi was approaching his jazz music as a scholar.' When as teenagers they showed an interest in jazz, I always told him that they were just going through a phase and things would balance out again. They could never lose their love of the music they were first exposed to. And it has turned out to be so, except for Lindi, who can tolerate only certain classical composers.

A.C. was a wonderful father, who loved his children and was proud of them. He had, like most fathers, hoped that his first-born would be a boy. But when Nandi, a daughter, came, A.C. was so excited that he forgot he had wished for anything else. Then when the boys came, his joy knew no bounds. Not that Nandi ever lost her place in his heart. Never! The achiever that he was, he expected great things from his children, greater than he had achieved. Why not? These children lived in a much bigger world; they had been exposed to a world of books, music and progressive ideas much sooner than he had and much sooner than most children. Whenever their parents had written something – a poem, article or essay – we all came together to critique it, each one having an input. This has borne good fruit, for all of them have a good pen and Nandi was writing good poetry before she died. These children lived in a world of ideas, in an intellectual atmosphere, and nothing was held back. The dinner hour, from seven o'clock every evening, was the best hour of the day for the Jordans at Thabisano, for during this hour we were always together, sharing the day's experiences. We talked, discussed, asked questions, had questions answered. This was our happy hour.

What a pity that A.C., owing to pressure of work, could not spend more time with his children in those early years, to appreciate fully just how they were shaping up. It was not until Madison, Wisconsin, that he could sit down for hours with them, especially the boys, and discuss jazz with Lindi, or economics, philosophy and history with Pallo. His girls astounded him also. Nandi had developed; besides writing poetry, her painting and her pencil work were very promising. And Ninzi, besides being an avid lover of literature, has a creative genius that can turn even the most mundane vegetable into the most tempting and tasty dish, and with chisel and paint can turn any piece of wood into a beautiful ornament.

I, who was close to them all the time, who took them to political meetings, distributed political leaflets with them, answered their questions on literature and history, and read to them their bedtime stories, knew that they were developing into the intellectuals that they are. I am glad they were so curious and inquisitive. That made me do my homework too. I had to know which books, encyclopaedias, or texts to refer them to when they came asking questions on literature, history, politics, or the meanings of words. They made me think. Even today, my children still keep me on track. When I espouse any reactionary, compromising ideas, they tell me: 'You are becoming very reactionary, Mrs J. I am surprised at you.' Or: 'I am shocked to hear *that* coming from you.' (I suppose this is what happens when people get old.) With such checks, I am bound to keep up with the latest trends in progressive thought.

People are perhaps surprised that I get frustrated sometimes when Lindi says to me: 'Yes, you taught me that: to argue until I get a reasonable answer.' Yes, it is my own teaching. But sometimes I wish he would just accept what I say. Perhaps too late for me now!

In Cape Town I was to experience something I had never found at home or when teaching, and this was the unwillingness of blacks to work for other blacks. I suppose the rationale is that when one leaves the country and goes to town, one is going to work for whites. The Coloured people, on the other hand, regard it as below their dignity and status to work for a 'Native'. For both groups, this is irrespective of what wages are paid.

Importing someone from the country involves a long process. It means an application to the local Native Affairs Department. This application is then processed through the Labour Bureau, which does not mean that the person will automatically be given the permission to proceed to Cape Town to take up the job. There is also the risk that when this person arrives, like the others, she may not want to work for another black person and was only using you to get permission to enter Cape Town. But if you are working and have children, it is almost impossible to keep your job unless you have help at home. Three times I imported people from the Transkei to come and work for me. Only one of them absconded when she got to Cape Town and sought work from whites. The law allowed me to have her tracked down and sent back to the country where she came from. But why bother? You shrug your shoulders and throw up your arms.

My first help from the local Coloured people was a small woman, Sophie, from Jakkalsvlei, on the other side of Welcome Estate. We called her 'Mpumpu' [Blindman's-buff]. She liked playing this game with the children. In Xhosa it is called *Mpumputhela*, but not being a speaker of the language, she remembered only the first part of the word. A very efficient person Mpumpu was, and very fond of children. The children were just as fond of her. Like some workers she wanted to do things only when *she* wanted to. I spoke to her several times about this, telling her I might as well have no help than have help I could not rely on. She always used the children, telling me that if she left they would be very upset and become sick.

Things reached a limit with me, and I told her I was terminating her services at the end of the month. She did not say anything. When she was with the children outside, she told them she had been dismissed. I was in the kitchen when a delegation of four entered and charged me: 'What do you mean terminating Mpumpu's services? Don't you know that she is the only person working in her family? How is her mother going to manage when Mpumpu is not working?' The subject of the delegation was sitting outside in the garden, pretending to be reading a paper, when, in fact, she was listening to what was going on inside. Confronted with so strong a case, I backed down and gave Mpumpu another chance. When I tell my children of that incident, we all laugh and they say: 'So we were Mpumpu's trade union.' Mpumpu left on her own, to work for a Malay couple who had just moved into our area. She had to remove herself from the stigma of working for a 'Native'. She was to regret it, for at Mrs Jacobs she ate servant's meat and servant's food. She appealed to the 'trade union' to take up her case with me. But not even the 'trade union' could help her this time. It was disgusted with her for it knew why she had left.

Then came Zubeida, a Malay woman of about thirty-five. She did not mind working for a 'Native'. In fact, where she lived in Thornhill, she preferred 'Natives' to Coloured or Malay. Actually Zubeida left us to marry a black man from Zimbabwe, who worked in Rondebosch. She had been married before to a Coloured man. At the time she came to us, this marriage was on the rocks. Now Zubeida wanted to try the 'Native' in the hope the marriage would work this time. Zubeida was another wonderful person. She liked doing things with the children, and from her they learnt how to prepare many Indian dishes.

After Zubeida came Maraldia, also Malay, married and with a lot of children. Maraldia would sometimes bring the smaller children with her to work. At first she feared I would complain and would ask me if she could give them something to eat. 'Of course, give them something to eat. How can we eat and they don't?' Maraldia had a beautiful daughter, just older than Nandi; Alice was her name. At every party in our house, Alice was the toast of the gathering and the white boys wanted to dance with her, much to the chagrin of the blonde Coloured girls who had come to the party to meet these white boys from the University of Cape Town. None of them ever thought that the white boys, perhaps, were tired of blondes; they wanted to meet some Coloured brunettes. And our Alice was just that, very beautiful.

Maraldia was with us to the very end. A.C. wrote to her when he reached London. I do not think there was a person in Lincoln Estate and in Thornhill who did not know that she had received a letter from the 'Doctor' in England. She kept that letter in her coat pocket to show those who, perhaps, had not seen or heard about it.

How can one forget such people? I often think about them and wish and hope that we will meet someday.

Talking of parties! Those in our house were a magnet that attracted all the people in our area and many from other parts of Cape Town. The children's friends from school would be there; their white friends from the University of Cape Town would be there; my nieces and nephews and their cousins from the African locations would be there; the street-corner boys in our neighbourhood would be there. The only condition was that they should dress up clean and tidy. I remember the first time the street-corner boys came. The party was just starting and people were arriving. They stood at the gate, debating whether to come in or not. A.C. saw them and went up to them: 'Are you not coming to the party, you fellows? Go back and dress up nicely and come and join the other kids.' They all ran home and in no time they were back, all spruced up. And did they enjoy themselves! What I liked most about them was that they saw to it that no riff-raff came to our parties. They always looked out for the boys from Gleemoor, who might come and cause trouble at the party at 'their' professor's house. With them around, nothing could touch us. It is when one sees free-mixing of people in Cape Town that one can understand fully the cruelty of segregation and apartheid in South Africa. Left to themselves, people know how to sort themselves out and live in peace and harmony one with the other.

One other person who lived with us was Oupa Booysen, an old Khoi, who helped me in the garden. And was Oupa proud of his work! If, when he came, he found that I had done some work, he would ask the children: 'Who plant that rubbish in the garden?' This question was never directed at me even though I was there – always at the children. Oupa grew up very close to nature. He could read the weather much better than the official weather forecaster. He would look at the clouds, their colour and the direction in which they were moving, and say: 'It's going to rain tonight,' or 'No, it's wind, no rain.' It always turned out to be so.

Commands from me he could take, but not from A.C. One time he was drunk and was making passes at the women passing by. A.C. went out to talk to him, asking him to stop. A.C. made the mistake (if mistake it was) of taking him by the hand to lead him inside. Oupa wrenched his arm off, and looking A.C. in the face said: 'No, man! I am no prisoner! You know, if you and I went to a white man asking for a job, the white man would give that job to me before he would give it to you. Do you know that?'

There was the status arrogance coming out. Our Oupa was a Coloured man, better than a Native. In the South African context, he was better than A.C., a professor. Relating this confrontation to us, A.C. laughingly said: 'I just wonder what job this would be for which I would be competing with Oupa.'

The bottom line in all this is: All employers are exploiters, no matter how liberal and generous they may be. It is just a question of degree. Take us for example. In both the Orange Free State and Cape Town, we tried to be fair, good and generous to our help, paying them what they would be getting if they were working in the white suburbs in Kroonstad or Sea Point. As they were people with families, their day with us ran from eight to six, or even before that, if they got the dinner ready or going by then. I made my children share the house chores with them. They could bring their young children with them and share with us whatever we ate. In fact, Maraldia's girls, who were the same age as mine, joined us whenever we went out picnicking, and at our house parties they came not to work but to enjoy themselves, as did the other kids. They were involved in the preparations because the party was at *their home*. Saturday was half-day and they were due back on Monday morning at eight o'clock.

Because of these advantages and privileges, if they could be called that, they all liked working for me and felt they were generously treated. I flattered myself too, feeling I was being good and generous to them. But for all that, I was underpaying them. In both the Orange Free State and Cape Town, the domestics were the least-paid workers. True, the wages in Cape Town were much better than those paid in the Orange Free State. All I did was to pay the same low, exploitative wage that the other exploiters of labour were paying.

This was once brought home to us rather forcefully. A.C. had asked Oupa Booysen to break up virgin ground in the vegetable garden. It was a hot day. The children and I watched him strain and sweat, turning over those sods. We were at dinner when Oupa came to A.C. to collect his money.

'All right, Oupa, wait for me in the kitchen. I'll be with you soon,' A.C. said. Then, turning to me, he asked: 'By the way, what is the rate for this kind of work?'

'I think you will have to give him more than the usual rate. That was hard work he did out there.'

'Oh, no! I'll pay him the usual rate,' said A.C.

He could not have said a worse thing. In one voice, his children in anger called out: 'You can't do that! You can't do that! Did you see how poor Oupa sweated and strained, the muscles in his short arms standing out, turning over those sods? You can't do that; you will have to give him more.'

A.C., not fully understanding just how serious they were, said: 'Oh, no! I'm going to pay him what he would generally get.'

Then Pallo saw red and dared his father to do it. 'Just do it! You will never again stand on any platform condemning exploiters when you are one of them. Just go do it! I'll expose you!' Pallo was nine years old.

A.C. thought the better of it and paid Oupa Booysen what his children felt was a wage he deserved for the hard work he had done. He said often afterwards: 'I am glad they are very sensitive to these issues. They will always keep us on the right track; with us and our set ways, it is easy to slide back and not match our deeds to our rhetoric.'

Involvement

At one time all the teachers, white and African, in the Cape Province belonged to the same teachers' association. The Transkei, though part of the Cape Province, was an exception; it had always had its own local self-administration, as if it were a province; and the teachers in Transkei had their own association. The Cape teachers' association was called the South African Teachers' Association, or SATA.

The African teachers in SATA were not pleased with their position within the organisation. They felt that they were treated as a 'kitchen' department, in that all matters pertaining to them were never given serious consideration by the organisation and were always tabled last on the agenda. They never came up in open conference, but were always dealt with by an expanded SATA executive, incorporating key branches of the African section. In 1925, the African branches of SATA, under the leadership of Professor D. D. T. Jabavu, broke away to form the Cape African Teachers' Association. Only a few branches in the north-western Cape remained with SATA. This break was a progressive step; the African teachers recognised that though they were all teachers under the same department, their problems were different. Shortly after this schism, the Coloured teachers broke away, too, to form the Teachers' League of South Africa.

Unfortunately, though the break itself was a progressive step, the Cape African Teachers' Association became elitist, drawing its membership only from the teachers in the African Ivy League schools, the big cities and a few friends of these elite in the rural areas. By the mid-thirties, the organisation had degenerated into a social club for the elite, and the important items on the body's agenda became receptions and tennis matches. True, the teachers still concerned themselves with increments to their salaries but nothing much beyond that. It became the home of the African graduates of Fort Hare, no matter what region of the Cape Province they were teaching in. Mr W. M. Tsotsi was the only Fort Hare graduate teaching in Transkei who remained with the Transkei Teachers' Association, all others joining CATA.

Overtures to link the two organisations – CATA and TTA – went on for some time, with the Transkei teachers resisting this merger, saying quite openly that their own organisation was not a social club but a place of serious business. Eventually, in 1940, the merger was effected and the United Cape African Teachers' Association emerged. Later 'United' was dropped and the organisation was known simply as the Cape African Teachers' Association, or CATA. When this happened, new blood and new attitudes were infused into the organisation and the teachers began to take their work seriously. Progressive elements emerged within CATA, members who saw the teachers as part and parcel of the community in which they lived and involved with issues of concern to the community. Such elements were becoming vocal by 1945 and some of them hoped that I. B. Tabata, a social scientist of note from Cape Town, would be given a chance to address conference at their meeting in Port Elizabeth. But the majority still felt that politics was something outside their calling as teachers and therefore outside their organisation. They were professionals and wanted to keep CATA that way.

In 1946 CATA met in Cape Town. They had invited, as their keynote speaker, the outgoing Chief Inspector of Education, Mr Hobson. As the theme of his topic, Mr Hobson took the CATA slogan 'Equal Pay for Equal Work'. He pointed out that it was understandable that professionals should have that as a slogan, more so teachers in the Cape Province, many of whom held the same qualifications as white teachers, and a good number of whom were teaching in the same schools and the same children. But while this was good as a slogan, it could not change things for the African teachers, whose salaries were based on the wages of the least-paid African workers, those on the farms and the mines. The white teachers in South Africa could always have their demands met, for their salaries were based on the salaries of the white workers in industry. To keep white teachers in the classroom, their salaries had to be competitive with wages in industry. 'What then can the African teacher do to better his condition? The African teacher has to work very hard for the improvement and a raise in the wages of African workers on the farms and in the mines, for not until those wage levels have improved will his salary ever be improved, no matter how highly qualified. What raises he or she will get will always be minimal, just a little more than the African worker is getting. That way he or she can always be kept in the classroom.'

This address was a shock to the teachers. Hobson had told them that their fate was bound up with the fate of the least-paid African worker and this was where the African teachers had to address themselves. It dawned upon them that afternoon at Langa High School that theirs was a political fight. After Hobson's address, the rest of the conference was taken up by discussion of what Hobson had said and how, as teachers, they could join the fight of the African workers. A committee of four, with A.C. as chairman, was appointed, to draw up guidelines which would be submitted for discussion and adoption or rejection at the next CATA conference the following year in Umtata. The guidelines called on the African teachers to come home, home to the African community where they belonged; it pointed out that the political fight of the African people was their fight, and as leaders of thought in the community, they could no longer stand on the sidelines and be spectators. Their organisation, CATA, had to join other African organisations fighting for the rights of the oppressed and exploited in South Africa. This was where CATA and the teachers should be.

When these guidelines were presented to conference in Umtata the following year, the whole house accepted them without dissension. They were not put immediately into effect because the north-western Cape teachers' branches that had remained in SATA had applied for admission as members of CATA, and asked for a year to study the guidelines. The guidelines were formally accepted as CATA policy in 1948 in Queenstown. The die was cast and the African teachers in CATA accepted the challenge. (In 1947 I had joined the Western Cape branch of CATA.) At the end of the conference, after the new policy had been accepted, CATA issued the following statement:

> It is clear that our struggle is inextricably bound up with the struggle of the African labourer. Even our slogan 'Equal Pay for Equal Work' is an old trade union slogan. It implies recogni-

tion of merit irrespective of colour. So anyone who makes the demand is fighting for the principle of full democratic rights. But we have already established the fact that it is futile to strive to obtain equality between White teacher and Black teacher unless there is equality between White labourer and Black labourer. In short, to seek equality between White teacher and Black teacher is to seek full social, economic and political equality between White and Black in South Africa. Our slogan therefore implies that our struggle is the general political struggle for the emancipation of the African. There can be no escape from this conclusion.

As if to test the determination of CATA, the newly formed Nationalist government of Dr Malan made clear its intention to appoint a commission of inquiry into the education of the Africans as a separate group. CATA decided not to appear before the commission, whose case was already clear-cut, but would instead submit a memorandum, rejecting the premise on which the commission was set up, and would continue to deal with the whole question of education for citizens of a country. To the commission's question, 'What do you consider should be the guiding principle and aims of Native Education?', CATA answered as follows:

> We repeat that the fundamental guiding principle in education should be to equip every individual to take his place in society according to his capabilities and make his contribution to it as a fully responsible citizen. All the inhabitants of the Union of South Africa should receive the same facilities for education. All the children, irrespective of race, colour or creed, should be regarded as its future citizens. Knowledge is the heritage of Mankind.

The CATA memorandum, dated 16 April 1949, which A.C. and his committee had been entrusted with drawing up, was submitted to the Eiselen Commission on Native Education.

These were exciting times! In the Western Province, we were not only campaigning against the new education system that was coming but also against the Van Riebeeck celebrations, scheduled for April 1952. Coupled with these were the new segregation laws that the Nationalists had introduced as soon as they came to power. The

Anti-Train Apartheid rally at the Grand Parade was one of the biggest rallies ever held in that city, with all the people's organisations coming together to oppose this measure. At the rally all the big guns from the progressive elements in Cape Town were on that platform, and the people resolved to oppose apartheid in all its forms.

Working together with the Teachers' League of South Africa, the Anti-CAD, the New Era Fellowship and SOYA, we held meetings throughout the Cape Peninsula, campaigning against both the Van Riebeeck celebrations and the coming of Bantu Education. The Society of Young Africa (SOYA) was a youth organisation, mostly African, launched under the auspices of the All-African Convention in the early fifties, to counter the rabid racism of the Youth League with its slogan 'Africa for the Africans'. SOYA spread rapidly throughout the African colleges, schools and townships, and brought logic and reason to the South African situation. SOYA taught young people that it was not the whites who were the enemy of the blacks, but the capitalist system which exploited both black and white workers; that the white workers had been, through concessions, co-opted and made to think that they were not exploited and their place lay with the white owners of capital; however, the day was not far off when white workers would know that their comrades-in-arms were the exploited African workers.

In Transkei, SOYA branches soon affiliated with the Transkeian Organised Bodies and they effectively worked with the peasant organisations, Khongo and Makhuluspan. It was the youth in SOYA who distributed *'uKwayo: isiKrweqe ne Khaka'* to the peasants of Transkei. This was my translation of I. B. Tabata's *The Boycott as a Weapon of Struggle*.

When CATA produced the pamphlet *Yenk' imfundo* [There Goes Education!] a cadre of young people from SOYA distributed it to the people. During the bus boycott in Alexandra township, Johannesburg, it was elements within SOYA, working with the organisations of the local people, that saved the day, when the Liberals collaborating with the Chamber of Commerce tried to persuade the public to ride the buses, buying five-penny tickets for four pence. The people saw through the trick and refused to ride the buses and decided to stay home. Dan Mokonyane, one of the heroes of that struggle, was a leader in SOYA. 'We Fight Ideas with Ideas' was the SOYA slogan. The youth tried to live up to that slogan.

In the Eastern Cape SOYA's strongholds were Fort Hare,

Healdtown, Lovedale, Queenstown and Lady Frere. As students at Fort Hare, young men like Vuthela, Cameron Madikizela, Bojana Jordan, Nota, Songca and others worked with peasant organisations in the Victoria East area, fighting the government's land rehabilitation scheme – *uMakatsha,* as the people called it.

When Fort Hare was closed in May 1954 because the students had boycotted the Graduation Ball, almost every student who was a member of or connected with SOYA was blacklisted and prevented from coming back when Fort Hare re-opened in July. The same happened to members at Healdtown. Most of these young men and women came to Cape Town to find jobs. It was a godsend, for they did a lot of work in the fight against Bantu Education and the boycott of the Van Riebeeck jamboree.

For the Van Riebeeck celebrations, our slogan was 'We Have Nothing to Celebrate!' We in CATA worked in the areas where there was a concentration of Africans – Langa, Nyanga, Simonstown, Retreat, Kensington, Elsies River, Eureka Estate and Goodwood. And the people were wonderful. There was one woman in Elsies River, a livewire, who would turn the audience around in the Eureka Hall, no matter what the quislings and collaborators tried to do.

It was at these meetings that I realised the versatility of the African languages: there is not a single concept that cannot be expressed in them. At one meeting in Nyanga, the speaker had been talking about the quislings in our midst when an African worker got up to make his comments. He had understood well the meaning of 'quisling' and in Xhosa referred to *Oo-Mpisekhaya* [the enemy within our ranks], which is what a quisling is. With so much response and understanding, who ever thought that thirty years later we would be still talking about the same things, covering the same ground?

The government went all out to make the Van Riebeeck celebrations a success. Money was available to all who were willing to participate, especially in making the Grand Finale in Cape Town a success. An area of about ten miles along the Foreshore was set aside for booths, depicting the history of South Africa from 1652, the year of Van Riebeeck's arrival, to 1952. The baThwa and the Khoi were to be brought down from the Kalahari and parts of Botswana for the world to see; African merchants in and around Cape Town were encouraged to take up booths, showing what they had done and were doing; the Coloured 'Coons' were to be there to entertain as well as the Malay choirs, both features special to Cape Town. But the people of the host centre declared: 'We Have Nothing to Celebrate,' and stayed away.

Even as 6 April approached, it was known that some merchants in Langa were taking up booths on the Foreshore. The people, in one of the meetings in Langa, had said: 'Let them go. But they might as well remain at the Foreshore, for they will not get us going to their shops again.' The people kept their word. To a man, those merchants who had booths for the Van Riebeeck celebrations went bankrupt. The lines were being drawn between those who would collaborate and those who refused. I. D. Mkize, principal of Langa High School, lost all the respect people had for him on the issue of the Van Riebeeck celebration. By the time he sold his soul to the government and went off to form the collaborating Cape African Teachers' Union, as a preparation for Bantu Education, he had been written off. When he died in Serowe on 12 April 1954, the day Bantu Education was introduced, people in Cape Town said that St Peter had called him to answer for his sins.

We had our biggest 'Boycott the Van Riebeeck Celebrations' rally on 4 April on the Grand Parade. It was our last call to the people to keep away and it was also a victory celebration, for only the previous Friday the last of the Malay choirs had decided to stay away too. I was on that platform. It was my first public speech at a political rally. When I. B. Tabata came to tell me that the committee was nominating me as one of the speakers, I pleaded with him to tell them not to.

'On the same platform with all you people, big guns, who have been speaking before big audiences here and other places! How can you do that to me?'

'We want an African woman on that platform, Phyllie. And you are that woman,' he said.

'Please get Mrs Siqwana, please, please.'

'No, Phyllie, the committee wants you. And it is going to be you.' So saying, he left me.

With me on that platform would be Goolam Gool, chairman of the Anti-CAD, Willem van Schoor, president of the Teachers' League of South Africa, Bennie M. Kies, editor of the *Teachers' Journal,* Miss Jane Gool of the Teachers' League, A. S. Jayiya of the Cape African Voters' Association, I. B. Tabata of the All-African Convention – all of them seasoned public speakers. What was I going to say to those crowds? But when I took up the theme 'We Have Nothing to

Celebrate' and related it to the position of African women, the exploited workers in the cities and the widows of the reserves, I was not at a loss for what to say.

Tata, who was coming to Cape Town that Sunday, 11 April, heard the report of the meeting in De Aar from some workers from Cape Town who were on their way home. They had forgotten the name of the young African woman on the platform. All they remembered was that she was said to be the wife of a teacher in a white school in Cape Town. When Tata asked me about it and told me what these workers were saying, he remarked: 'I thought it might be you, Phyllie. But I told myself not to feel elated, just in case there was another black teacher in a white school here in Cape Town.' He was so proud of his Gqaza.

Of the participants from up-country who were pouring into Cape Town for the celebrations, the Africans were supposed to be housed in the barracks in Langa, but they had to be removed for fear of their lives. As they alighted from the trains and walked down to the barracks, people stood on either side of the street, booed and jeered at them, calling them quislings and collaborators. They knew they could not sleep there and those who had lured them to Cape Town knew that they had to be removed. In the dead of night they were transferred to some army barracks beyond Windermere, where they lived for those two weeks. Some had hoped to see Cape Town while there. They never did. All they saw was the Foreshore. On Tuesday, 6 April, the march past took place in front of an empty grandstand. The people were not there. What a flop for the government that had put up this show! What a success for the people's boycott!

The Campaign Against
Bantu Education

We could not go ahead in full force with the campaign against Bantu Education until the Eiselen Commission had made its recommendations. These appeared in 1951. But the people had been prepared for what was coming, for we all knew it was not to our benefit. Our first task was to acquaint each other with the recommendations and their implications. In time the African people of the Western Cape were fully educated and they knew what to do.

I. D. Mkize, principal of Langa High School, had, at the instigation of the Native Affairs Department, launched his Cape African Teachers' Union, collecting around him all the collaborating elements to form this body. The excuse used was that CATA had affiliated to the All-African Convention which, according to their reasoning, did not represent all African organisations. Somehow Brian Bunting, arch-enemy of the All-African Convention and the Unity Movement, and editor of *New Age,** thought that he could make common cause with Mkize. So, every action of Mkize that was anti-CATA found coverage in Bunting's *New Age*.

Mkize had tried to take control of the local branch of CATA in 1951, not by convincing the other teachers that his course was right but by taking over the CATA funds and account. The treasurer happened to be one of his henchmen, and Mkize thought that, assisted by the bank account, he could build his CATU. Little did he know that when his friend had gone home on holiday in June, he had left the books with his assistant, a staunch CATA member. When we held our first branch meeting in August, the books were still with Siyaya, the assistant treasurer, and not with Mabali, Mkize's man.

* A newspaper of the Communist Party of South Africa, published in Cape Town.

Mkize's motion that the branch disaffiliate from the All-African Convention was lost; he staged a walk-out, calling on his fellow followers: 'Come, let's go, we have got the books.' Mabali, the treasurer, did not know whether to follow or not. As he was going out, he said to Mkize: 'No, Siyaya still has the books. I left them with him when I went home on vacation.' Mkize was stunned.

As soon as they were gone, we regularised the situation, appointing Siyaya treasurer of the local branch. Even after that, Mkize still tried to maintain that his body was the Western Province branch of CATA. He wrote several letters to Victor Siwisa, as ex-secretary of CATA Western Province. Every time these letters came, Mrs Siwisa gave them back to the postman, telling him that there was no ex-secretary of CATA at that address. He tried sending letters by registered mail to be signed for. Nontando returned them unsigned, until Mkize gave up. His last attempt was made at a meeting we had in Langa towards the end of 1952. We had enjoyed a very successful CATA conference in June, as a result of which the people of Cape Town saw CATA for what it was, and had held a good joint meeting with the TLSA, also assembling in Cape Town that June. Mkize was determined to smash this unity between Coloured and African teachers and, with the help of Bunting's *New Age,* he thought he could do it. For this meeting, Mkize organised some old women to disrupt the meeting, and alerted *New Age* that we would never again hold a meeting in Langa.

The meeting opened and A.C., who was the main speaker, walked onto the platform. Mkize's 'women' would not allow him. He was not one of the teachers of their children. They wanted teachers in the Langa schools to address them on the question of Bantu Education. A.C. did not live among them; he must go and speak to the Coloureds among whom he stayed. As a result of the disruption the chairman had to close the meeting. The next issue of *New Age* carried the following front-page news: 'The Unity Movement Driven out of Langa.' As we read this we wondered if Brian Bunting realised, even in his hatred of the Unity Movement, who his bedfellow was.

We stayed away from Langa for about four months, working quietly among the people, holding small house meetings, teaching each other about the tragedy of Bantu Education that was about to befall us. When we returned in May, we came back in full force. Our young workers had canvassed every house in Langa and every worker's place of residence. We organised our bouncers, too, as we knew that this was going to be *it*. Mkize had sent out a leaflet, distributed throughout the location by the children in his school. In it he said: 'Here they come again, the misleaders. You have shown them before when they were here. Show them again; drive them out through that door.' He invited *New Age* to send a reporter to the meeting. *New Age* sent Mary Turok, who came with Thomas Ngwenya, a member of the Liberal Party.

The hall was full. The air was charged. As I walked in I knew it was our day. All the young supporters to whom I had given leaflets were there, ushering people in, standing along the sides of the hall, expectant. Khwebulana, the chairman of the local branch, opened the meeting and called upon A.C. to come up and speak. Maphisa, one of Mkize's men, a teacher in Langa, rose to object. A big, stout, strong woman got up and looked at Maphisa: 'Dougie, sit down. We have children and we are not here to listen to your nonsense!' She gave Maphisa just one more look and he knew he had to sit down. When Mkize saw this, he tried to get up himself. Magodla, his assistant, who had realised on coming in that they stood no chance at this meeting, pulled him down. Then the meeting could proceed.

It was a very good meeting and the people, for the first time, had the opportunity to discuss the resolution that had come out of the ANC conference at the end of the year, namely that all children, except those already in Standard 5 and above, should be withdrawn from school. Johnson Ngwevela, a strong ANC man, had introduced the resolution and had asked the people of the Western Province to adopt it at this meeting. But the people replied: 'No, we have to discuss it first and arrive at our own decision.' This was what one liked about the people of the Western Cape. They discussed issues thoroughly and arrived at their own decisions.

Three women got up to speak on this resolution. One was a young woman, Francina Mamfanya, a mother of three. Francina said: 'What I would like to know is: Whose children must be doomed to no education while other people's get education? The resolution asks us to withdraw our children from school, while other people's children, already in Standard 5 onwards, will get educated. You see me standing here, my first-born is due to go to school only this coming year. I want her also to go to Fort Hare some day. Why should my children be condemned to ignorance, while other people's are not? Who has any right to tell me that mine must remain uneducated, while other people's get education? I want my child, due to start school only next year, to go to Fort Hare too someday.'

Another woman to speak was Mrs Winnie Siqwana, veteran of protests in Cape Town, member of the Communist Party and the ANC. Mrs Siqwana said: 'I am amazed that the ANC, an organisation of the African people, which should know, if it does not, that education is the only hope the African people have, through which they hope to liberate themselves some day, could ever come up with such a resolution. I have lived in this location for years and I think I can say I know the wishes of the mothers here about the education of their children. I can say the same about all those fathers in the barracks and bachelors' quarters. Every one of them wishes to see his children educated. Go to the mines, the farms, the rural areas, there is not a single African parent who does not wish to see his or her child educated, to be in a better position than the parent. How, then, can the ANC, an organisation of all these people, call upon them to do what they know the people will never do?'

The third woman who spoke from the floor was Dinah Mapille, also a member of the Communist Party and the ANC, who said: 'The fight is for us, the parents, not for our children. Who ever heard of parents putting their children in the forefront, in the front lines in battle? We want our children educated. But we can refuse to co-operate with Verwoerd in the school boards and committees he wants to set up. That is our role. That is our fight.'

After a full discussion, the chairman called for a resolution. Moses Molelekoa put forward the following resolution:

> After a full discussion of the merits and demerits of the resolution of the ANC at its conference, this meeting of parents and teachers of the Western Cape, held in Langa Hall, resolves:
>
> 1. That we shall continue to send our children to school, for a child with even Bantu Education is better than a child with no education at all.
>
> 2. That we call upon our teachers to stay in their posts, teaching our children what they know should be taught, as they have been doing over the years. Our teachers are our hope, for they and they alone will counteract the poison of Bantu Education. We call upon our teachers to be vigilant, watching out for any signs in the content of what is to be taught that are not in the interests of our children.
>
> 3. That this fight is for us the parents. And as such we, the parents, will refuse to co-operate and collaborate with the

government in the elections of school boards and school committees to run the Bantu Education schools. We further resolve
that all collaborators and quislings be ostracised.

Put to the house, the resolution was carried without any dissension.
Mary Turok, the *New Age* reporter, left before the vote was taken,
even before Molelekoa finished reading his resolution. As she was
going out, the young people, standing along the sides of the hall,
called to her: 'Vote, Madam, vote!' She was so embarrassed. There
was not a line in *New Age* about that meeting.

The people of the Western Cape kept their resolution, and for the
first fifteen years of Bantu Education, those who served on the
school committees and school boards were appointed members,
who did not have the confidence of the people. This was the beauty
of involvement in the Western Cape. The people worked together,
examined the issues, discussed them and arrived at a consensus,
irrespective of which organisation led the fight. There was hardly
any rivalry among the different popular organisations. The people
understood that, even though they belonged to separate bodies, the
enemy was the same and their fight was the same fight. What was
important was defeating the ends of the enemy. *Agents provocateurs*
there certainly were. But the people of the Western Cape never
allowed themselves to be led astray. They knew who the quislings
and collaborators were, and these were ostracised and shunned.

When Sobukwe held his February meeting in Langa a month
before the PAC launched the pass campaign in 1960, the throngs
that came to the meeting were not PAC members. The PAC as an
organisation was young and hardly known among the people.
Those who attended were the people who had stood together in the
fight against Bantu Education and in the Van Riebeeck boycott, and
they came from the active organisations in the Western Cape. The
people of the Western Cape lauded and followed the PAC call on 21
March 1960, because it struck a chord in their hearts; they were
ready to take the fight forward. The women in Langa, who shamed
the men going to work on 21 March, were Annie Silinga, Nellie
Malindi and Dinah Mapille, all of them ANC members. To them, this
was a national call and had to be supported. This is how mature the
people of the Western Cape were in their politics. One wishes that
our people in the other areas, too, would take a leaf out of the
people's unity in the Western Cape and act together, to defeat the

ends of the enemy. The enemy is not a member of ANC, AZAPO, BCM, UDF or any of the people's organisations. The enemy is the oppressive system of South Africa, the government that has imposed it upon the people, the lackeys who operate the machinery. That is the enemy.

On 14 December 1953, CATA called an All-In Conference of all teachers from the four provinces and invited teachers from the sister organisation, the TLSA. All teacher bodies, except the Orange Free State African Teachers' Association, now in the control of collaborators, responded to the call. The Bantu Education Act had just been passed in October of the same year, and April 1954 was scheduled as the start of the new system. Eiselen, as Secretary for Bantu Education, had on 13 December, the day before the conference, issued a stern warning that all teachers who attended the conference would be dealt with severely by his department. But the teachers came in their numbers in spite of this threat.

The question facing teachers and parents was 'What now?' Everybody knew what was in store for the African people and their children in the new system. Mr Leo Sihlali, president of CATA, took as the theme of his address the CATA motto: 'Where There Is No Vision, the People Perish'. Mr Sihlali made it quite clear to his audience that there could be no turning back. When CATA embraced the new policy, it was because the teachers had a vision of what they wanted the education of their children to be, and what they, the oppressed of South Africa, saw as their future – a future that gave every individual an opportunity to develop to his or her highest potential, a future in a new society where exploitation and oppression would be unknown, a future of a South Africa of equals.

'This is our vision,' declared Mr Sihlali, 'and nothing is ever going to blot and blur that vision for us. This is our vision of a new South Africa and to get there, we, the teachers, we, the parents, must gird ourselves for the struggle ahead, a struggle which all the forces of reaction, the power of the state, are bent on diverting, thwarting and sabotaging.'

Conference agreed to adopt the resolution of the Parent–Teacher Organisation of the Western Cape, namely, that teachers were to remain at their posts, forever vigilant, teaching as they had done before and watching out for indoctrination; parents were to refuse to serve on the proposed school boards and committees; and parents were to keep their children in school.

A number of young people at the conference had been asking me to speak, saying that if I did, that would give courage to the other women in the conference. Though many women attend conferences of this kind, few ever speak. The idea that these are the affairs of men is still present and the women always hold back. So when we convened in the afternoon, I thought I would oblige. I had come as representative of our local Western Province CATA–Parent Association, and I spoke on their behalf. I always used Xhosa at such meetings and would relate my theme to the experiences of the people.

> A flock without lambs is doomed. A herd without calves has no future. A people whose children are doomed to ignorance has no future. It is our children who are, by this Act, condemned to a world of darkness and ignorance, who will never fit in anywhere in the world after being shut away from the rest of humanity by Bantu Education. If we all realise that, we cannot, no matter what the odds, stand idly by and let that happen. Where are the mothers in this hall who will say: 'Never! Not to my child!'? Where are the women of this nation who will say: 'Never, not to our children!'? Have we less courage than the mother-hen, that will dare the falcon that swoops down on her young? I do not think so. Let us take a lesson from those mothers in Hitler's concentration camps, who, in a desperate situation, tried to save their children. We will do the same too. We will tell Verwoerd that over our dead bodies will he condemn our children to ignorance. We will tell him: Never, not to our children.

To me, the fight against Bantu Education was a fight for the mothers of the nation. If they stood firm, we could defeat the ends of this measure. Perhaps this conviction was borne out of my experience in the Western Cape, where it was the mothers, the women, who were our great support in CATA.

For three full years, 1955 through to 1957, the authorities tried without success to get the people to elect school board and school committee members. Then in 1958 they decided to call a meeting for elections throughout the Cape Peninsula for all schools, on the same day. In addition, the parents were to be admitted to the meetings if

each had an invitation as a parent with a child in that particular school. Police were posted at the doors to check identity
papers, because they were under the impression that certain
elements opposed to Bantu Education would float around on election day to oppose the elections. They were to learn that this was
the decision of the people, the parents, and no 'pressure groups'
were responsible.

The meeting at St Cyprian's (the Anglican school in Langa) was
presided over by Mr Mama, ex-principal of the Methodist school and
now court interpreter in the Cape Supreme Court. After the people
were assembled, Mr Mama asked anyone for a prayer to start the
meeting.

Moses Molelekoa responded and prayed as follows: 'Dear God,
please help us to remember the decisions we, as parents, have taken
on this question. Help us not to waver now but to abide by the
decision of the people of this area. Amen.'

Mr Mama knew that there was going to be some trouble. In a few
words, he explained the reason for the meeting and called for nominations for members, first of the school board.

Silence.

Then Annie Silinga, a veteran fighter and opponent of every anti-
African law, rose: 'I dare anyone, quisling or collaborator, to get up
now and tell us to elect. He or she will soon know of what stuff we
are made.' She sat down.

'Any nominations?' called Mr Mama.

Silence.

The meeting closed.

From St Cyprian's the women walked over to the Methodist
school. Here the municipal police were still checking the parents'
identity notes.

'What are you waiting for?' asked the matrons from St Cyprian's.

'The police are still checking if we have children in this school,'
was the answer.

'Who says? Who does not know that every mother is every child's
mother?' So saying, they pushed their way in and the police could
not do anything.

Chairing the meeting here was Mr Parsons, Chief Native Commissioner in Salt River. After Mr Parsons had opened the meeting, Mr
Myathaza asked if Mr Parsons had a child in the Langa Methodist
school (which, of course, as a white person, he did not).

'No.'

'Why are you here then? Don't your children go to the University of Cape Town?'

Everyone at the meeting wanted to know what Mr Parsons was doing at a meeting of parents whose children attended the Methodist school in Langa. When Mr Parsons explained that he was the Chief Native Commissioner, the people told him: 'We all know that. What we want to know now is why you are at this meeting, when your children attend the University of Cape Town?'

He could not get past that question and the meeting had to close, and no elections were held. He never again went to any meeting. Where the chairman was a local person, who had the right to be at the meeting, the people dared the quislings and collaborators to tell them to elect.

In the Cape Province we had decided to send the children to school, but to boycott the machinery for running the schools. This we did. There was a lot of talk that in Johannesburg the children were going to be withdrawn from school, following the ANC resolution. Ambrose Reeves, Bishop of Johannesburg, decided to close all fifty church schools in his see rather than rent them to the Department of Bantu Education. This meant that children from these schools would have to find accommodation in other schools or stay at home. I went up to Johannesburg for an on-the-spot assessment of the situation. The Liberal Party was interested in the situation and asked me to give them my report. On 12 April 1954, the first day of Bantu Education, there was an air of something about to happen. Most of the parents I spoke to were saying: 'Who has a right to tell me whether to send my child to school or not? I dare anybody who is going to stop my child tomorrow.' I thought of what Mrs Winnie Siqwana had said at our meeting in Langa when this was brought up.

Just two blocks from my cousin's house was a big Presbyterian school, under the principalship of Mr G. Jolobe. That morning, 12 April 1954, fathers with sticks under their arms were escorting their young ones to the school, daring anybody to stop them. After watching this for an hour or two, my cousin drove me to Holy Cross, down the road. It was the same scene – fathers with their children, seeing to it they went in. Thinking it was perhaps Orlando where the parents were not in favour of withdrawing their children from school, we went to Benoni and Germiston the next day. Here we found the same scenes. The children from the Anglican schools that had been closed were there with their parents seeking admission in those schools that were open.

On our way back, we stopped at Mr Ntombela's, our nephew, who was principal of the Albert Street School, Johannesburg, to find out what the position was at his establishment.

'Any boycotts?' I asked.

'What boycotts? I have more children than I can take. The Anglican parents are clamouring for room for their children because Reeves has closed all his big schools. But we can take only a few. We were overcrowded even without that.'

'Who then is withdrawing his children?' I asked.

'Nobody! If there will be any children not in school, it will be mostly those from the Reeves' schools; they, too, because they cannot find a place. My aunt, this is Johannesburg, a place of big talk.'

The next day we went to the Far East Rand – Springs and Brakpan – and here too the children were in school and the parents were saying: 'We are not fools. We, too, want our children educated. They exempt from this withdrawal all those in Standard 5 and up, because their children are already in those Standards. Who do they think they are fooling?'

The school boycott! Could it have succeeded? *No.* Because as one observer wrote in the *Cape Times*: 'This could never have been a decision of the African parents, who were so keen on educating their children and would go to any length to achieve that. This was a rash decision of the elite who purported to speak for them, a publicity stunt, so as to appear tough.'

And it was just so. None of the ANC elite had even prepared the people for this school boycott, nor were they prepared to educate the people on how it could be achieved, even at this late stage. And neither did they understand all the things implicit in the Bantu Education Act, for if they had, they would have known that the South African government was by this Act trying to solve *for all time* the labour problems of South Africa. The Bantu Education Act of 1953 relegates the majority of African children to a position of hewers of wood and drawers of water, even before they are born. What could better suit the mine magnates, the farmers, the industrialists, than to be provided with this army of illiterate workers? Secondly, the Act made it a crime for anyone to teach African children without the permission of the Minister of Education. So African parents who in the past had taxed themselves and built schools for their children could not do so any more. The children withdrawn from the schools would be roaming the streets with nothing to do. And the Act had foreseen such an eventuality in that it included a clause that empowered the Minister to collect all children who were not in school when they should be and send them to youth camps, which the government would establish for that purpose. The mass arrests of schoolchildren we are witnessing today take place under that clause of the Bantu Education Act. The only difference perhaps is that instead of being sent to youth camps, a euphemism for youth jails, these kids are being sent to the ordinary jails.

Those elements who were for the school boycott would have us believe that it was a success, and to support this they cite the 'cultural clubs' that were set up in areas like Benoni. They make sure not to tell us that most of the children who came to these 'cultural clubs' were from the Anglican schools, now closed. Bishop Huddleston makes this point clear in his book *Naught for Your Comfort*.

When, after the Soweto student rebellion in 1976, some teachers on the Reef resigned in protest, parents were worried and demanded to know from these teachers who was going to teach their children in the right way; who would be the watchdogs, seeing to it that government propaganda did not poison their children. It is interesting to me that the lessons of non-collaboration and the boycott thus came to be espoused by the very children who started school when these words were first used. The ideas behind them took root, and since 1976 it is the children who are teaching these lessons to their parents. Today's children seem to have drunk with their mothers' milk the meaning of these words and have come to understand that the 'boycott is a weapon of struggle', which, as I. B. Tabata says, a people without arms can use to halt the machinery of the state.

Writing

Early in 1957, a friend, Ronnie Segal, asked me to write an article for his recently launched magazine *Africa South*.

'I want a story of an African woman, Phyllis, and it must be in your maiden name, for A.C. is already a contributor to the magazine and I don't want another Jordan in it.'

'When do you go to press?' I asked.

'Middle of March. This will go into our April–June issue of the magazine.'

'OK, I'll do it. How much editing do you do?'

'Just dotting the *i*'s and crossing the *t*'s. No change whatsoever, except to correct a sentence that is wrong.'

'That suits me fine. I do not want anybody changing the way I write.'

'No problem there, you may be sure.'

There were so many women whose profiles I could draw, those success stories of women who had done this and that and are now 'pillars' of their society. I thought: 'To hell with them all'. We have heard enough about them and are going to hear more, for they are the beloved of those who write anything on the African. I decided to write about those other women whom nobody ever hears about, whose story has never been told, because they are not the 'pillars' of their societies. These were some of the girls I had grown up with, now married and living the lives of widows, as their menfolk were away in the cities. Their faces came flooding before me – Ntombemnyama, Buyiswa, Nozengazi, Nobantu, Nomawo, Mkamlungu and my cousin Nontuthu, whose husband was somewhere in Cape Town and had forgotten that he had left a wife and two children at home. People do not even know that these women exist.

And if they do, who cares? Turning this over and over in my mind, I decided that the best way would be to begin by providing some background and telling the story of the tragedy of the African people before I drew the profile of any African woman. 'African Tragedy' is the article.*

> It is the sad story of a whole people, 15,000,000 souls, land-less, homeless, destitute; a people who have been ruthlessly uprooted from the country, but not allowed to develop roots in the towns, victims of a vicious worked-out system to render them homeless, propertyless and poor so that they can be pushed into the labour market to still the economic cries of the industrial age. The Native Reserves have them by the thousand, those young men who have never known life; husbands and fathers who have never known what home is, what family life is; fathers who do not even know their own children. It is the tragic story of thousands of young women who are widowed long before they reach the age of thirty; young married women who have never been mothers, young women whose life has been one long song of sorrow – burying one child after another and lastly, burying the husband, that lover she has never known as husband and father. To them, both men and women, adulthood means the end of life; it means loneliness, sorrow, tears and death; it means a life without a future because there is no present.

This is the tragic story of our people! I had seen it in the rural areas; I had seen it in the cities. I had seen it only three years back, in its ugliest, here in Cape Town in the transit camps that the Divisional Council had set up twelve miles east of Cape Town, when they were clearing the settlements that people had made among the sand-dunes and bushes throughout the Cape Peninsula. The winter of 1954 had been one of the coldest in Cape Town, with floods that swept away people's shanties in the bushes, taking everything with them and leaving some with nothing but the clothes they stood in. It was during this winter that people were removed to bare bush, without even the semblance of shelter, *nothing*.

Early in the year personnel of the Divisional Council had gone round all the settlements where Africans lived informally, giving each household a number, their lot when they moved. A month

* *Africa South,* Vol. I, no. 3, April–June 1957.

before the removals, the Council again came round, leafletting these areas, telling the people when they would be moved and advising them to be ready on that particular day. On the said day the vans came, collected the people with their belongings, drove to the 'transit camp' area, dumped them in the open, each family on its designated spot. The places they had lived in were bulldozed. Moreover, if people were not there when the moving vans came, their possessions inside were bulldozed along with the shack. It was May of a very cold winter when all this was done. It is only when one sees such things that one can realise the callousness of white authorities when they deal with Africans.

I went during the second week of the removals to see for myself. A friend, Mrs Jilana, who lived in Nyanga East, not far from the school, took me, and what I saw begs description. There were the people with their children, dumped on wet sand, in the bush, in the rain, without any shelter. Some had cleared trees, put hessian over the bushes and were crouching underneath, round an open fire. Others had set their pieces of furniture down, put hessian around them, and pieces of cardboard and zinc on top. Everybody was coughing, the children's noses were running, and many had pneumonia. Children died. There were no shops, no water, *nothing!* What provisions most had brought with them had already run out. The nearest shop was usually two miles away through bush, and it was possible that if one walked to it one would not find the way home, for there was no recognisable way home. For four days I was there talking to and meeting those people in the transit camps.

Here I met a man who told me that he had been at work when the moving vans came. When he came back, there was no 'home'. Except for the street, he could not even recognise where his house had been. He headed for the transit camp on foot for there were no buses going that way. He was going to find his family. Where? He did not know. 'Nkosazana, I ran, I prayed, and I cried. It was getting dark and I did not know in which area people from Eureka would be. I was guided by the fires in the bush. As I approached a group, I would call out: *"Nivela kwa Qhobosha? Ngaba bakuliphi cala abakwa Qhobosha?"* [Do you by any chance come from Eureka? Which way would be people from Eureka?]'

That man trudged through that bush, in the cold, hungry and tired, until three in the morning when he came upon his family. 'They offered me food,' he told me. 'But I could not eat. I was just glad I had found them.'

Many children were separated from their parents and stayed with other groups completely unknown to them. But the people took them in until their parents showed up.

I went back again in September of the same year and it was then that I met Mrs Dumani, the subject of my article. Things looked much better than they had been when I first went there. This was the result not of the authorities but of the people.

My second article for *Africa South* was 'The Widows of the Reserves', which has enjoyed a lot of publicity and has been translated into French, Flemish and Dutch. I am glad I opened the window on these women. Before that no one had thought their story was worth telling. Langston Hughes wrote to congratulate me after reading it and later included it in his anthology *An African Treasury*. It is in that volume that many people in the Americas read the article. Other articles of mine in *Africa South* included the series 'An Abyss of Bantu Education'. A variation of these appear in *Fighting Talk*, edited by the late Ruth First, under the title 'Five Years of Bantu Education'. This series appeared also in *Contact*, the Liberal Party magazine.

Sometime in the mid-fifties, I. B. Tabata produced a booklet on the boycott entitled *The Boycott as a Weapon of Struggle*. It was felt that because of the situation in Transkei and other rural areas where the peasants were protesting against stock limitation, the rehabilitation scheme and Bantu Authorities, this booklet should be translated into Xhosa. I was asked to do it. Reading it in Xhosa, no one would ever think it was a translation. It was also while working through the booklet in Xhosa that I realised that there was not a single concept expressed in the European languages which one could not express in African languages. If anything, it is the European languages that fall short of expressing concepts found in the African languages, for example, the Nguni *'uBuntu'* or the Sotho *'Botho'*.

Those peasants in Transkei who read the booklet adopted it as their bible. At the meeting in Bizana, chaired by the Chief Native Commissioner of Ciskei, to inquire into the causes of the 1960 disturbances in Pondoland, the peasants quoted concepts from that booklet in Xhosa, in putting their case. And A.C., the scholar, writer, critic, translator and linguist, declared that I had produced a classic.

UCT and My Work

In 1957 I decided to attend the University of Cape Town to do a Diploma in Native Administration. I wanted to understand this network of laws that binds the African people hand and foot. When I got to UCT I found that the programme was much wider and more interesting than I had thought, for it embraced Comparative African Government and Law, drawn up and given by a very able professor, Dr H. J. Simons. The programme covered three areas of colonial Africa – British, French and Belgian Africa – and compared the administrative systems of the three powers. It was an eye-opener, for basically the purpose of all three in Africa was the same, namely, to exploit Africa's resources and the labour of her people. When we turned to South Africa it was then that I understood that, in fact, the basis of apartheid was laid by the English, before the turn of the century.

Reading the correspondence between the Colonial Office in Britain and the government in Cape Town, as well as debates in the Cape parliament, was very revealing. On one occasion Cecil John Rhodes, then prime minister, warned his fellow whites: 'I have just returned from Transkei and found there huge institutions, where they are teaching the native Greek and Latin, producing excellent fellows, parsons by the dozen. But they are overdoing it. Those men will soon agitate against the government.' On the question of imposing taxes on Africans, Rhodes again did not equivocate: 'We want to get hold of these young men and make them go out and work. It must be brought home to them that in future nine-tenths of them will spend their lives in daily labour, in physical work, in manual work.' In 1899, three years before Dr Verwoerd was born, Lord Milner spelt out the aims of Britain in South Africa in these words: 'The ultimate aim is a self-governing white community in control of the economy, supported by well-treated and justly governed black labourers.' Of course it would be Lord Milner and other whites who would determine what good treatment and government would be, and not the African labourers.

By the end of my two years working towards my Diploma, I knew every law in the statute-books governing the African people, and every loophole. It was just as well, for the following year I went to work in the offices of the Institute of Race Relations in Cape Town.

The South African Institute of Race Relations had been inspired by Dr Aggrey of Ghana on his visit to South Africa in the mid-twenties. It never had any popular support among the African people, even among the intellectuals. Initially it was joined by men on the Advisory Boards in the big cities and the first layer of Fort Hare graduates, Z. K. Matthews, Ngcobo, Moerane and a few others. But by the mid-forties, not even the 'respectable' Fort Hare graduates were attracted to it. Among whites, the same held. It was the home of the Liberals of the Cape, Johannesburg, Natal and particular places like Fort Hare, Lovedale and St Matthew's.

The Institute is mainly a research body, carrying out projects on race relations in South Africa. Every year it produces a survey from highly selected reports from the quality papers in South Africa, though never from the *Guardian, Torch,* or other progressive papers in the country, and also very little from the Afrikaans press, except perhaps *Die Burger.*

Our office in Cape Town, because it was located in the legislative capital, dealt with legislation that was coming up before parliament in that particular year, interpreting it for the layman and making our research known among the public through the media. Whoever was handling a project in our office had to do a lot of research into past legislation and consult with some lawyers in town; we always dealt with D. B. Molteno S.C., the father of the Institute in Cape Town – it was such a pleasure working with him. Besides this, our office handled all the cases of Africans who had problems with their passes, men and women, new arrivals and old workers who thought they would get into trouble under the pass laws and influx control. They came to our office for free help. My knowledge of Native Administration and the laws affecting Africans thus came in handy. And how does anybody handle a case of one who has no rights under the laws of the land? One looks for all the loopholes and uses these; one also taps the tender feelings of the administrators who have to apply these laws. This meant knowing just which chord to touch when writing a letter to Mr Palmgren, Mr Worrall or Mr Rogers, the Superintendent in Langa. One had to know what things not to include in a letter to the Chief Native Commissioner in Salt River and, to some extent, what sort of man he was. One had to learn all these tricks and to lie where and when it was necessary – to lie to save a man or woman from being turfed out of an urban area – and to be sure that all the same the story hung together. One had to consider all the possibilities of where and how this seemingly neatly sewed-up story could be punctured.

What could one do in a situation where the people have no rights under the law? All I required was that when they came, they should give us the true story, hide nothing from us, for we were there to help them and get round the law if we could. But not knowing all the facts we could not build a case. Give me all those ugly facts and from them I could proceed. It was a heart-rending job. But I am glad to say that in many cases we succeeded in obtaining for the people who asked our help what they wanted, which was often not much at all – a woman wanting to have her stay in Cape Town extended so that she can conceive; a mother asking that she be allowed to bring her children into Cape Town because the relative she had left them with has died and now there is no one at home to look after them; a worker who wants to change his category for he has an offer for a better-paying job; a woman coming to Cape Town, smuggled in the boot of a car, to look for her husband. All these were human desires and human requests. Yet in a better society, people should not even be required to refer such questions to others. They are private personal issues and no third person should know about them.

The State of Emergency

The events of 21 March 1960 and those of 4 April, when hell's fury was let loose on the African people, were to bring me closer still to my people. After 21 March and the shootings in Langa and Sharpeville, the African workers in Cape Town downed tools and very few of them reported for work. After the big funerals on 26 March there was virtually a complete work stoppage in the African townships in and around the Peninsula. One of the provocations that made Africans march to the centre of the city on 30 March was the police raids on their living quarters, unleashed in an attempt to drive the people to work.

The 30 March walk to Caledon Square, the central police station, was not pre-planned; it developed spontaneously as the police were driving workers out of their quarters into the centre of Langa. When thousands had gathered near the iNkundla, they all decided to proceed to parliament, and on they marched. I was at work and did not know about this until lunchtime, when the people were already converging on Caledon Square. A.C. and Pallo were at the university at Groote Schuur, Nandi was downtown at the Little Theatre, Ninzi and Lindi were in school in Athlone.

When Pallo and the other students heard that African columns were approaching Mowbray, they flew down and joined the marchers, just as the first column was entering De Waal Drive, and marched with them to Oranjezicht. A.C. had followed in his car with one or two other professors. He did not know that Pallo was with the marchers. He only saw him later, resting with the others under the trees, as they debated whether to go to the House of Assembly or to Caledon Square. A.C. called out to Pallo to let him know that he too was there. I was on my way to lunch in the Cape Town

Gardens when, as I crossed Long Street, some white woman told me that Africans were reported to be marching to the Houses of Parliament. I flew through those gardens, heading for the House. As I came out, I saw other people streaming past, running towards Plein Street. I followed and got to the area around Caledon Square, just as the people were coming in and taking their places. In no time, the whole area filled up and there was nothing but a sea of black faces all around. The few whites, Coloureds and Indians were hardly visible in that sea of black. A helicopter was already droning above us. It was a tense moment. Nobody knew what was going to happen. All stood there, silent and determined. Now and again, through the din of the helicopter above us, came a lone voice: *'uSana olungaliliyo, lufel' embelekweni!'* [A baby that does not cry dies in its mother's back-strap.] Whose voice this was, no one knew. We were to learn later that this was Vernon February, A.C.'s Coloured student in his Xhosa II class at UCT.

Patrick Duncan limped past us and headed for the door of the police station, asking: 'Where's Kgosana? Where's Philip Kgosana? Did anyone see him go past here?' I do not know if he received any answer to his question. We all stood there, silent.

After a wait of about two and a half hours in that hot sun, Philip Kgosana climbed on a police van to address the crowds. But as his voice could not carry, and because he did not speak the language of the majority of the people gathered here, Mlamli Makhwethu got up next to him to tell the people to go home, their grievances had been noted and would be passed on to the Minister in charge; passes were suspended and the police would not harass them anymore.

The people quietly turned round and went home, 30,000 of them! They had come to town on foot, marching fourteen miles over De Waal Drive, orderly and quiet, reminding each other 'No violence, Ma-Afrika!' Others had followed by bus and train and caught up with the marchers in front of Caledon Square. Those from Nyanga, on hearing of this, followed on foot. But by the time they got to Claremont train station, the crowds were already going home, and they turned to go back with them.

Where I was standing, some Africans doubted the wisdom of going home, saying it was all a trick. This was just a way to defuse the situation. They were right. By the time the crowds reached the townships, the government had declared a State of Emergency, giving the Minister of Justice and any officer in his department arbitrary powers to deal with Africans. In terms of the State of Emergency of 1960, the South African government did away with *habeas corpus*. That suspension was to be incorporated later in the General Law Amend-ment Act of 1963.

Pallo had marched back with the people, all the way from Caledon Square to Langa junction, where he took the bus home to Sunnyside. A.C. and the other faculty members had driven back to varsity to collect their bags and they too headed home. It had been an exciting day. Passes suspended! Does it really mean a change in policy? Yes, suspended they were for more than two months. The State of Emergency would have stopped any black stampede into the towns. It covered the whole country; it was ruthless. Under it, men, women and children, especially boys, were arrested for all sorts of infringements of the laws, real and imaginary. That same evening after the State of Emergency was put into effect, the whole PAC executive in the Western Cape was arrested for incitement, the same charge that had been levelled against Sobukwe and others in the Transvaal and against Chief Albert Luthuli, after he had burnt his pass in public. By the morning of 31 March all entrances to the locations were sealed, with army units in fours, standing at each entrance, with instructions to shoot anyone leaving or entering.

As soon as I got to work, I told Mrs Matthews, the secretary, under whom I worked, that I would like to check what the situation was like in Langa, whether it was possible to go in through the foot-paths. She agreed that I leave as soon as I could. I left at eleven o'clock. The suburb of Pinelands is separated from Langa by only a broad boulevard, running from east to west. There are many foot-paths from Pinelands into Langa, which many workers from Langa use. I thought I would try one of these. I knew that going through the gate was well-nigh impossible, and I did not want to answer any of the questions at the gates, still more go through that barrier of armed soldiers. From town, I took the bus to Pinelands, and got off at a spot just below the Langa Hospital where I knew there was a footpath. I crossed the street, walked through the bushes towards Langa, and right there, in front of me, among the bushes were the soldiers. Another woman coming from Paarden Eiland and going home to her children joined me. We stood there for a few minutes and both of us decided not to try this entrance. Further on, east of us, there was another footpath, near Thornton. We decided to try that one, even though we figured we would find the same situation.

At this one, too, soldiers were standing guard. I gave up and went home. That Saturday, A.C. and I tried another path through Bridgetown–Kewtown into the barracks and zones south of Langa. The soldiers were there too. They were so young; they looked bored, standing there with nothing to do, defending white supremacy.

The African workers were home, doing their domestic chores for a change. All the industries where Africans worked were losing money. Managers were getting desperate and something had to be done. By the morning of 4 April more army units were called in, flown into Cape Town the previous night. That morning and right through the day and the next and the next hell's fury was let loose on the African people; they were beaten out of their houses, beaten in the streets and driven to work. This was the day a seventeen-year-old white boy, a policeman, assaulted A.C. in Rondebosch. He had gone to the post office to send off some examination books, and was returning to his car. The young policeman ran across, telling him to stop. 'I did not even think he was calling to me,' said A.C. When the young officer reached him, he demanded to know why he did not stop.

'Me?' asked A.C.

He had his cigarette in his hand and the officer knocked it out with 'Yes, you!' and a slap across the face.

At that point another officer, older, ran towards them calling: 'Stop it! Stop it!' When he got up, he said: 'I am sorry, Sir. Sorry!'

A.C. went back to the university, and made a report to the head of his department, informing him he was going home and would remain there until the university guaranteed him safe passage to and from his work. His nephew Bransby, who was serving articles with a firm of lawyers in town, called home on the off-chance that his uncle might be there.

'You are home early,' remarked Bransby.

A.C. told him what had happened that morning. He had just finished writing an official letter to the head of his department. At once Bransby called Donald Molteno S.C. and reported that his uncle had been assaulted by a young white officer in Rondebosch. Mr Molteno at once called Mr Harry Lawrence, MP for Salt River, and told him to bring the matter up at once. All these were people who respected A.C. and felt outraged that such a thing could happen to him just because he was black. Only two years before, Lawrence's son had been in A.C.'s class and the young fellow had nothing but praise for his professor, both as a person and as a teacher. Lawrence was furious and raised the matter at once, demanding a public apology, to A.C., to the University of Cape Town and to the African people at large. The House adopted such a motion.

Sometime during the State of Emergency, the Commandant of the Wynberg Police came to our house, with a written apology to A.C. from his department, the Department of Native Affairs and the Department of Justice. It was Lindi who answered his knock at the front door. After he had introduced himself Lindi made him stand on the stoep while he went to the study to call his dad.

Many people sent messages of sympathy to us. Only one person, a member of staff in the English Department at UCT, a friend of A.C., thought he had made an undue fuss for other 'Natives' were also being assaulted. Why should he have imagined an exception would be made of him?

After calling Mr Molteno, Bransby had phoned me at work. I called home at once and A.C. answered.

'Are you hurt?' I asked.

'No! No! Don't worry. I am all right. I am not even angry any more. I'll tell you when you get home. Please, don't worry!'

It was only in the evening that I heard the whole story.

Yes, hell's fury was let loose on the African people that 4 April. This was the day the police shot and killed Mkhwane in Nyanga West. They had driven him and other men out of their shacks and as they ran round the fence, the police opened fire and killed Mkhwane on the spot. His wife was the first to reach him, just as he was gasping for his last breath. I met Mrs Mkhwane a week after, still in shock. Another worker, Nkohla, of Nyanga East, had been shot while running away and had caught a bullet with his forearm as he cowered to protect his head. When he fell, the police took him, threw him in the van, and sent him to Worcester jail where his broken arm was attended to some ten hours later.

Under the State of Emergency, people disappeared into thin air. A boy who had run an errand for his mother after school would not come home; a man who had gone to Langa to renew his pass would disappear; a worker waiting for his train at a railway station would not be seen or heard of again. Nobody knew what had happened to them. All had been taken under Article 4 *bis* of the Emergency Regulations. Their relatives came to our office in Bree Street to help them find their loved ones. This was my assignment. It seemed a hopeless task, for we had nothing to go on; the police precincts in and around Cape Town did not keep any records of such people. Under the Emergency Regulations a 'mock' court was established in Cape Town where those arrested appeared before a magistrate, were sentenced and sent to goodness-knows-where. It was to this court that I directed my inquiries. It was not much help to us. All I could obtain was the name of the person arrested (in most cases misspelt), the date of appearance in court, the date of departure from Cape Town, the train the said person was put on, the destination, and the last train station on the other end. Where the person landed up nobody knew or even cared to know in the 'mock' court. Mrs Kathleen Rose Matthews, then secretary of the South African Institute of Race Relations in Cape Town, was just marvellous. Somewhere I have said of this woman: 'I shall never forget the humanity and the courage of Mrs Kathleen Rose Matthews, then secretary of the SAIRR office in Cape Town, under whom I worked, for though we had so little to go by, she held on doggedly, and we followed every lead, checking and rechecking every bit of information. It was the sympathy and courage of this woman that comforted those who came to our office for help and gave them hope that something would someday turn up.'

Putting bits of information together, little by little, we were able to trace most of the people who had disappeared. I was in the townships on Tuesdays and Thursdays and later every weekend. Here with some good news perhaps, or here to check on a name. To this very day I can still see the happy faces when the news was good, but how sad they looked when the news was bad. When they cried, I cried with them and, locked in their embraces, I knew that the situation we were all in had bound us together. It was during these trips that I met in Nyanga West a tall black man, a six-footer, muscle all over. His whole body was covered in weals, his legs were swollen up to the waist and he told me that for a whole week he had urinated blood. He had been beaten with sjamboks and truncheons by the police on 4 April. 'There were six of them,' he told me. 'If only I had had two to face, I would have shown them.' I believed him. He was a giant. 'Nkosazana, I was not in this campaign. But the police beat me into it. Now I am in it heart and soul.'

I learnt a lot from the people during those days and months. One thing was that no matter what the odds, how long the road, they were determined to walk it to the very end. One had to be in the magistrate's courts, where batches of them were facing trial. The people were defiant and unafraid. The Xhosa call them *amaDela-kufa* – those who defy death. Those to be charged would be called up to the well of the court, before the magistrate – six or eight of them. The charge would be read out: Guilty or not guilty? 'Not guilty!' would be their response, and they would be remanded for some later date. Then they would turn round to go to the basement where they had been kept and where others were waiting. As soon as they left the well of the court, each would call out *'iZwe Lethu!'*, and from the basement came a thunderous response: *'Afrika!'*

'Amandla!'

Response: *'Ngawethu!'*

There was nothing that any court orderly could do to silence them.

The African people knew that history was on their side. They still know it today.

After 30 March my brother Mzukie was one of the few contacts that the PAC members in Langa had with the outside world; through him they could send and receive messages. This meant he had to go through that cordon of armed units, with bayonets at the ready, every time he entered Langa. Was I scared for him! Would Mzukie know what to do and say when asked questions? I would ask myself. A.C. always told me that Mzukie would handle the situation much better than I ever could. I could not believe it. For all the serious discussions we had had, to me he was still that small, innocent boy, shooting marbles on the stoep or moulding clay cattle under the table in the kitchen at home, who would be fed up with me when I said: 'No clay in the house; clay belongs to the side of the cattle-fold, not inside the house.' So I always breathed a sigh of relief when I saw him enter our gate, cool as ever, calm and controlled. Running to meet him, I would say: 'Nqoko, you are here! How are you? How are things?' Then I would think to myself: 'Perhaps A.C. is right; Nqoko is no longer a child.'

This anxiety for him never left me. I remember in 1961, when he and five others were arrested in Langa for 'furthering the ends of a banned organisation, the PAC' and were under interrogation for more than two weeks, I was all torn inside, fearing they would beat him up, wondering if he would give a consistent story every time he came up for questioning. Knowing that the police would search his room in Crawford, I went there, looked through his bookcase for any books that might be thought subversive and removed these, as well as papers he had in his dresser, and left these in the custody of the family in the next room, great friends of his, whose three-year-old daughter just adored him. When the detectives brought him to the house to search his room, this three-year-old, I was told, seeing his hair unkempt, came out with a brush and comb and started combing him. Mrs Plaatje, the mother, said: 'I was so glad when Ntuthu did that, to show them that he was a good man who would not hurt anybody.'

'Is this your child?' the police had asked.

'No, she is my friends' and we are good friends,' he had told them.

To me Mzukie will always be my little brother, the baby I prayed for when I was five years old.

Throughout those six months of the State of Emergency, a black Dodge police car always parked at the corner of Unity Road and Covington Road, right in front of our house. Mr Forbes, our next-door neighbour, alerted us to its presence there every night. For three months I could not sleep. I, too, stood by the window, watching them. The car would come up our street at about eleven o'clock, slowly go down to Port Jackson Road, then back again at about midnight, up the road; at about one o'clock, it would stop just before the light and remain there until four in the morning. After three months of watching, I decided I might as well get my sleep. I am certain now that after three months of watching our house, they knew that no people came to us by night. But they maintained their vigil, just to keep us on tenterhooks.

The Siege

Determined though the African people may be, their economic condition and their settlement in segregated locations, often many miles from the centre of the cities and white suburbs, make them very vulnerable. An African township is easy to surround and blockade. In fact, the powers-that-be do not even have to spend a bullet on the people, they can bring them down on their knees just by shutting off the water supply, which is, in many cases, controlled from the city. Because of their poverty it is difficult for Africans to store up anything for a long siege. This was the case in 1960.

After the big Sobukwe meeting in February in Langa, the PAC cadres had gone round, holding meetings, advising people to store up foodstuffs, as nobody knew how long the campaign would last. A friend of mine, Thembsie, who lived in Langa, told me about these meetings and one day, with her, I went to a meeting at the North Barracks, next to Langa Hospital. As these were meetings for men, we went there dressed as men with scarves round our heads. It was dark and no one could recognise us. I wore my brother Mzukie's overalls, which I had been using while painting at home. We made sure that we sat apart and at a distance from the rest of the men. Norman Shuba and Manelisi Ndibongo were the speakers. They told the men of the coming campaign, what was to be done, emphasised that it was going to be non-violent and disciplined, and above all exhorted the people to start storing up foodstuffs – samp, beans, sugar, tea, coffee, oil and dripping. They stressed the importance of dry foodstuffs.

We left as soon as the meeting began to break up. After seeing Thembsie to her house in Mvambo Street, I took the bus home to Sunnyside. I never said anything to A.C. at that stage. I believe the people stored some foodstuffs, but by 26 March appeals were already out for food for the people in the townships. The weekend before the big march, Hudson Gila and one other on the PAC Cape executive stopped at our house. *'Udl'amahashi, mfo ka Jordan!'* [The army has run out of food and is now eating the horses.] We responded at once with cash, and the following day we went round to our friends in the neighbourhood asking for food donations. We were still puzzling over the question of a food depot when we learnt that Sayed & Sayed, an Indian business concern that supplied African traders in the townships, had accepted the responsibility for being a depot. This was the best arrangement, for the Sayeds delivered orders to the townships. The response from the non-African community of Cape Town to this appeal was tremendous. People flooded the Sayeds with groceries – bread, vegetables, sugar, tea, dried milk – you name it. The Indian fruit vendors on the Grand Parade were big contributors and almost every merchant on the Cape Flats that I know of contributed, and this was besides the contributions of ordinary people, Coloured and Indian. I remember housewives in Lincoln Estate stopping by my house, saying: 'I understand the people in Langa are out of food. What can I give?' We directed them to the Sayed & Sayed depot.

I am always saddened when I hear people, especially Africans, speaking disparagingly about Coloured people – shifty, irresponsible, snobbish and good-for-nothing. They speak like that because they do not know Coloured people nor understand them. If one wants to know the Coloured people, one has to get to know those in the Western Cape, where it could be said there is a Coloured tradition, for it is here that as a group and a community they started to emerge. The Coloured people, I mean the ordinary people or workers, are a fine people who have a healthy suspicion and distrust of all government institutions and all those who operate them.

They showed this in Cape Town during the State of Emergency and even before that, after the shooting in Langa. When the bullets began to fall, people ran in all directions, to Bridgetown, Kewtown and Bonteheuwel, and hid among the Coloured people there. When it was not safe for some Africans to sleep in their houses, because they were wanted by the police, the Coloured people of Athlone, Crawford, Bridgetown, Thornhill, Bonteheuwel and Salt River took them in and hid them for as long as it was necessary. Some were smuggled out of the country from these hide-outs. There was no fear that these friends would betray them. My brother Mzukie, with a price of one thousand rand on his head, dead or alive, eluded the police for three months, hiding among the Coloured people.

Many of the ordinary young Coloured men were very sorry they had not joined the campaign in 1960. They told the Africans that they did not quite understand until the big march into Caledon Square and the State of Emergency. They were determined to be counted in the next campaign. In 1976, the students of the University of the Western Cape were the first to come out in support of the students of Soweto.

1961 and 1962

After the State of Emergency was lifted in August 1960, one would have thought that things would improve in South Africa. Not in the least. If anything, they got worse. There were arrests throughout the country, in the cities and rural areas. The blacks had called for a Convention of the People, all the people of South Africa, but the government ignored this demand. The ANC then called for a stay-at-home in protest against celebrations of South Africa's new status as a Republic after it withdrew from the Commonwealth. Leaflets were distributed all over the country. The state machinery was set into motion to crush any protest on the part of the people.

Nandi and Pallo, now at the University of Cape Town, were caught up in these activities with other students. If there was anything that my children liked, it was leafletting and distributing political propaganda. This is not surprising: they had started quite early with their mother. Coming home one afternoon, after distributing leaflets in Rondebosch and Newlands, they told me that somewhere in Newlands the police saw them and followed them for some two or three blocks. But they eluded them.

At two o'clock that night, a call came through: 'Nandi, scram! The police are after us!'

A.C. had taken the call in the study.

'Who is that calling at this time of night?'

'I do not know. All he said was: "Nandi, scram! The police are after us!"'

A.C. was getting back to bed.

'But we have to wake up the children and get them out of here,' I said.

'Where are they to go in the night?' he asked.

'I do not know. Let's take them to the Nobles for tonight and think of where to hide them tomorrow. But those police must not find them here.'

A.C. dressed and went down the road to the Nobles. In the meantime, I woke up the kids and told them of this call. 'Who could it be?' I asked. They did not know. By the time A.C. came back from the Nobles, they were ready, and their dad took them over. We could not sleep after that. We expected the heavy police knock on our door. Where were we going to hide them for a few days, at least? was the question. We decided to ask our friend, Mrs Birt in Rondebosch, to take in Nandi for a week. Though Pallo had many friends in Lincoln Estate in whose homes he could sleep, we thought it was not safe for him to be in the neighbourhood. All the other friends we could think of were not safe; they could be raided too. Anyway, we had the whole day to figure out something. After breakfast at the Nobles, they came home and drove with their dad to the university. At work I called Mary Birt and asked her if she would have Nandi for a few days. No problem; she would collect Nandi at home in the afternoon. Nandi should just call her when she was ready.

When we were all home in the afternoon, the kids said: 'Strange! none of our co-workers had got any such alert the night before.' Anyway, we decided that Nandi should go to the Birts in Rondebosch and Pallo would sleep at the Nobles again. On the third night Pallo refused to go. 'If the police take me, they will take me from here. I am not going anywhere. I am not going to run away from them.' I thought this was childish and silly, but it was his decision. We respected it, A.C. saying: 'Let him, if he feels that way.' No police ever came. After a week Nandi came home. To this very day, we do not know who played this cruel joke on us.

A similar trick was to be played on me again in 1962 at two o'clock one morning. I had not seen my brother for a few days. I was not worried, for the last time I had seen him he had told me he was going to Lesotho for a meeting there.

'This is the Langa Police Station. Are you Mrs Jordan?'

'What do you want? Who are you?' I asked.

'I am the police sergeant, Langa Police Station.'

'What do you want?'

'Is your brother's name Reggie?'

'What do you want?'

'We have him at the police station. He was arrested this evening at a PAC meeting at the Flats. You can come and see him tomorrow.'

'Thank you!' and I put down the phone.

Good God! Could it be so? When did he come back from Lesotho? Why did he not come round to tell me he was back? Why have none of his friends called to let me know? Should I go out in this rain to his place in Crawford to find out if he was back? It was pouring out there! I decided to sweat it out until morning and only then try to find out the truth. From work I called one of his friends, Sifanelo.

'When did Nqoko come back from Lesotho?'

'He is not back yet. Who tells you he is back?' he asked.

After I had told him of the call of the previous night, Sifanelo said: 'That must be So-and-so (a fellow who was once chairman of the Western Cape branch, the first layer of the executive). He must be wondering where he is and wants to tell his bosses that he is out of town. Malumekazi, don't worry, if anything happens to Malume, I'll be the first to tell you.'

What do people get out of playing such cruel jokes on others?

People were still being swooped upon by night. The police had taken Lettie Sibeko in mid-autumn 1962. I had seen her in Nyanga not long before that and she had told me that since Archie, her husband, had left, the police were harassing her, wanting to know where he was.

'They are going to *endorse me out,* Sis' Phyl, that I know. I do not know what they want from me or want me to say. I really do not know where Archie is. That is a fact,' she had told me.

Lettie Sibeko was three months pregnant when she was arrested. She was let out just two weeks before her baby was born. I was already in England when they released her. What thoughts went through Lettie's mind, sitting there alone for six months, with her unborn baby? Lovely Lettie! I am hoping to see her again someday.

University Apartheid

In 1959 the South African government passed the Extension of University Education Act, commonly known as 'University Apartheid'. In terms of this Act, four ethnic universities were set up: the University of the Western Cape in Bellville, fourteen miles east of Cape Town, for the Coloureds; Westville on Salisbury Island in Durban, for the Indians; Turfloop in the northern Transvaal for the Sotho–Tswana group; and Ngoye in Kwa Dlangezwa, Zululand, for the Zulu. Fort Hare in the Eastern Cape, which had hitherto been the only college for blacks, was to be exclusively for the Xhosa.

Under this Act, those predominantly white universities, like the University of Cape Town, the University of the Witwatersrand and the University of Natal, which had hitherto accepted blacks, could no longer do so without the permission of the Minister of Education. Permission would be granted in special cases where the courses the students wanted to pursue were not available at the ethnic universities.

This meant that our children could not go to the University of Cape Town where their father was teaching. Nandi alone had managed to beat the Act when she entered the Drama School at UCT in 1959. The Act excluded Pallo just at the end of his high school, Ninzi by two years and Lindi by three years. The policy at UCT was that all children of parents who were on the UCT payroll obtained an 80 per cent rebate in fees. This included the children of janitors and everyone else employed on the campus. The 1959 Act would thus deny our children this benefit.

We were then faced with sending Pallo either to one of the ethnic colleges, something we were not prepared to do, or overseas to continue his education. Not only Pallo, but Lindi as well. Ninzi had chosen to go into nursing and she had started her course at Baragwanath, Johannesburg, in 1961. To get into a British university, Pallo had to have credit in courses at A-level. He needed two courses to convert his Cape Senior Certificate, and fortunately for us, two of his father's colleagues offered to help him in these subjects, English and History. The university was also gracious enough to allow him library privileges on campus. So for two years, Pallo was up at varsity to use the library. There he had an opportunity to meet and rub shoulders with other young people. It was a good experience for him and he liked it there. In no time he became well known on Freedom Square and among the Modern Society group.

Early in 1961, A.C. had been awarded a Carnegie Travel Grant to tour American universities and colleges. These grants are given to noted scholars from all over the world to enable them to become acquainted with higher education in the United States. The University of California in Los Angeles seized upon this opportunity, and invited A.C. as a visiting professor for a year after the Carnegie tour. A.C. then applied for a passport to leave South Africa to take up these assignments. I was to remain behind with the children.

A.C. was to have left early in July, but he was refused a passport. This he got to know just three days before he was due to leave. The Vice-Chancellor of the University of Cape Town went up personally to Pretoria to push for the issuing of the passport. Even his effort did not help. We were to learn later that the Department of Native Affairs, which in fact is the Department that decides these matters as far as Africans are concerned, had recommended that he be allowed to take up the travel grant, but the Department of Justice was still fed up with him for the storm that had brewed when he was assaulted by the police officer, and vetoed the recommendation.

When this happened, everyone who knew A.C. – friends and students – urged him to leave the country and take up this opportunity. Even if it meant never coming back, he, an eminent scholar, would always find a suitable post outside South Africa. In addition, there was the question of his children who, it seemed, could no longer receive a good education in South Africa. Why not leave? And with university apartheid, how long would he keep his post at UCT?

There was also the question of Group Areas. The whole of Athlone, Crawford, Sunnyside and Rylands, right up to Bellville, had been declared a Coloured area. Inspectors from the Group Areas Board had already come round to assess and value the properties of those who would have to leave. For us, this meant going to live in a location – Nyanga or Gugulethu – which we had avoided in the first place. It seemed that even if A.C. could keep his post at UCT, there was no future for us in Cape Town. Why not leave?

I was all for him leaving too. After much thought, A.C. decided to leave without a passport. Why not take Lindi with him? Lindi had just one more year to finish high school, and could finish his schooling in England. It was not an easy decision to make, to send Lindi off at fifteen. We discussed this for days among ourselves and when Lindi accepted the idea, we decided that he would leave with his dad. Only his brother, Pallo, was against the idea, arguing that Lindi was too young to be sent to strangers in England. How I wish I had listened to Pallo's advice. That year and a half alone in England was devastating for Lindi. The experience left him angry and bitter.

Even as we approached the time for them to depart, I was not certain if Lindi's going away was the right thing for him. I said to A.C. that, should Lindi at any time during their journey say he wanted to come home, he should put him on the first train, boat or plane home. I was to learn that in Botswana he cried one day saying he wanted to come home. His dad comforted him and talked things over with him, and Lindi was then willing to go on. They had left home at the end of September, with stops in Botswana and Dar es Salaam, reaching London in October. From Dar es Salaam, Lindi sent me this message: 'Keep on smiling,' and another one when they reached London. We all missed him, particularly Pallo, his brother and protector. They had been very close and perhaps I should have known that his life would be a void without Pallo. Lindi enrolled at Kingston High School in Hull, Yorkshire, and stayed there with an English family, working people, whose daughter we had met in Cape Town. At the beginning of the following year, A.C. left him and proceeded to Los Angeles.

It was a struggle for A.C. to get to California. He had imagined that with an invitation from an American university it would be easy for him to obtain an American visa. Not at all! He had no passport and he had to have that first before the American Embassy would consider his application. The British authorities in those days were sympathetic to South Africans leaving the country. It was easy to be granted citizenship on the basis that one had been at one time a British subject or one's parents were once British subjects. This was how A.C. obtained citizenship in Britain within a matter of three days. This right of citizenship covered me, his wife, and his minor children.

A.C. had written from Los Angeles advising us to apply for British citizenship and passports. By then it had been decided that we would all leave South Africa for Britain. The British Consulate in Cape Town was not very keen to issue passports to us, advising that we try the South African government first. The children did. The South African government, after a long delay, refused my children passports, sending both Nandi and Pallo this message: 'Passport applications denied. Department will consider applications for Exit Permits.' We all then applied for exit permits.

England

Only those who have had to leave home know the unspeakable pain involved. No words can describe it. Much as the situation was ugly in South Africa, and still is ugly today, South Africa is my home. I love it. No place in the world is like that country to me. For all its ugliness, it is my home, the place where my roots are, and I love it. This is what is so painful. Even now it is still my hope that I'll go back to live there. It is the only place where my soul can find rest and peace.

A.C. had returned to England from Los Angeles in the summer of 1962 to prepare for our coming and to meet us there. As Lindi was in school in Yorkshire, he bought a cute semi-detached house in one of the better suburbs of Hull. Pallo, who was entered for college in England, was the first to leave, in September 1962. Ninzi was now training as a nurse. After she left us to go back to Baragwanath, Nandi and I waited for our papers. And we waited and waited. In a situation like this one cannot even plan. Early in October, Nandi's exit permit came. At least she could go. We started selling some of our belongings and packing our library, and booked a passage for Nandi and me on the *Pendennis Castle* for the end of the month. One weekend, we drove home to Idutywa to say farewell to Tata, my family, my sisters Granny and Ntangashe and their families. I did not tell Tata and Ntangashe that I was leaving. Granny was the only one I told. I feared to tell these two, for I did not know how I or they would have taken it. There were never any farewells between me and Ntangashe: we had always avoided them.

When we returned to Cape Town after the weekend at home, the travel agency called to say that there were places for us on the boat leaving that Friday. I at once called Mr Thorpe, Chief Native

Commissioner in Salt River, to whom I had referred the question of my exit permit.

'Any word from Pretoria about the exit permit?'

'No, no word yet.'

'I am leaving this Friday, with or without that exit permit, Mr Thorpe.'

'But you cannot do that,' he protested.

'Mr Thorpe, I am leaving this Friday. I cannot let Nandi go alone. She will not know how to handle this exit permit thing when she gets to England.'

'Hm! Chip off the old block?' he said.

'Yes, chip off the old block, Mr Thorpe,' I returned.

Mr Thorpe had worked in the Idutywa Magistrate's office with Tata when my father was a clerk there. He knew him very well.

Though we had applied for British passports, at this point we did not know whether we would get them. They were aware of our situation, but were waiting to see how the South African government was going to handle the matter.

Nandi had already spread the word around that we were leaving that Friday. On Wednesday, the neighbourhood kids, who had formed a band, threw a party at our house and invited another band from Gugulethu, whose organiser was my cousin Allen. He brought crowds from both Gugulethu and Langa. Our neighbours and friends were there in full force, and we all had a good time.

That Wednesday was my last day at work. I called the British Consulate and told them I was leaving on Friday, and that the exit permit had not come yet. They advised me to call back the following afternoon. When I called, it was to be told that the passports would be ready on Friday morning; I could pick them up any time after ten o'clock. So we picked them up on our way to the boat on Friday afternoon.

I was sorry things had happened this way. I had not been able to see my many friends in the townships and suburbs; I had not been able to see my Ninzi in Johannesburg. This really hurt me. We had already boarded the boat when looking at the crowds on the quay-side, I saw Sis' Annie Silinga, Dinah Mapille, and Sis' Sanase Zali. I ran down the gangway to meet them. We hugged and kissed. 'It was only at mid-morning we heard you were leaving today,' Sis' Annie Silinga said. 'We thought that you, at least, we must come and see off. We missed Titshala [A.C.] when he left, as you know.' My dear sisters in the struggle! I was sorry they had come after visitors were no longer allowed for I would have gone on board with them into 'this thing, whose insides they had never seen', as Sis' Annie told me. Many other friends were there. I still carry in my memory the sight of those three solid African women, standing there, come to say farewell to me. Nothing comforts me more than to know that I am loved. I have always basked in love, warmth and acceptance.

That boat journey! So boring and tedious. Even though there are lots of things to do, just the thought of being confined is enough to drive one crazy. At last we got to Southampton. I do not know why but I expected the boys to be there to meet us. From London we took the train to Hull. What a long, tiresome journey. The English never speak to each other on trains or buses. Everyone is looking at his or her paper or book. I was tired of all this silence; so getting up to go to the washroom, I started singing one of the popular songs of the townships in those days, moving and swaying to it: *'Nal' iNyasa libhokile; selisithi lingumXhosa!'* I then laughed and ran off to the washroom. When they heard the music, everyone's eyes popped open, thinking, I suppose, that the 'Coloured' woman was going crazy. Nandi was in stitches, laughing. She told her brothers as soon as we met and we all laughed. When A.C. came that December and Nandi told him, he could not believe it. Nandi then would say: 'But you know Mama. She is capable of doing such a thing.' Now and again A.C. would call Nandi aside and ask her: 'Nandi, did Mama really do that?'

Throughout the boat journey I had not been happy at all, thinking of my child, Ninzi. How lonely and lost she would be without us. Even though her older sister, Ndileka, was in Johannesburg, she did not know her as family. I wrote her as soon as I had arrived, apologising for our failure to come up to Johannesburg, explaining that we had had to make on-the-spot decisions towards the end. I promised that as soon as I was settled, I would look around for good training schools for nurses and would send her all the available material. This I did.

I sent letters to Tata and Ntangashe, too, apologising for not letting them know before I left. I told both that my short trip home was, in fact, a goodbye trip, but fearing to upset them, I had said nothing about that. Tata wrote back to tell me he was glad I had joined my husband. When he heard that A.C. had left, leaving me and the children behind, he did not know what to make of it. He had never suspected or heard of any trouble between us 'but, Phyllie, one never knows these days'. Ntangashe also wrote to tell me that Granny had informed her after we left. She understood and accepted my explanation. I knew she would.

My first few months in England were spent settling in and providing comfort for my children, and picking up the threads of our life. I found Lindi very uptight and bitter. He had withdrawn into himself, something that was not like him at all. When he did open his mouth, it was to say something cruel and hurting, especially about his father and those connected with him. I knew that my child had been scarred and I had to heal those scars.

We had a very happy reunion in Hull that Christmas. When A.C. left again for California, Nandi decided to try London for her theatre work. There was just nothing for her in Hull. I remained with the boys; Pallo was at the Hull College of Commerce and Lindi at school. Hull! What a hole; nothing to do and nothing going on; nobody anywhere near that we knew; just ourselves. The boys could not wait to go down to London at Easter, leaving me alone. I did not mind that; I did not begrudge them that; they had to go and meet people whom they could communicate with, and London was where their friends were.

One weekend, I went down to London to see Nandi and other South Africans who were there. Nandi had told Professors Westphal and Tucker at the School of Oriental and African Studies (SOAS) that I was coming, and by the time I arrived there, there was already a lunch invitation at SOAS. Nandi came with me, and we had lunch with the staff. What a stuffy crowd they were. I was thinking, as I sat there with them: Is this what is going to happen to A.C. when he gets here? And when he is here, where will I be? Just a housewife at home? There's nothing I fear as much as being a housewife. If I am going to be one, I must be one by choice.

And then the other South Africans, blacks! What a terrible plight they were in. No work; no places to stay. Our people could not get work even in those organisations that hired blacks, and in Britain there were not many of them in those days. And what of the South African whites who were there too as refugees? Most of them had jobs, in Defence and Aid, Anti-Apartheid Movement and other positions for which they qualified just on the basis of their skin colour. It was then that I understood the racism of whites, including those who came from South Africa and posed as anti-racists. Those in organisations like Defence and Aid and Anti-Apartheid had their jobs lined up for them by their friends in Britain even before they left South Africa. To my knowledge there were only two blacks working in those organisations at that time. When I went back to England in the mid-seventies, there was one black woman. I do not know if the number of blacks has ever increased. I hope it has.

The United States of America

Early in May, A.C. wrote from Los Angeles to tell us he was going to give a talk at the University of Wisconsin, in Madison, at the end of the month. In June he wrote again to say he had been offered a post at the same university, to help them structure their African Studies Program, due to be launched the following year. He had accepted the offer. He added: 'Much as I like English institutions and their education system, I think the universities are too conservative and not flexible enough. I like the flexibility of American institutions. They give scope for creativity.' He had had an offer from the School of Oriental and African Studies at London University and another from the University of Copenhagen in Denmark. On why he had turned down this too, he had this to say: 'I was very much attracted towards this offer. But I thought of you, Phyllie, on the language question. I feared you would be isolated and would not be involved even in a rummage sale. In America, this would not be the case, especially now. There is a lot of interest in South Africa and you will be able to mix with other political activists.'

We decided to move together to the United States, to start afresh there and then spread out to whatever place the children wanted to go to. Nandi did not want to come. But after her dad convinced her that there might be greater opportunities in theatre for her in the United States than in England, she was persuaded to come. Little did we know then that American theatre wanted blacks with a black American accent, not with an Oxford accent. Blacks were still playing as blacks in theatre, and not as human beings, artists. Even broadcasting and television did not have blacks, least of all black women. When Nandi went to do a course in communications in 1964, she hoped to get into broadcasting and TV. But she was ahead of her time. Even the 1964 affirmative action project did not help her, because she was not an American black for whom these token programmes were set up in the first place. This was to be my Nandi's frustration in the United States.

We left England at the end of September. The boys had gone ahead of us, to be in time for the start of the term. They liked that. We had hoped that they would find room in the university dorms, but there were no vacancies. So they stayed at the YMCA until we came. It was just as well, for their money was running out. Under the circumstances, we decided to rent a house or perhaps buy one. All this was on the understanding that those of the children who wanted to go and live in an apartment or dorm would do so, as soon as something convenient was available.

A.C. was the only black on the faculty of the university. The other black member who had been there left just as A.C. arrived. We were the second black family to live in the area where we moved to. There was some concern on the part of the university about our safety. I remember Dr Philip Curtin, director of the African Studies Program, who had recruited A.C., went round our immediate neighbours to find out if they minded blacks as neighbours. All had said no. 'Possibly the family immediately behind them might,' Mr Marlett, our neighbour, had told Dr Curtin. Even this family did not mind as soon as they knew we were not American blacks; we came from Africa. But even with this assurance, the university posted its security cars in the parking lot at the shop just across our house every night to make sure no harm came to us.

We moved in. On our third day a black man, Mr Marshall Colston, then chairman of the Madison chapter of the NAACP (National Association for the Advancement of Colored People), arrived at our door. After introducing himself and asking a few questions about where we came from, he told us that he had not known we were there until only that morning, when some white person called him at his office.

'So you have brought other niggers into our neighbourhood? You have a nerve.'

'What do you mean?' he had asked.

'Aren't you responsible for those niggers who have just moved into Midvale?'

'Get lost!' he told the caller.

'Then it dawned upon me that there might be a new member of

faculty at the university,' he said. 'I called the university, and was told a Dr Jordan had just joined the university staff and had moved into this house in Midvale Heights. This is how I got to know you were here. That is America for you.' He laughed. 'My house is just about eight minutes from you, in the hollow in Westgate. We were the first blacks to move there and you are the second.'

It was Mr Colston, in fact, who told us that the university had posted its security to watch our house every night. Those security remained there for the first three months of our stay in that neighbourhood. After that they came past occasionally. The Colstons became our best friends in Madison, right up to the time they left for Sacramento, California.

Two days after the Colston visit, a woman rang my bell. As soon as I opened the door her face lit up in a smile and her eyes sparkled. 'I am Rozah Meyer; I live down the road; I thought you might like this,' handing me a plate she had in her hand. It was a pumpkin pie. I invited her in and we sat talking. She was a housewife with four children, a girl and three boys. Her husband, Earl, was in atomic research in the Physics Department of the university. She had seen A.C. on the bus one morning and was told he was a new professor at the university. She asked me where we came from. I found she had some idea about South Africa and about what was going on there. Rozah Meyer and her family became our friends from that day until they left for Los Alamos, New Mexico.

Anne Curtin, wife of Dr Curtin, director of the African Studies Program, went all out to make our entry into Madison, especially the university community, smooth and easy. She not only sent us titbits of this and that, and helped find the house we were living in; she also took me out to the various shops in Madison for groceries and clothing. She and her husband had been to South Africa in 1963, so she was not altogether unaware what type of person an educated black woman from South Africa, and wife of a professor, would be.

Unlike other Americans, especially American women, Anne Curtin was not surprised to discover a modern African woman in me. She had seen quite a few when in South Africa, though she may not have spoken to or met any of them. The African Studies Program of those days had a small, tightly knit staff, all members of one family, who knew each other and became friends. The students, too, were few. It was still possible to know each other. I think things have changed now after so many years.

We were very well received in Madison, by the university community, by our neighbours, professional and small business people, and by the Madison community at large. Just before Thanksgiving, in November, there was a reception for all new faculty at the university in Southside Madison, where the few blacks in Madison lived. This was sponsored by the Madison chapter of the NAACP. Most of the white enthusiasts of the NAACP and Civil Rights Movement were there. On that day we had an opportunity to meet the leaders of the black community in Madison. There were not many, for this is a small community.

South Africa was still very much in the news – the Rivonia arrests, Neville Alexander's arrest, and the general counter-attack by the state. People in Wisconsin, particularly in Milwaukee, were keen to hear first-hand from South Africans. A.C. and I were often invited to house-meetings, where we would meet groups of people – progressives – who wanted to know more, and what they, as ordinary citizens of America, could do. It was at these gatherings that I first won recognition as someone who could also speak on issues pertaining to South Africa and the world.

The boys were enjoying their classes at the university. Both were popular in the circles they moved in. As at home, they tended to have friends in common but this time the circles were wider. Pallo, being more mature politically than Lindi, was in great demand among the progressive student groups, all of them interested to know more about the South African situation. He also became a contributor to the students' paper, *The Cardinal,* on aspects relating to Africa. As a student of history, there was not a thing he did not know.

The boys were lucky not to have come on American scholarships or grants. We soon found that American universities, even those like the University of Wisconsin which prided themselves on being progressive, were in agreement in discouraging foreign students from dabbling in what they deemed 'politics', even politics of their own home countries. There was always the threat of the scholarship being withdrawn and the student thrown out of the country. When foreign students arrived, the Foreign Students' Office warned them against 'politics' and also against American blacks. But the university could not hang this sword over my boys' heads. We were paying for their education.

In the summer of 1964, Pallo had moved out to an apartment in

Mifflin Street, the street where the university radicals lived. It was then that we got to know most of his friends whom he brought to the house with him. What a bunch of lovely kids, lively, determined and with high goals in life. We enjoyed them. Lindi was the only one at home. He, too, brought his own friends, much younger than Pallo's, mostly students interested in jazz, which was now his love.

Many people in the United States have remarked to me: 'You must be glad you are in this country and not in South Africa.' This is especially so when there has been some upheaval there. They are surprised when I tell them 'no' and I go on to explain that in South Africa I lived as a black person, and in the United States of America I am also a black person. So I look at things from a black person's perspective. The racism and discrimination I encountered in South Africa, I find in the States too. It may not be as blatant but it is there nevertheless. In South Africa, in the Cape Province, I enjoyed some measure of freedom and respect among those I met and lived with, and it is the same here. But in both countries, the potential for a black person to be harassed is always present. And, while as an individual I was perhaps privileged, there were all those others, my people, who are at the bottom of the pile. The difference between the two countries is that here in the United States there is a constitution that guarantees equality, liberty, and the pursuit of happiness to all her citizens; and those in power, mindful of this, are often aware that what is happening is wrong and try their best to right it. In South Africa, there is no such idea, and the various governments of that country have always thought that they, and the whites who elected them to govern the country, are the only Chosen People.

The USA in the Sixties

The sixties was a period of revolt and protest in the United States of America. The air was charged and there was a feeling that something really big was about to happen. This was an era of promise.

What started it all was an individual act of defiance by one Rosa Parks, a seamstress in Montgomery, Alabama, who, tired at the end of her day's work, refused to give up her seat on the Cleveland Avenue bus to a white man, after the bus conductor ordered her to do so. Rosa Parks was arrested. News of her arrest infuriated the other women in Montgomery and they called for a boycott of the buses. Fearing the boycott might not succeed, the people gave themselves until Monday, 5 December 1955 to launch it, and also called upon all the pastors to galvanise their congregations. On Sunday, the people – three thousand of them – gathered at a church to plan for the boycott the next day. Here twenty-seven-year-old Martin Luther King, Jr., a pastor newly arrived in Montgomery and one of the speakers at the meeting, announced: 'There comes a time when people get tired,' and the people responded with: 'Yes, Lord!'

'We are here tonight to say to those who have mistreated us for so long, that we are tired.'

'Help him, Jesus!'

'We are tired of being segregated and humiliated.'

'Amen!'

'Tired! Did you hear me when I said "tired"?'

'Yes, Lord!'

Martin Luther King was expressing the feelings and the mood, not only of those gathered there that evening, but of many others throughout the South. When the buses rolled by on Monday morning, 5 December 1955, there were no people to ride them. The

Montgomery Bus Boycott had begun.

This spark that lit the fires of protest and revolt in the sixties also threw up the young Martin Luther King, Jr., as leader of the forces that would challenge and confront segregation in America, South and North. The Negro Revolt was on!

In 1960, black students in Greensboro, North Carolina, began sit-ins at lunch counters, setting a pattern that was to spread throughout the South. In 1963, students launched the Student Non-Violent Coordinating Committee, to work on voter registration and also to challenge the legitimacy of governments in the South. This registration drive drew thousands of young people, mostly white, from the North, who went to the South to help blacks register as voters.

As the protest grew and spread, so did hate groups – the K.K.K., the White Citizens Council, the John Birch Society. They attacked and killed blacks and all others associated with the protest; they fired and bombed black churches in the South, in one instance killing four children attending Sunday School. When the Student Non-Violent Coordinating Committee moved into Selma to register blacks, the local sheriff recruited civilians and armed them with billy clubs and cattle prods, to increase his force. Three young SNCC volunteers, two whites and a black, were murdered and their bodies were buried in a dam.

The local and federal governments seemed unable to protect the demonstrators. In the South, in fact, there was a lot of collaboration by local government with these hate groups. And where they did not collaborate, they turned a blind eye and a deaf ear to what was happening. Even the federal government seemed paralysed and in many instances dragged its feet. This was why John Lewis, chairman of SNCC, asked in anger: 'On whose side is the federal government?'

President Kennedy, for all his election campaign promises and his rhetoric, always acted after the fact. It was Lyndon Johnson who passed the Civil Rights Act in 1964 and the Voting Rights Act in 1965. And not only that, Johnson shored up the Civil Rights Act with affirmative action, which opened some doors to a few blacks.

The truth of the matter is that no American president is ever likely to sacrifice white Southern votes for black votes. This was quite evident at the Democratic Convention in Atlantic City in 1964, when the Convention refused to seat the Freedom Democratic Party from Mississippi that came to challenge the seating of the all-white delegation from that state. Moreover, those in the centres of power are never likely to brook any challenge from people calling for a change to the *status quo*. By 1968, the demands, especially on the Northern campuses, had gone beyond civil rights for the Negroes, to the question of the poor, black and white. Students had adopted the slogan 'We don't want it! Tear it down!'

In 1966, Dr Martin Luther King moved his forces north to lead a campaign for open housing. He started in Cicero, an Irish suburb of Chicago. It was racial incidents and death threats that were to expose the hypocrisy of the North. The King forces were not only pelted with rotten eggs and tomatoes, not only jeered at and their cars overturned and burnt, they were faced with certain death if they did not get out of Cicero. Federal marshals had to come in to escort them safely out of the suburb.

Near to Madison, in Milwaukee, a city that boasts of having had a socialist mayor for over twenty years, in a state that is one of the most liberal in the Union, Father Groppi led an 'open housing' campaign in the Polish neighbourhood. Here, too, were ugly racial confrontations and Father Groppi had to withdraw.

It was at the height of these demonstrations in Milwaukee that two Molotov bombs were thrown at our house. The first came early in the evening and fell on the driveway, just short of the garage. Fortunately the car was inside and the door was closed. The second, a week after, came before midnight, as A.C. was leaving the study to retire. This fell on the lawn, about five feet away from the study window. Then two weeks after, a swastika was burnt on our lawn in front.

I am certain these must have been the work of some racists in sympathy with the anti-Open Housing demonstrations in Milwaukee. They could not have come from any of our neighbours. When the incidents became widely known in the community, I received a letter of sympathy and solidarity from the wife of one of the university deans, assuring me that they must have been the work of some naughty kids up to pranks. My question to her and all others who thought so was: 'What kind of society is this that breeds children who know that it is houses of blacks that Molotov bombs may be thrown at, and lawns of blacks where they can burn swastikas, that symbol of hatred? If these were acts of "naughty" children, they are all the more disturbing to me.'

Dr Martin Luther King, whom the liberal press had built up into a folk hero, by now realised that it was not only the blacks who were deprived in America, but all the poor, black and white. In 1967, he joined the Anti-Vietnam Mobilization Protest in New York and spoke against the war. He was preparing to lead a March of the Poor to Washington D.C. in the summer of 1968. In April he went to Memphis, Tennessee, to join the protest of the garbage workers there who were on strike. He was 'becoming too dangerous', and for that they killed him.

There were other voices of protest in the USA in the sixties, voices much older than those of the Civil Rights Movement. In the early twenties, there had been Marcus Garvey, who taught black Americans to be proud of themselves, to hold their heads high, for they had a great heritage, the African heritage. This message was to be repeated by the Black Muslims, followers of Elijah Mohammed. The voice of the Black Muslims became more strident during the period of the Civil Rights Movement. Their most articulate advocate was Malcolm X, an ex-convict, who had embraced the Muslim faith while in prison. A remarkable man Malcolm X was, with a sharp mind and great eloquence, who thought on his feet. He would make mincemeat of reporters, interviewers and opponents, all of them hostile. Malcolm X was perhaps the only black American who had his finger on the pulse of the black community, the only one who understood their anger and frustration, could articulate their hopes and aspirations. Malcolm X saw capitalist America for what it is, that whatever reforms were brought about were only cosmetic, to co-opt the vocal elements, the better to exploit the rest. Because of this stance he was feared by the Establishment and hated by the middle-class blacks, who were the focus of this co-option and whom he exposed as the sell-outs and collaborators that they were. Malcolm X was among the first to denounce the war in Vietnam, questioning the involvement of blacks in defending a 'democracy' in Vietnam which they did not enjoy at home. Because he spoke to the hearts of the masses, telling them why they were catching hell and what to do to get the 'man' off their backs, Malcolm X found a real place among the oppressed blacks of America. They loved him. He was their folk hero.

After his break with Elijah Mohammed, he began to speak out against US imperialism at home and abroad and saw clearly that the fate of black Americans was bound up with the fate of the African nations, suffering under the stranglehold of the former colonial powers. He was just starting to organise an American version of the OAU, to be called the Organization of Afro–American Unity, when he was killed in New York in February 1965. Only after his death did middle-class black Americans admit that Malcolm X had been one of the leaders in the black community and that it would take some time before another like him would emerge.

The sixties was the decade of the long hot summers – New York and Philadelphia in 1964, Los Angeles (Watts) in February 1965, and then Detroit in summer of 1967. The blacks turned their anger and fury on all those they felt or thought were responsible for their plight and deprivation. They torched and looted business places in their ghettos, burned down the rat- and cockroach-infested tenement buildings they lived in and for which they were paying such high rents. None belonged to them but to the 'man' downtown or out in the suburbs. Watts, the Los Angeles black ghetto, was almost razed to the ground.

'But what I can't understand is why they burned down even the places they lived in,' said one white social worker friend of mine in Los Angeles.

'Because those places do not belong to them and never will,' was my response.

In Detroit, the protest forces used a church in the riot-belt whose congregation was exclusively 'High-Yellow Niggers'. Its headquarters were in New York. These respectable High-Yellow Niggers did not like the idea of the 'riff-raff' using their church for strategy meetings. They appealed to headquarters to do something about this and about the minister who had allowed it to happen. Headquarters cautioned 'go slow'. These 'respectables' withdrew from the church and left the minister with the blacks who had led the protest. Little did they know that these would form the nucleus of Detroit's famous Shrine of the Black Madonna. Discontented young blacks found a haven in the Shrine of the Black Madonna. Here drug addicts, alcoholics, people who had reached rock-bottom and saw no purpose in life, found that they were accepted and their lives could be turned round. Like the Black Muslims, the Shrine of the Black Madonna has done a tremendous job in rehabilitating people who thought there was no purpose in their lives. It has made them useful, decent people, proud of themselves as human beings and proud of their African heritage.

The University of Wisconsin

From 1964 through the seventies, the campus at Madison, Wisconsin, was alive with political activity. It was here that the anti-Vietnam campaign gathered momentum. It was here that, even after the campaign had been dubbed communist-controlled and many liberals withdrew from it, the fires were kept alive. When things were in the doldrums, it was the University of Wisconsin, Madison campus, and University of California, Berkeley campus, that saw to it that the protest did not die out. Early in 1964, the Anti-Vietnam Committee was inaugurated in Madison. Pallo, though not up front in it, was very much involved behind the scenes. At the very first meeting of hand-picked people – students and faculty – Pallo had written a note to the chairperson of the meeting, advising him that 'no notes were to be taken at the meeting'. This note's contents were to be quoted to him when he went to the Immigration Offices in Milwaukee for an interview. The interviewing Immigration Officer knew the day, the date, the room where the meeting was held, and he quoted Pallo the contents of his note to the chair. To this day, the kids do not know who could have been there planted by the CIA among them.

1964 and 1965 were the years of the Johnson teach-ins, when teams of experts were sent to the various campuses to tell the 'truth' about Vietnam. Whenever these teams came to the Madison campus, the students drove them away and would not even hold the meetings scheduled for them by the university. One such meeting was in the lecture hall in the Social Science building. The members of the team were already on the stage, but the students refused to hear them and told them to leave. When they left, the meeting was turned into a people's meeting, an anti-Vietnam meeting. All this activity on campus reached out to the people in and around the university, and they rallied to the call and the momentum grew again.

In February 1965, after the mining of the North Vietnam harbour, the Madison Anti-Vietnam Committee, with committees in the neighbourhood, called for an all-night vigil round the State Capitol. It was one of those very cold February nights – and all who have lived in the Midwest know just how cold February can be in this part of the United States. I knew Pallo would be there, and that there was also the possibility of the police coming to break up the vigil. I was going to be there, to be there if and when the police came, to grab my child by the wrist and run away with him. It is strange that I should have felt this way. When I took my four children to the political rallies in Cape Town, where there was also always the possibility of police raids, I was never afraid for myself and my four kids; it never occurred to me to ask myself: What will I do with four kids, the oldest of whom was eight years old and the youngest four? But here I was afraid for Pallo, a grown-up man!

When A.C. turned in to go to bed at half past twelve he found me dressing warmly in the room, wrapping myself up.

'You seem to be going out. Where are you going to?' he asked.

'To the vigil around the Capitol,' I said.

'Phyllie, in this cold? Why not go in the morning?'

'If it is cold for me, it is cold for the other people too. And they will be there,' I replied.

'I'd go in the morning if I were you,' he said, and got into bed.

I took the last bus just across the street at half past one and by two o'clock had joined the crowds round the Capitol. It was cold! Even the coffees and soups, set up at strategic points where we could help ourselves, did not seem to help. I kept moving around, trying to get to a point where I could spot Pallo. I would stay at a good distance from where he would be, keeping an eye on him all the time. It was not until about half past two that we spotted each other.

'P, you are here in this cold!' he exclaimed.

'Well, if it's cold for me, it is cold for these others too and for you.'

'I thought you would come in the morning,' he said.

'No, you are here now and I am here.'

Pallo quietly laughed at me, understanding why I was there.

The police never came. I was there until midday the next day when I went home, soaked myself in a warm bath and went to sleep.

In the fall of 1965, two weeks after the start of term, John Shingler, another South African in the Department of Political Science at Madison, called one afternoon, wanting to talk to A.C. As A.C. was not there, he said, 'I might as well tell you, Phyllis, what I was going to tell A.C. One of the faculty in our department had just told me that the CIA is here investigating one of your boys.'

'Which one?' I asked.

'He did not say,' was Shingler's reply.

'Could you please find out?'

'I will and will get back to you tomorrow.'

When A.C. came I told him. At least we knew that one of them was being investigated by the CIA. We both felt it must be Pallo, who was more active in political groups on campus than Lindi. When Shingler called the next day, he said that it was Lindi. I thought surely he was making a mistake. It must be Pallo. 'It is easier for a foreigner to remember a name like Lindi than a name like Pallo, which is not that common even among Africans.' In November of the same year, both Pallo and I received letters of invitation from Immigration in Milwaukee – he in connection with his request for an extension to his student visa, and I in connection with my application for alien residence.

When the boys had come to the States they were on student visas. Pallo's had expired sometime in August of that year. He had sent in his application and his passport, requesting an extension to his visa. No reply had come from Immigration. This letter, requesting an interview, was the first response to his application. I had been paroled into the country, as the University of Wisconsin was keen to have A.C. come to them and they knew that he would not come without his wife and family.

On the appointed day, I went down to Milwaukee in the morning alone; Pallo was to come down in the afternoon for his appointment. It was a very interesting interview with a gentleman who seemed to know almost everything I had been involved in back in Cape Town, particularly my activities in CATA and our campaign against Bantu Education. He was interested in our opposition to Bantu Education and the Van Riebeeck celebrations – in the reasons for this opposition. Then he asked me about my views on American involvement in Vietnam. What did I think of it? When I told him that as a non-American I was not prepared to express my views, he replied: 'You must have some opinion; you have been involved in protests in South Africa.'

'Yes, I have been. But here as a non-American, whatever views I have do not count. I do not see why I should even express them.'

Then he went on to ask me about Pallo and his friends – if I knew his friends; if they came to the house. I told him I knew them and that they came to the house. He then asked why Pallo was not staying at home with us. I told him that our plan from the first was that the children would stay in a university dorm. But when they arrived in Madison, there were no vacancies open. We rented a house on the understanding that as soon as there was something suitable, any one of them who wanted to move out would do so. Then I went on to remind him that I was amazed that in America, where children leave home and are out on their own at the age of sixteen, he should ask me about my son, over twenty, not living with his parents at home. 'I thought this was something accepted in the United States – that children live on their own.'

Then he wanted to know why Pallo had spent his summer holiday in New York.

'Why not, if he wanted to go there and could afford it?' I asked.

'Didn't he go to Cuba?'

'Now look, if he did, Immigration would be the first to know about that, for the simple reason that he would have to go through your checkpoints in and out of the country.'

'Are you sure he didn't?'

'Why didn't your people catch him when he came in? You know he did not.' I was getting fed up.

'Well, Mrs Jordan, you will hear from us soon. Thank you for coming in.'

As I was leaving, Pallo arrived. I told him some of the things they were likely to ask him and what they had asked me about him and what I had said. He went in. For four full hours they kept him in that interview, during which the officer questioned him about the contents of the note he had written to the chairperson at the inauguration of the Anti-Vietnam Committee, about two articles he had written for *The Cardinal,* the students' paper in Madison and about the YSA and the Du Bois clubs whose meetings he had addressed on South Africa. When he asked Pallo for the names of the members of the YSA and the Du Bois clubs, Pallo told him he was there to answer questions about himself and not about other people.

Then the officer said to him, 'Seeing that you want us to extend your visa, don't you think you could help us with these names?'

Pallo said 'no'. The interview came to an end.

I was furious when I heard his last question to Pallo. Who did he think my child was? A traitor, a sell-out? It was just as well I saw him before I knew that.

Waiting out there, I was imagining all sorts of things they were doing to my Pallo. I called after three hours to find out if he was still there and how long they would keep him.

'We are almost through, Mrs Jordan. He will soon be out,' they had told me.

Half an hour after that I called again, and again just a few minutes before he came out. By then I was waiting outside the room where the interview was taking place. They had to know that I was there.

Neither of us heard anything from Immigration after those interviews, until November 1966 for Pallo, and March 1967 for me.

Selective Services had been sending letters to Lindi. I had never asked Lindi what they wanted from him. But when one came with 'Final Notice' on it, I thought I should ask. He showed me the letter. They had been requesting him to report to their office in Monroe Street. I called Professor Price, a retired law professor, asking him if the US had any right to draft a non-citizen. He told me that as an alien resident, Lindi could be drafted. I told Professor Price: 'Over my dead body.' Then one afternoon I took the letter with me to the Selective Services offices in Monroe Street. Getting there, I presented their notice to the man at the desk, wanting to know what it meant. He told me that Lindi was liable for the draft.

'Over my dead body. He is not a US citizen. Send your US citizens first to go die in Vietnam for a war that is not theirs. Not my child. He will not go there.'

'Well, lady, that is the law.'

'Law or no law, he is not going. Let the McNamaras, Johnsons and the rest of them send their children first before they send mine. He is not going.' So saying, I put that notice on his desk and left.

When I got home, I asked A.C. if he knew anything about the notices that Lindi had been getting. He was not aware of them. I told him I had just been to Selective Services, to tell them not to send Lindi any more notices as he would never go to Vietnam.

'But, Phyllie, you cannot do that.'

'Joe, I am from there already and have told them to send their sons to Vietnam before they send mine. If it means walking to

Washington D.C. to tell Johnson that, I am prepared to do it. No Vietnam for Lindi.'

A.C. knew there was no getting past that. He left me alone. That summer, Lindi married Casey, a girl he had been dating since he arrived in Madison. So that marriage saved him from Vietnam and saved me a walk to Washington D.C., I guess.

In 1966 the University of Wisconsin embarked on an all-out campaign to recruit blacks. They brought in Mr Marshall Colston to head the drive. He did a good job. Most of the blacks on the faculty now came in under that drive and so did the students, especially students from the South. Because it was known that most of the students from the South would come in with very poor academic skills and would never be able to compete with others on the college level, Mrs Doyle, an administrator in the Madison school system, established with her own money a programme to upgrade the skills of these students and any others who needed the service. This in-between programme has now become a permanent feature not only of the University of Wisconsin but at most universities throughout the country.

By 1967 black students in the Northern universities were clamouring for Black Studies programmes, complaining that what they were being taught was irrelevant to their lives; they could not relate to it. To some extent, perhaps, they were right. They could find no folk heroes or heroines in the characters in Literature, History, Art or Music. But for all that, the students were not certain what they meant by Black Studies. All they knew was that they wanted a bit about themselves too in what was being taught. This demand coincided with an era of prolific writing, particularly poetry, by blacks, poems written in the language they speak in the black ghettos. This was what they could relate to, the students said. This was how they wanted to write and saw no reason why they should not be allowed to write that way. Sympathetic though one was to these views, the language they insisted on could not be allowed because it was not English.

The demand for Black Studies reached a climax in the late sixties and early seventies. In Madison, the black students drew their support from radical white students. To bring attention to their demands, in 1969, for five days in a row, the students rampaged through the campus and State Street, smashing and destroying property. They smashed almost to rubble the all-glass Math building on campus. At a faculty meeting in the midst of this destruction, the University of Wisconsin faculty decided to accept the students' demand for a Black Studies programme, even though none of them had any idea what it was going to be like and how and where it was going to fit into the whole structure.

In 1970 the University of Wisconsin opened its Black Studies Program, creating the faculty from the blacks already there and bringing in new recruits. It seemed 'blackness' was the major qualification, irrespective of area of expertise. A black doctor with a private practice in Madison and a black nurse on the staff of the university hospital were brought onto the staff. It is not clear what these two medics taught on the programme.

The university also opened up a Black Students' Center, with a director and staff. The students had demanded this for, as they complained, they were not comfortable in the Students' Union with all 'them honkies' around. This was going to be their centre and no honkies would be allowed in. The black students demonstrated their resolve when Congressman Charles Diggs, from Detroit, came to Madison at their invitation and brought his 'honky' secretary with him. The students who had gone to the airport to meet the Congressman were shocked to find he had a 'honky' secretary. They called the others at the centre to alert them to this travesty. On recovering from the shock, the women resolved that no 'honky' would be allowed to cross the threshold of their centre. They would block her entrance. They tried, but the Congressman told them he would not go in without his secretary; he would go back home to Detroit.

The University of Wisconsin had set up all this under duress and ironically under the name of integration. The white radicals who had supported the blacks in their demand were alienated. They could not go to the centre they had helped bring about. Try as the director might to tell them the university would never allow this segregated facility on campus, his fellow blacks would not listen. My children and I – Lindi and Nandi – tried to convince those of them who were close to us that the director was right, the university would not allow that facility on campus if they insisted on segregating it, and if they insisted, the whole facility would be closed down. That was exactly what happened. Early in 1972 the university notified them that the centre was going to close. The university did not dare, the students said. They would picket and keep their centre open. Then, one morning in February, they found they were locked out. After a few days of picketing in February, even the die-hards gave up.

Of these Black Studies programmes throughout the country, one does not hear much any more. Many died a natural death, their courses having become part of a department within the university structure – Literature, Art, Music, History or Philosophy – as should have happened in the first place. Through these Black Studies programmes, a number of blacks obtained positions in the universities because they were black, positions they never would have had otherwise.

Pallo Is Endorsed Out

In summer 1966, Pallo moved to New York to the New School for Social Research, where he hoped to do his Masters in Economics, History and Philosophy. He liked it at the School and had some excellent professors who in turn liked his approach to his courses. Then about the middle of November, he received a letter from Immigration telling him to be out of the country by the end of the month, as the purpose for which he had entered the United States had been accomplished and he was prolonging his stay unnecessarily. And yet the School had submitted all the relevant information on Pallo as a registered foreign student. At once Pallo took this letter to the Office of Foreign Students, who contacted Immigration. At first Immigration denied having had any information on Pallo's status as a student, whereupon the School sent them a registered letter with the relevant papers. After that all was quiet, and we thought matters were settled.

Pallo called me on my birthday in January and told me he was to go to Immigration on 21 January about his visa application. They had asked him to come for an interview. It was just as well he had the presence of mind to take a lawyer with him, for when he got there he was put under arrest for having ignored the notice ordering him to leave. He called us from behind bars, telling us he was to appear in court the next day. When he appeared in court, the lawyer pleaded contest and he was allowed out on $1 000 bail, to appear in court sometime in March. Even at this stage, we all thought that Immigration had no case. They wanted Pallo out of the country for the wrong reasons. He was a registered student and they knew it.

At the court hearing in March, his lawyer brought along all the evidence that Pallo was a student at the New School, and two of his professors testified on his behalf. Everybody thought he had a tight case. Just the previous Friday he had called us, excited about the draft proposal for his thesis, which his professor was greatly pleased with. But the court he appeared before that Tuesday in March was not the court that had remanded his case. It was a different court, an Inquiry Court, and from the beginning the presiding judge explained that he had no jurisdiction over the question of why or why not Pallo had not left the country. All that his court was going to look into was whether an order had been given and whether the order had been obeyed. So the whole case they hoped to argue fell by the wayside. He was ordered to leave the country forthwith.

'I will give you a choice, Mr Jordan. You can either leave voluntar-ily and pay for your departure, in which case there will be no record of your having been deported, or you can leave by deportation and this will go on your record. Which do you choose?'

Pallo chose to take 'voluntary departure'.

'You were wise, Mr Jordan, for if you had chosen deportation, you would from henceforth be under the care of the Immigration author-ities. In that case you would have to give me authority to appoint somebody to wind up your affairs in this country, while you would be waiting in detention until such time as Immigration would send you off. How long do you think it is going to take you to wind up your affairs?'

'About two weeks. I would like to visit my family in Madison, Wisconsin.'

'No, I am afraid I cannot give you two weeks. We'll make it next Monday. You are to report to this court by twelve next Monday, with your ticket and date of departure. Only then will you have your bail bond released and your passport given back. Should you fail, I'll issue a warrant for your arrest.'

When Pallo called us that evening, neither his father nor I could believe it. He came home on Wednesday and together we discussed the whole case, all feeling there was something wrong somewhere. We decided to seek legal advice. The next day we went to Roy Anderson, our lawyer. He knew very little about immigration laws – this was what I found with most law firms in this country of speciali-sation. We then contacted Pallo's friend Don Bluestone, now teach-ing at Roosevelt University in Chicago, to find us an immigration lawyer. It was not until Saturday that Don landed one, Mr Orlekoff, who was unfortunately out of town and expected back on Saturday night. He was kind enough to set up an appointment with us for Sunday morning in Chicago. We drove to Chicago that Sunday morning to see him. From Chicago, Pallo was to fly to New York. He was uptight, as one can imagine. Whatever happened, he was to report with his ticket on Monday to avoid arrest. Before we left Madison, he had asked his girlfriend in New York to book a seat for him on any plane out and buy his ticket so that it would be ready when he reached New York. Mr Orlekoff accepted the case and was to get in touch with Pallo's lawyer in New York the next day. Pallo was not interested in all this. His mind was on the order to report, with the ticket, by noon the next day. We put him on the plane to New York at five o'clock and came back to Madison. When we got there, I called a friend, Philip Hart.

'You sound very tired,' he said.

'Yes, I am. I should say we both are. What with the authorities throwing our child out of the country just as he is starting his M.A. in New York!'

'What! Let me come over to hear it.'

When he came, A.C. told him the whole story right up to our visit to Chicago that same day.

'I must get it out in the papers tomorrow,' Philip said.

True enough, the first issue of the local newspaper carried the story as headline the next day. Then people throughout Wisconsin and beyond started calling us, wanting details and pledging support, telling us they were asking their Congressman, Kastenmeir, and their Senator, Gaylord Nelson, to take up the matter.

Both Senator Gaylord Nelson and Congressman Kastenmeir called A.C. for more details and to assure him that the matter would be taken to the highest court in the land. 'We have been deluged by calls from Wisconsin,' Kastenmeir told A.C. We were to learn later that as the calls came pouring in, Kastenmeir asked one of his staff: 'Who is this Pallo Jordan?' Now the matter was in the hands of the Congressman, the Senator and the lawyers in Chicago and New York, and all were advising that Pallo should not leave. Such massive support encouraged A.C. and me, and we too felt he should not go. Up to that Wednesday it seemed that he was not for leaving. Then on Thursday he called and spoke to his dad, telling him he had decided to leave on Friday.

'Why, Pallo, when everybody is so supportive and thinks that this order can be reversed?' A.C. asked.

'I'll forever move in the shadow of the CIA and I will not be safe,' Pallo had told him.

Pallo left that Friday for England. Both A.C. and I still thought he should not have gone. But events of the following month proved that he was right in leaving when he did. His room-mate was shot by an unknown gunman just as he was stepping out of the stairs in the building where they lived. Who knows if the gunman did not think he was killing Pallo? I shudder to think of it.

We were to learn later that, in fact, Immigration had wanted to throw Pallo out of the country in 1965 or 1966 while he was still in Wisconsin. But they had been advised against it as Pallo was so very popular among the students. If they moved against him, they were advised, the whole place would go up in flames. So they waited until he moved to New York and struck before he had established a base there.

It may have been coincidence, I do not know, but the same Tuesday that Pallo was being endorsed out of the United States of America, the Regional Immigration Office in Chicago wrote to me rejecting my application for residence. The reason? I had refused to answer some of the questions put to me. My application had been lying in their offices since the spring of 1964. This was March 1967.

If there was anything that hit A.C. hard it was the expulsion of his son on the eve of his starting his Masters programme. Many things had disillusioned him about the United States since first seeing it at close quarters, but I think this drastic action against Pallo was the last straw. If he had had an offer of a job anywhere else at that moment, he would have left there and then. Unfortunately for him, he could not handle a crisis; it immobilised him. It took A.C. a long time to gird himself and pull out of this crisis. In fact, when the cancer that hit him came, he had not completely overcome the pain he suffered when Pallo was expelled from the USA.

In the spring, I went to New York to pack and send away some of Pallo's belongings which he could not take with him on the plane. My visit to New York coincided with the Spring Mobilization, the big protest against the war in Vietnam. Thousands of people from all over the United States were there, mothers with their young children, carrying banners, protesting and condemning the killing of innocent American boys and Vietnamese people. It was at this gathering of thousands of people that Dr Martin Luther King joined the anti-Vietnam forces for the first time and spoke on the theme 'Why I oppose the war in Vietnam', a theme he later fully developed as his last sermon at his own church, the Ebenezer Baptist church in Atlanta, Georgia. It was a good and impressive demonstration and reminded me very much of our demonstrations back home, except that I find American demonstrations lack the seriousness which characterised ours; there is more of a picnic atmosphere. I must say, though, that this Spring Mobilization was very different from the march on Washington of August 1963. We had seen this march on British television and we wondered why so many people would come all the way to Washington for a picnic. Even Martin Luther King's famous speech 'I have a dream' was lost in the atmosphere of picnicking. But this mass protest of 1967 was something different. It had to be. American boys were coming home by the hundreds, in caskets, while many more were being blown to bits in the jungles of Vietnam. The general populace had woken up to the fact that this war was one the United States could never win, and that it was unjust and had never been their war in the first place. The anti-war feeling was very high in the country by 1967. I was glad to have been there to experience the impact of the people's feelings on me. I came back to Madison very much refreshed.

Now that we were all by ourselves, A.C. often took me with him when he went on lecture tours. I did not quite enjoy these visits as much as I did the house meetings where both of us would be invited to speak. At academic lectures, the professor's wife is regarded as an ornament, a beautiful flower the professor is wearing in his buttonhole. And if anything is referred to her, it is a question about exotic African cuisine – if she comes from Africa – or how does she like her American house, American foods and shops – if she is a foreigner. I have never been able to understand this attitude, especially coming from American university people whose wives are well travelled and well educated. One would have thought that in their travels, they had met other university professors and their wives. Or do they not?

Tired of this condescending attitude, to a question: 'Where did you learn English, Mrs Jordan? You speak it so well', I replied: 'On the plane between London and New York.' The lady felt quite a fool for having asked me the question. And I was glad. I hope she never asked any foreign woman that question again.

Illness and Death

Even as I walked in through the front door that Friday evening, I knew there was something very wrong. A.C. was at his typewriter on the dining-room table with his back to me. He turned round, saying: 'So you are here already! Where are the others?', and came towards me in the living-room.

'They are just opening the garage. I am coming to open the door to the basement from this end, for I think it is locked.'

He came with me to the kitchen and to the door from the garage. 'Hi, Nandi! How was your trip?' and he went back in.

I had gone to Chicago to fetch Nandi's belongings. She had decided to come home, feeling that her marriage was not going to work unless her husband assumed some responsibility and found her a decent place to live in Chicago.

A.C. had not accompanied us to Chicago as he had to go to the doctor for booster shots. He was preparing to attend an Africanist conference in Senegal and was due to leave by the middle of the following week. This was Friday after Thanksgiving. When he saw that I was ready for bed, he said: 'By the way, I did see the doctor today. He wants me back on Monday for further tests. He said my X-rays this time show a spot on my right lung which was not there when we took X-rays in October. This could mean my going to hospital.'

'How big is this spot?' I asked.

'Very small. In fact, the doctor said if he hadn't had that October X-ray he would not have spotted it. It was only when he compared the two plates that he could spot it.'

'Well, let's wait till Monday, it is only then we will know.' I crossed my fingers and went to bed.

On Monday I took him to Madison General Hospital where he was going to have the further examination. As soon as I got to work, I called Dr Giles and asked him what he thought this spot was. 'It could be cancer, Mrs Jordan,' he said. 'That's why we are going to do a biopsy today to determine what it is exactly. Call me again in the afternoon.'

When I called in the afternoon, it was to be told that A.C. had a cancerous spot on his right lung, no bigger than the point of a pencil. The doctor asked me to meet him at the hospital about seven o'clock and to bring other members of the family. A.C., he told me, was already admitted as a patient. He gave me his room number and telephone number. When I called the hospital, he did not sound too depressed – something that I had very much feared.

'Well, it looks as if there will be no Senegal for me. These fellows want me to go into treatment straightaway. When you come, please bring me this book and that book,' recounting what he wanted. I called Lindi at work and told him, and asked him to pick Nandi and me up from the house on his way from work. Lindi found us waiting for him at home when he came and we all drove to the hospital. We found A.C. quite cheerful and resigned to his being away from home for some time. I was really relieved about that, for if there was anything he could not stand, it was to be away from home. I remember he would go away on research, intending to spend six months in the field, but after four or five months he would send a telegram saying he was coming home. He was tired of sleeping in strange places away from home. But he took his stay in hospital well and never complained.

At seven o'clock we three – Nandi, Lindi and myself – met Dr Giles in his office at Madison General Hospital. He told us what I had already heard over the phone and the course of treatment they were prescribing for A.C.

'There is a good chance. It is seldom that cancer is spotted at so early a stage. We are lucky,' he said.

'Can't you operate on it?' Lindi asked.

'I am afraid not. It is too near the big vein. But with the therapy and the radiation, we should be able to kill it before it spreads.'

Then Dr Giles suggested that a senior member of staff in A.C.'s department should be told. We all suggested Dr Curtin, director of the programme.

Reaching home that night, I wrote five letters before I went to bed. These were to Pallo in London, to Dan Kunene, A.C.'s under-study at the University of Cape Town, now at the University of California in Los Angeles, to Tata and my sister Granny back home in South Africa, asking my sister to break the news gently to Ntangashe, and to Tshutsha Honono, A.C.'s best friend from the same home area and now an exile in Dar es Salaam. I let all of them know that the doctors were hopeful that they could arrest the cancer before it spread.

A.C. responded very well to the treatment – chemotherapy and radiation – and in a month there was no trace of the cancer in his lungs. He came home on Christmas Day, and it was a good Christmas for all of us. He could go back to work, the doctor told him, but he had to take things slowly and not overwork himself. This he did. He was fortunate in having Gideon Mangoaela as his Teaching Assistant. Gideon was a South African from the University of Natal, whom A.C. had recruited when he got to Wisconsin.

Then in March, A.C. went down with pneumonia on the same lung. This time he was very sick. For three days it was touch and go. But he pulled through. As it was still cold in Madison, I thought a warm climate might do A.C. some good. I suggested to Dr Giles that I would like to take him to California to recuperate there. The doctor agreed, and in April we flew to California. I stayed with A.C. for two weeks and then came back to work, leaving him in the good hands of a wonderful woman, Selina Kunene, Dan Kunene's wife. A.C. improved, even the coughing that he had when we left disappeared, and in June he came home.

It was on a Tuesday, 13 August, that I received a call from Dr Giles at work, informing me that A.C. had just been wheeled across to hospital from his office with a severe heart attack. I drove up to Madison General Hospital and arrived there just as they were putting A.C. under oxygen. He was conscious and alert and recognised me when I came in. When I saw the doctor, he told me that A.C. had been brought in by one of his students in great pain with a severe attack of angina pectoris. It was not until the next day that his heart stabilised, and by night-time it was back to normal.

We thought things were getting better when all of a sudden his chest became congested and he could not breathe. The doctors had to drain four pints of pleural fluid from his chest cavity before he could be himself again. It was the chest congestion and the need to drain this fluid that kept him in hospital all those months. The attacks came suddenly, without warning, and A.C. would struggle for breath.

When A.C. went down with pneumonia, Nandi insisted that we call Pallo from England to come see his dad. Knowing how difficult this could be, I asked the doctor to send a telegram to the American Embassy in London, while I sent one to Pallo, which, I told him, he should take to the Embassy when he applied for a visa. Pallo did as I told him. When he reached the Embassy, they informed him no such telegram had been received from Dr Giles. Pallo called and in turn I at once contacted Dr Giles, who not only sent a copy of his telegram to the American Embassy in London, but also got the university to send a similar one: 'Dr A. C. Jordan very ill. Grant visa to son, Pallo, to come at once.' It was only when this copy and the telegram from the university arrived that the Embassy acknowledged receipt of the messages. They gave Pallo a two-week visa, and he came at the end of August. But when at the end of two weeks his father was in no position to come home, we asked the university to support his request for an extension. We drove to Milwaukee and he was granted extension to stay.

As a heart patient, A.C., though ambulatory, had to have the bed railings up at night. He hated this. He would climb over the rails and go to the bathroom, and the nurses would hear the flush of his toilet or the tap running. Going to him they would call out: 'Dr Jordan, Dr Jordan, how did you get out of bed? Please do not do it, ring your bell.' He never did. So they would put restraints on him. This made him very sick and agitated. I was forced to engage a private nurse to sit up with him at night. This proved very expensive. After two weeks I had to dismiss her and sit up with him myself. His hours of getting up were between one o'clock and three in the morning. I would be there with him from twelve-thirty to three-thirty; then I would go home, and sleep from four-thirty to about seven, when I would have to get up and prepare for work.

I was doing this when Pallo came. He was furious with me. 'You can't do this, P. You are going to get sick yourself,' he argued.

'But what can I do? I do not have $135 every week for the private nurse. Do you remember what happened to Mrs Sasman back home, when she was found dead on the floor at Groote Schuur because there was no one there to help her out of bed and she tried it herself? The hospitals are understaffed and they cannot keep an eye on every patient.'

Then one morning in September, towards the end, A.C. on waking up saw me and asked: 'Phyllie, what are we doing here?'

'You are in hospital and I have come to sit up with you.'

'Oh! Harold and Dr Giles brought me here. My goodness, it is two months then. No, these fellows must get me out of here.'

'If you improve they will get you out of here. They want that too, you know.'

I was told that when the doctor came in the morning, A.C. said he wanted to go home and the doctor had informed him that if he got better, as he seemed to be doing, he soon would. From that Friday morning A.C.'s condition so improved that by Wednesday the following week Pallo could go back to England. His visa was expiring on the Saturday, and A.C. was discharged the following Friday. At home he continued to recover. Was he pleased to be in familiar surroundings, playing his music, sampling this book and that at leisure! I had resigned my job when he came home, just to be there with him.

In the week prior to the opening of the university in October, A.C. asked for his correspondence so that he could update himself on things, particularly his work. Among the letters was an invitation from Atlanta University for the end of November. As they had heard that he had not been well, they left it open to him to come when he felt well enough to make the trip. He was looking forward to it: it was to be his first trip to the South.

Waking up on Saturday, he complained of a pain in the left shoulder. I called Dr Giles, who advised that I bring him in on Monday for a check-up. He soon forgot about the pain during the day. Lindi and his wife, Casey, were there. We all had supper in the living-room, and they left a little after nine o'clock. When I suggested we go to the bedroom, A.C. said: 'It's cooler here. Let us remain here.' I made him comfortable on the couch and he fell asleep. At about 12.30 Lindi came back to check on us. 'You see, we are camping out,' said A.C. He slept on and off after Lindi left. His chest was getting congested and I had to suction it every half hour. I called Diah (Mrs Mangoaela) and she was there in no time. A.C. saw her when she came in. 'Diah, so you are here already?' Diah sent me soon afterwards to the kitchen for something. When I came back, A.C. was gone. Gone, relaxing there on his couch in the living-room. It was three in the morning, Sunday, 20 October 1968.

Diah went to the room, stripped the bed, put on clean sheets, and between the two of us, we carried A.C. to his bed. Diah laid him out and covered him with a sheet. After that she called the doctor, Gideon and Lindi. All three came within minutes of each other. The doctor went into the room and came back to pronounce A.C. dead. He gave me some tablets which I put in my pocket and forgot, to discover them months later. While I was standing alone in the room looking at A.C., for the first time I saw Lindi in him, with his face now calm and peaceful. People had always said that of his two boys Lindi looked more like his father than Pallo. Nandi came in while I was standing there. Tiptoeing, she gently put her hand on my shoulder and said: 'P, I'll look after you!'

Again the Madison community rallied round us, giving us support. The Rev. Klyve announced A.C.'s passing at the morning service in his church. Many of the parishioners came to express their sympathies with us. For the whole week, we never had to bother about cooking. On the day of the funeral, our neighbours asked that we leave the house open. When we returned, the tables were laid out with food, food enough to feed those people who came. This I will never forget. They did the same when Nandi died in 1971.

Back home in South Africa people were shocked and saddened by the death of A.C. Some had heard he was ill, but none expected him to go. The message to Cingo, our principal at Kroonstad High School, reached him at the Methodist Church Annual Conference in Bloemfontein. The announcement was made there, and conference suspended their deliberations for that day and held a memorial service instead. Many of the Methodist ministers, laity and other delegates, and ordinary people in Bloemfontein knew A.C. from his days as a teacher there and from Fort Hare. Memorial services were held at Kroonstad High School in November and drew thousands from the surrounding areas. His colleagues and students gave tributes. In Transkei, a memorial service, which drew crowds from as far afield as Port Elizabeth, East London and Queenstown, was held at St George's Mission in Mt Frere, his grandfather's church.

That was the most difficult period in my life. I am glad I had the strength to pull through. From March 1967, when Pallo was expelled from the United States, we went through one crisis after another. First, the death of Nandi's baby in July, Nandi who so loved children. Then A.C. hit with the cancer that finally led to his death. The only bright star during the period was the birth of Lindi's daughter, Samantha Lee, at the end of 1966.

And yet, the fact that I remained strong drew upon me some criticism from certain quarters, especially Africans. I do not put this down to cruelty and unkindness. To me it was due to lack of under-standing, pure and simple, people failing to understand that I had to be strong for all of us to make it. Here was A.C. fighting for his life; for him I had to be strong. Here were my children and me, all away from family and friends, friends who had given us anchor and stability. I was the only anchor that my children could have in a situation like that. If I had fallen apart, all would have been lost for them and they would not have known what to do. We had friends in the States, true. But they were not the same friendships we would have had were we back home. In this crisis, we were all alone. To those who thought I seemed not to care much, I can only say: little did they know that my pillow was drenched with tears every night when I went to bed, during all the time that A.C. was in hospital, when he came home, right up to the end. When he was in hospital, I debated every night whether to take the phone off the hook or not, for fear of the call from the hospital telling me all was over. People forget that in some cases the situation is so grave and the responsibility so great that one's tears dry up. It is the only way to survive.

Staying On

Even before A.C. died I had made up my mind to regularise my stay in the United States. I had told him that I would tackle this through Congressman Kastenmeir. I now wrote to the Congressman about my problems and asked him to assist me in getting my stay regularised. He did. Just before the end of the year he sent me a reply from the Immigration offices to this effect: 'As Mrs Jordan had been paroled into the country, the Immigration Service had already taken a decision on her, namely that she leave the country, now that her husband is dead.'

I could not believe it – hardly a month after my husband died. True to their word the Service sent me and Nandi letters, ordering us to leave the United States by 16 February 1969. If there was anything that nearly devastated me it was this order. I thought to myself: Not even four months after A.C.'s death? They can't even give me time to raise a tombstone over his grave. Where would I go? I nearly fell apart. I started crying all over again and for a month I could not act or think. Congressman Kastenmeir had written that he was sending the letter to the university to let them know. Even the university was shocked and embarrassed. They resolved in their Council meeting to refer the matter to Senator Gaylord Nelson, asking him to introduce a Bill in the Senate to stay the execution of the order, so as to give me time to regularise my position, and wind up my affairs. It was the Senator Nelson resolution that has made it possible for me to be here still.

Then started my long battle with the Immigration Service to obtain residence as an alien. The university referred the matter to their lawyers in Milwaukee and paid for the bulk of the expense. The firm assigned my case to a young fellow who was very patient and understanding. I had to submit sworn statements to Immigration of my assets showing that I would not be a burden on the country, as well as my certificates and credentials showing I could work and support myself, with supporting statements from people who knew me, testifying to my character. All this information was to accompany an affidavit that the lawyer drew up. After some months of waiting the reply came from the Immigration Service, turning down my application on the grounds that the areas where I could find work were already full and I was not likely to get the necessary work permit from the Department of Labor.

The lawyer then looked for some other loophole in the Immigration laws. This time he used the fact that I am a freelance writer and as such I would not need a work permit from the Labor Department. Even this was not good enough and the application was turned down after some months of waiting. At this point I told the lawyer that I was not going to send another affidavit. It was ridiculous to allow myself to play a game with Immigration in their own court, with their own men as referees, and according to their rules. It was for me a no-win situation, and I was not going to play it any more. If they wanted to throw me out, let them. We had reached an impasse. My lawyer tried to get me to agree to drawing up another affidavit. I refused. Then sometime in 1971, he called to tell me he had just found another loophole in the law, which he thought he could still use.

'Please, Mrs Jordan, let's try this one for the last time. Let's put ourselves in a position where we can say we have tried everything and the onus is on them to respond favourably. Please, Mrs Jordan,' he pleaded.

I am not even sure what this loophole was. But I think it had something to do with my being a British citizen. I told him I would think about it. I never called. He came over to Madison to see me in April and I told him to go ahead. So he did; I was still not interested. Then in March the following year, he called to say that he had heard that my name was on the British quota for that year and he hoped this meant I would be accepted as a resident alien under the quota. And, lo and behold, in September of 1972, I received a card from the Immigration Service with the message, 'Welcome to the United States of America'. I thought they must be crazy. I had been in this country since 1963; didn't they know that? I threw the card away. It was not until the Green Card came in October of that year that I realised what the 'Welcome to the United States' was for. At last I was accepted as a resident alien. I took my first trip out of the country in November, going to Toronto to visit friends who had been asking me to come over the years.

Death Strikes Again

I was having lunch downtown with a friend, Mrs Taliafero, one of the mothers in Madison who just adored and loved Nandi. That whole hour we talked about her, Mrs Taliafero asking where she was and what she was doing.

'She is in California, Laguna Beach, and likes it there. She seems to be getting her act together, organising an artist's studio, which she hopes to open in October,' I told her.

'She is a wonderful and clever girl – very artistic. She should make a success of anything she undertakes,' Mrs Taliafero said.

We parted. When I came home I found a note stuck in my door. 'Call Police Department and ask for Policeman So-and-so.' Why should I call the police? I wondered. I phoned as soon as I got inside. I was told to contact the Santa Ana Police Department. I knew it must be something about Nandi, but nothing serious. She must have been trying to reach me and, being unable to, had called the Madison Police Department, thinking this was the fastest way of reaching me. Only Nandi would do something like that, I thought. I called Santa Ana, to be told to call about seven o'clock, California time. It was only three o'clock in Madison. Those four hours seemed like a year. Still, I was not apprehensive. When I called it was to be told that she had been struck by a car on the highway, and was dead.

'How do you know it is Nandi? Are you sure?' I asked in disbelief.

'From her fingerprints,' the sergeant said.

I could not believe it. I called Lindi, and told him that I had just received a message from the Police Department in Santa Ana, that Nandi was dead.

'I can't believe it, Lindi, it can't be true!' I said.

Then I contacted the Kunenes, who were now in Madison. Selina came to the phone. 'Selina, I have just been told that Nandi is dead in California.' I could not say anything more. I hung up.

I do not know what I would have done without Dan and Selina on that occasion. Dan took things over and made all the necessary arrangements with the local funeral home to bring the body over to Madison; and he was at the airport when it arrived and saw it taken to the morgue. Between Dan and Lindi, they called friends and sent messages to people at home and in England. In fact, all the arrangements were in Dan's hands. Of all my children, Nandi was his favourite. Nandi had adopted Dan the very first time he came to Cape Town, and there was a lot of love between them. When Selina came, Nandi took her as a sister.

We were fortunate this time that we had people very close to us, the Kunenes. We had to go through the same motions again to get Pallo to come to his sister's funeral. The death of Nandi was one blow that has been very difficult to get over, particularly for her brother Lindi. It immobilised him. On this occasion, too, the Madison community rallied round us, giving us all the support we needed. Nandi's friends were just great. It is on occasions like these that one really sees the largeness of heart of people in this country. In that way they are like Africans back home. Again, the South African community in this country – mostly students – were very supportive. Vel Nongauza and Mxolisi Ntlabathi brought them down to Madison to bury their sister.

Nandi had moved to California in November 1970, after the death of Bruce, her husband, in Chicago in the previous month. First she worked in the Los Angeles area and then moved to Laguna Beach where she was planning to open an artist's studio. The Monday before she was hit by the car, on 19 July, I received a letter from her, telling me of her plans. She hoped to open her studio in October. She was all enthusiasm about what she was doing. The Friday before, I had received a letter from Pallo, telling me about Nandi's plans and urging me to give her all the support she needed, reminding me: 'You know Nandi needs and wants our unqualified support in everything she does.'

That fall I registered as a student at Madison Area Technical College to do a course in Pre-school Education. As part of the course, I had to be attached to a day-care centre. I obtained placement in Children's Village, a centre on the southside of Madison, housed in the local Lutheran church. This was the best thing I could have done for myself at this period. It was good therapy for me. Surrounded by those lovely two-year-olds, I forgot my woes. How could I not, when two-year-old Todd Delane would come and sit on my lap, put his warm little arms around my neck and say to me: 'Phyllis, I don't like you, I love you.'

Coming Through

Now that I was alone people began to see me for the person that I am, as a person in my own right. I was no longer the appendage of the great man, A.C., the beautiful, smiling doll, basking in his glory. This has been good for me, and for people generally. True, there are still those who are interested in me because I am his widow, people who have never read anything that I have written, or having read it, have never thought it as important as the fact that I was A.C.'s wife. What a pity many women are placed in this position, to live vicariously through their husbands. As a result there are many whose contributions to mankind have been stunted, and the world is the loser. One such African woman was the late Florence Thandiswa Jabavu, née Makiwane, wife of Professor Jabavu of Fort Hare. Here was a woman whose brilliance was far above that of her husband, a brave woman who was prepared to fight for those things she believed in. How many people know about her or have even heard about her? There are many others I could cite.

People began to remember that they had read some article by me in a magazine or paper, or had heard me speak at a meeting. The house-meetings that I had addressed and spoken at began to bring results. Those who heard me arranged meetings for me to address on South Africa. My trips to Chicago when Nandi was there, and where I had spoken to groups of Afro-Americans, either at her mother-in-law's place or at some picnic for progressive elements, mostly Garveyites, also began to pay off. Mxolisi Ntlabathi and his wife, Nzwakie, were eager to get me publicity too. In fact, my first meeting was in March 1969, when I was invited to speak at a Sharpeville memorial meeting under the auspices of the African Program Bureau. Mxolisi had set up this bureau the previous year, and my talk was its first public sponsorship. This was my first visit to the South and it opened the way there for other meetings. It was on that visit that I met Mrs Coretta King, Andrew Young, and some of the civil rights activists living in Atlanta. It was a very enriching experience for me and the response was very good.

In April 1969, coming back from Atlanta, I found an invitation from Loop College, Chicago, to speak to their staff and students on South Africa. I chose as my subject 'Apartheid, a system of internal colonialism'. Loop College was an all-black college in those days. My analysis of apartheid struck a chord with those black staff and students, as I drew parallels between the position of blacks in America and those in South Africa. In a good analysis, it is easy for the audience to draw those parallels and to see that the struggle of the South African people is intricately bound up with the struggle of blacks in America and the other exploited and oppressed people the world over. The response was terrific.

One of the trips I enjoyed was a trip to Spelman College, Atlanta, at the invitation of Dr Florence Mahoney of the Department of History. Dr Mahoney came from the Ivory Coast and had read my articles in *Africa South*. She wanted to know who Phyllis Ntantala was. In her inquiries, she traced me to Madison, and invited me to Spelman to run a seminar on 'African women, south of the Sahara'. I divided my subject into three: 'Women in society', an introduction; and secondly, 'African women in traditional society', stressing that though in traditional society women had no political rights, they were not totally dependent on men for they had property rights, and that even in the political sector there were checks and balances to see that women were not abused. The last section was 'African women under colonialism', under which system they are stripped of every right they once had, and made to depend totally on the men, who are themselves exploited and oppressed. Under colonialism, the African woman is triply oppressed. The discussions after each session were the most stimulating. Students and staff came from all the colleges in the Beckwith complex – six of them. Travelling through the United States, I have met students who saw me then at Spelman, and when I meet them again, they still talk about that seminar.

When I was in England in 1974, some South African women wanted me to speak to them on the problems of women in South Africa. I thought we had had enough of that subject; we know our problems. To me there is one major topic that we in the Liberation Movement have to face, and that is the question of women within that movement. I took as my theme 'Women and the Liberation Movement', a subject the movement has not begun to address and yet, unless we face this question and do so honestly, the movement will not succeed; it will have failed the women who have given so much of their energy, time and in some cases their lives to the struggle for liberation in their country. As this is a topic close to the hearts of women, it generated a lot of discussion, with all those there agreeing with me that, unless the 'woman question' and her place in the movement is solved, the movement is bound to fail. I pursued this question in my article in *Sechaba* (the magazine of the ANC) in December 1984 which I called 'Black womanhood and national liberation'. The ANC had declared 1984 'The Year of the Woman', and the questions I posed there are the questions I felt we should be asking ourselves at the end of that year.

Since I moved to Michigan, I have been busy for, almost twice every year, I have been invited to speak on issues that concern my people in South Africa. I have been as far east as Albany, New York, as far west as California, as far north as Toronto, and to almost every state in the Midwest as far as Memphis, Tennessee. Everywhere I have been, I have been received well. I have met some very good people, genuine and interested in the plight of our people in South Africa. I am hoping that in my talks I have changed some minds and converted some people.

And yet for all this, there are times when a feeling of guilt overwhelms me. Such feelings hit me on those occasions when I have had a very good response to my talk on South Africa, or when I have been standing for hours on the picket line or walked for miles in a demonstration against apartheid. A tiny voice whispers to me: 'For all your eloquence and rhetoric, your bravery and stamina, you are a coward, a coward who ran away when things began to heat up in South Africa, ran away, leaving all those people with whom you shared platforms, walked in demonstrations, stood on picket lines, to face the music alone.'

I left because the ground in which I could operate was shrinking, getting smaller and smaller. I felt it was better to carry on the struggle outside, rather than risk going to jail to rot there doing nothing. This I have done. But the struggle for liberation cannot be carried on outside the country; it is inside the country. That is where the battle is and where it will be won.

When Fikile Bam came out of Robben Island after ten years, in his first letter to me he wrote: 'Mama, we have decided to remain in the country. The struggle is here and not outside.' This was in response to my efforts trying to get him out of the country. Fikile was right.

I Have Survived

Our move from Cape Town to England and then to the United States, all within a space of three years and all at personal expense, was a real upheaval. It drained our resources. But we always told ourselves that with health on our side we would recoup this loss. It was not to be.

Because of the way he left the country, A.C. lost half his pension benefits, and this after sixteen years of work at the University of Cape Town. But even with that loss, we still were fortunate in that we could work; we were not in the same position as many of our fellow South African exiles, who found no work after leaving South Africa. From 1967 to 1974, our life was one crisis after another – Pallo's expulsion, the break-up of Nandi's marriage and then A.C.'s illness – all these had drained our resources further. At the time of his death A.C. was under the care of six doctors – a heart specialist, oncologist, radiologist, surgeon, chest specialist and his personal doctor. True, he had catastrophic insurance which took care of three-quarters of all bills, but the one-quarter I had to pay came to quite a good bit. He had not been long enough at the University of Wisconsin to accumulate any large pension benefits and his life insurance was new. And by the time of his death, there was not much left of the children's education insurance either. So I was in pretty bad financial shape when he died. Going back to school to further my studies was completely out of the question. Pallo had lost two years of his studies and I had to see him through; Nandi had to be assisted in re-establishing herself, now that her marriage seemed not to be working. Fortunately, Ninzi had a scholarship and Lindi was working. I had to go out and work. This was exactly what I did.

My friends and relatives were all concerned about my plight.

Mxolisi Ntlabathi wanted me to move to Atlanta when they were there so as to be near them. When he moved to Detroit, he engineered my coming to Detroit to take up a job with Metro East Child Care Services. This was something I learnt: he did everything to introduce me to the notice of people and institutions that could make use of my knowledge and expertise. All this has paid well.

My friends and relatives back home wanted me to return to South Africa. They were concerned and wanted me near them where they could help me. Every time Mr Cingo wrote, he ended his letter with: 'Nkosazana, please come home. We are worried about you. Here you will not be stranded. We are still there to assist you. Come home.' When K. D. Matanzima, my cousin, came to see me in 1972 during his visit to the United States, he too advised that I come home. 'Dad'ethu, come home now, while we are all still there. The thought of you stranded here alone worries us. Please come home.'

I had always told them that emotionally I was not ready to leave this country, especially Madison. After my trip to England in 1973–4, the thought of going back has been constantly in my mind. But every time I planned to go, something drastic happened in South Africa.

Most of the people who are dear to me are now gone. First, Tata in 1972; then Ntangashe in 1978. My dear aunt Nosithe disappeared in Nigeria in 1979 and has not been heard of to this very day. My brother-in-law Rhodes, my sister Granny's husband, passed away in 1980; then in 1982 it was my stepmother, Edwina; in 1984 my sister Granny. Now I ask myself: To whom am I going back, if I go? I know that there are many others, family and friends, who will welcome me with both arms and give me that love and warmth I need.

In all these painful experiences, I have been blessed in having friends who have been very supportive and were there whenever I needed help. All my children's friends, who have now become my friends, have been wonderful to me. I have basked in their love and friendship.

There are three girls who came into my life through marriage. They are Casey, Lindi's ex-wife, Carolyn, Pallo's wife, and Nzwakie, Mxolisi's wife. All three have adopted me as a mother. I am no longer a mother-in-law. I am their mother. They have been wonderful daughters to me, and with them around I know I'll never be without help. Through them I have been blessed with two beautiful granddaughters, Samantha Lee and Nandipha Esther; with two great-nieces, naKazi Xolisa and Ujamaa Loyiso; and a great-nephew, brother to the two girls, Sipho Uhuru. These five kids have been my joy and comfort. Through them I have experienced grandparenthood. They have brought me joy, fun and love.

At the ceremony that marks the rite of passage from boyhood to manhood in my part of the world, one of the obligations stressed upon the young men entering adulthood is: *'Ukuze ihlala lika nyoko lingomi, kwedini'* [See to it that your mother's ointment jar is never dry]. My Pallo has heeded this exhortation, observing it from across the Atlantic Ocean. He has always been a considerate person, my Pallo. I remember, even before he left hospital after the injury from the bomb that killed Ruth First and nearly killed him in Maputo in August 1982, he wrote: 'Knowing how anxious you must be, I thought this letter should be in my own handwriting, to allay your anxiety about my condition.' I cried when I read that, for that was Pallo all over.

Lindi has been with me throughout, giving me support. He has always been the first to share with me any bad news we had, been there when I needed someone to help me pack in my many moves in this country. His father gave him the name 'Lindikhaya' [Homeguard] in the hope, I think, that he would always be there to guard the home. Then there is Bojie, A.C.'s nephew. Of all the Jordans I can say that Bojie is the one who accepted me fully; with him there were no 'ifs' or 'buts'. I was just his 'Ma'. Bojie has a heart of gold and has been a wonderful support throughout the years.

I have been in Michigan now for twelve years. I have not developed any roots here and I do not think I ever will. This area is not like any other place where I have ever been. I still regard Madison, Wisconsin, as home, for from there I had hoped never to move away again. But, for all that, people have been good to me in this area. I have made lots of friends, though perhaps not the kind of friends I made in Madison, and never those that I made in Cape Town.

It is amazing just how much goodwill there is out there. I know this from my own experience. Without that goodwill, I do not think I would have made it. It has been a lonely life, a struggle in which sometimes I lived off the smell of an oil rag. But with the support of my children, and my friends, I have come this far and can say: I have survived.

(Continued from p. 238)

Palmer and Neil Parsons (1977)

26. *The Soul of Mbira: Music and Traditions of the Shona People of Zimbabwe,* by Paul F. Berliner (1978)

27. *The Darker Reaches of Government: Access to Information about Public Administration in the United States, Britain, and South Africa,* by Anthony S. Mathews (1979)

28. *The Rise and Fall of the South African Peasantry,* by Colin Bundy (1979)

29. *South Africa: Time Running Out. The Report of the Study Commission on U.S. Policy Toward Southern Africa* (1981; reprinted with a new preface, 1986)

30. *The Revolt of the Hereros,* by John M. Bridgman (1981)

31. *The White Tribe of Africa: South Africa in Perspective,* by David Harrison (1982)

32. *The House of Phalo: A History of the Xhosa People in the Days of Their Independence,* by J. B. Peires (1982)

33. *Soldiers without Politics: Blacks in the South African Armed Forces,* by Kenneth W. Grundy (1983)

34. *Education, Race, and Social Change in South Africa,* by John A. Marcum (1982)

35. *The Land Belongs to Us: The Pedi Polity, the Boers and the British in the Nineteenth-Century Transvaal,* by Peter Delius (1984)

36. *Sol Plaatje, South African Nationalist, 1876–1932,* by Brian Willan (1984)

37. *Peasant Consciousness and Guerrilla War in Zimbabwe: A Comparative Study,* by Terence Ranger (1985)

38. *Guns and Rain: Guerrillas and Spirit Mediums in Zimbabwe,* by David Lan (1985)

39. *South Africa without Apartheid: Dismantling Racial Domination,* by Heribert Adam and Kogila Moodley (1986)

40. *Hidden Struggles in Rural South Africa: Politics and Popular Movements in the Transkei and Eastern Cape, 1890–1930,* by William Beinart and Colin Bundy (1986)

41. *Legitimating the Illegitimate: State, Markets, and Resistance in South Africa,* by Stanley B. Greenberg (1987)

42. *Freedom, State Security, and the Rule of Law: Dilemmas of the Apartheid Society,* by Anthony S. Mathews (1987)

43. *The Creation of Tribalism in Southern Africa,* edited by Leroy Vail (1989)

44. *The Rand at War, 1899–1902: The Witwatersrand and Anglo-Boer War,* by Diana Cammack (1990)

45. *State Politics in Zimbabwe,* by Jeffrey Herbst (1990)

46. *A Democratic South Africa? Constitutional Engineering in a Divided Society,* by Donald L. Horowitz (1991)

47. *A Complicated War: The Harrowing of Mozambique,* by William Finnegan (1992)

48. *J. M. Coetzee and South Africa: Contemporary History and the Politics of Writing,* by David Attwell (1993)

49. *A Life's Mosaic: The Autobiography of Phyllis Ntantala* (1993)

PERSPECTIVES ON SOUTHERN AFRICA